T0270997

WORLD TRADE ORGANIZATION

DOHA AND BEYOND

The Future of the Multilateral Trading System

Edited by

MIKE MOORE

CAMBRIDGE
UNIVERSITY PRESS

CAMBRIDGE UNIVERSITY PRESS
Cambridge, New York, Melbourne, Madrid, Cape Town, Singapore,
São Paulo, Delhi, Dubai, Tokyo

Cambridge University Press
The Edinburgh Building, Cambridge CB2 8RU, UK

Published in the United States of America by Cambridge University Press, New York

www.cambridge.org
Information on this title: www.cambridge.org/9780521833431

© World Trade Organization 2004

First published 2004
Reprinted 2005

A catalogue record for this publication is available from the British Library

Library of Congress Cataloguing in Publication data
Doha and beyond : the future of the multilateral trading system / edited by Mike Moore.
p. cm.
Includes bibliographical references and index.
ISBN 0-521-83343-4
1. World Trade Organization. 2. Commercial policy. 3. International trade. I. Moore,
Mike, 1949–
HF1379.D64 2004
382′.92–dc22   2003065200

ISBN 978-0-521-83343-1 Hardback

Transferred to digital printing 2010

CONTENTS

CONTRIBUTORS

Robert E. Baldwin is Hilldale Professor of Economics at the University of Wisconsin–Madison. He is also a Research Associate at the National Bureau of Economic Research and at the Centre for Economic Policy Research.

Jagdish Bhagwati is a University Professor at Columbia University.

Peter Eigen is Chairman of Transparency International, based in Berlin. He is also Adjunct Lecturer at John F. Kennedy School of Government at Harvard University.

Koichi Hamada is Professor of Economics at Yale University and President of the Economic and Social Research Institute, Tokyo.

Patrick A. Messerlin is Professor of Economics at the Institute of Political Studies in Paris, Visiting Fellow at the Institute for International Economics and Director of the Groupe d'Economie Mondiale de Sciences Politiques (GEM) since its creation in 1997.

Sylvia Ostry is Distinguished Research Fellow at the Munk Centre for International Studies at the University of Toronto.

T. Ademola Oyejide is a Professor in the Department of Economics at the University of Ibadan, Nigeria.

LeRoy Trotman is former President of the International Confederation of Free Trade Unions. He is currently the General Secretary of the Barbados Workers' Union.

Konrad von Moltke is Senior Fellow at the International Institute for Sustainable Development, Winnipeg, Canada.

INTRODUCTION

In July 2001, I appointed a panel of experts to advise me on the challenges and opportunities confronting the World Trade Organization (WTO) and the global trading system. The members of the WTO advisory group included distinguished individuals from a variety of backgrounds. What they share in common is a keen interest in international trade issues and their distinguished involvement in these matters over many years. I asked these talented individuals to examine how the WTO should respond to the needs of member governments and their citizens in an increasingly integrated global economy. Related questions were how to ensure the fullest possible participation of each member government in multilateral decision-making on trade matters as the WTO expands to near-universal membership, and how a more effective partnership could be established with civil society.

The Doha Ministerial Conference was a significant step forward in defining the tasks facing the WTO. At the same time, the negotiations and work programme set out in the Doha Declaration mirror the many challenges faced by the international community in the trade field. While agreement in Doha has provided much-needed momentum, this does not reduce in any way the need for serious thought to be given to the problems confronting the institution.

This volume offers ideas from the members of the WTO advisory panel on how the organization should move forward to address these challenges in terms both of substance and process. Each of the individuals who has written for this volume comes from a different background and sees the world from a different perspective. But each shares a common desire to see a strengthened and representative WTO serving all its member governments and their people more effectively. Some of the ideas elaborated in this volume are provocative. But addressing the issues confronting this organization calls for fresh thinking and creative suggestions. A healthy debate which examines these institutional issues needs to offer a variety of perspectives for consideration by the owners of the WTO, the member governments.

While the contributions bring to bear the differing expertise and interests of the advisory panel, they also share much in common. First, the contributions emphasize the value and achievements of the multilateral trading system and the WTO. The members of the panel believe that the multilateral trading system has been instrumental in the unprecedented expansion of global trade and investment since the Second World War. It was a process that allowed a large number of developing countries and millions of people to escape poverty. Second, the contributors recognize that there has been a substantive shift in the coverage of multilateral agreements, from the traditional focus on border measures to a far more intrusive involvement in policy-making on a broader front. Third, they believe that because of its success in promoting international economic relations, circumstances now conspire to impose new demands upon the organization. Pressures to incorporate a range of new issues within the purview of the WTO – such as labour standards, environment, corruption, competition policy and international governance – are unlikely to diminish. Great clarity of thought is called for in addressing these pressures. Finally, the contributors to this volume recognize the importance of ensuring that the current WTO negotiations contribute in a meaningful fashion to the development prospects of poor countries.

1 Challenges

The challenges identified by the advisory panel include several well-debated issues such as the divide between developed and developing countries, the demand by civil society groups for transparency and greater participation in the WTO process and the vexing question of how to grapple with issues such as the environment, investment, competition policy and labour and their interaction with trade. But the panelists also identify less familiar issues, though no less important ones, such as corruption, improving the WTO dispute settlement mechanism, the impact on the WTO of EU enlargement and China's accession to the WTO.

Robert E. Baldwin in chapter 4 looks at the major challenges faced by the WTO and discusses various proposals for successfully meeting them, including the decisions taken at the Doha Ministerial Conference. Jagdish Bhagwati and T. Ademola Oyejide in chapters 7 and 5, respectively, offer their views on the development dimension in multilateral trade negotiations and how best to assist poor countries. Sylvia Ostry in chapter 6 talks about the need for greater external transparency of the WTO and offers a proposal for a series of initial steps. Konrad von Moltke in chapter 1 examines trade and sustainable development issues and provides us with his assessment of how effectively Doha's mandated negotiations in trade and environment address the issues. Peter Eigen in chapter 8 builds a convincing case regarding the dangers of corruption and explains how the WTO can make a contribution in combatting it through the negotiations on transparency in government procurement. While the WTO does not involve itself with labour standards, LeRoy Trotman in chapter 2 argues that this is a major omission, and suggests a way of advancing such discussions in the WTO. Koichi Hamada in chapter 3 contributes his insights on China's accession to the WTO and what this implies for the institution. Finally, Patrick A. Messerlin in chapter 9 ventures his thoughts on what kind of impact enlargement may have on the EU's negotiating stance in the current multilateral trade negotiations.

A degree of convergence emerges in terms of the solutions offered. The members of the advisory panel are almost unanimous in the importance they attach to the WTO's decision-making process and the need to improve upon it. Almost all of them have called for increased transparency of the WTO, both internal and external, and for meaningful participation in the WTO process, not only on the part of all member governments, but also other stakeholders such as civil society groups. In terms of substantive suggestions, the members of the advisory panel have given us a number of realistic and practical proposals for how to move forward. In many of these suggestions, further trade liberalization is a key component. To the extent that this is true, we can see scope for addressing at least some of the growing challenges to the system through the WTO's core business of promoting profitable trading opportunities. But our authors would never claim that this is the answer to everything.

2 Development and the WTO

Since the mid-1990s, developing countries have been increasingly vocal about what they perceive as an imbalance in the sharing of the benefits from the Uruguay Round negotiations as well as the increasing number of complex issues under negotiation in the WTO. The Uruguay Round negotiations produced new agreements in intellectual property (IP), investments and services where they felt that the substantial gains have been enjoyed by the developed countries. In those areas such as textiles and agriculture where they expected to get something in return, they have been disappointed with the progress of implementation of the Agreement on Textiles and Clothing (ATC) and the continuing levels of domestic support for agriculture in the developed countries. At the same time, new issues such as the environment, competition policy and government procurement are being discussed, for which they feel they do not have the appropriate technical capacity to respond.

The Doha Ministerial Conference was important in putting the development dimension at the heart of the current WTO negotiations and therefore responding to developing countries' concerns. But what should be the content of this development dimension in the WTO? Two members of the panel, Jagdish Bhagwati and T. Ademola Oyejide, give often contrasting but always insightful answers to this important question. Both believe that for poor countries, development is the ultimate objective and that trade is a policy instrument to help achieve it. But Jagdish Bhagwati argues that the development dimension in the current negotiations means that poor countries will have to take substantive steps to liberalize their own trade and open up their economies. On the other hand, T. Ademola Oyejide believes that poor countries should not liberalize too hastily and should not be subject to many of the same trade rules as developed countries. They also differ with respect to the value of special and differential (S&D) provisions in WTO agreements and non-reciprocal trade preferences (such as the Generalized System of Preferences, or GSP) given by rich countries to poor countries.

Bhagwati begins by dismantling what he believes are misconceptions that plague many policy-makers from developing countries. These include the beliefs:

(a) that the world trading system is 'unfair' with the poor countries facing protectionism that is more acute than their own;
(b) that the rich countries have held on to their trade barriers against poor countries while using the Bretton Woods institutions to force down the trade barriers of the poor countries; and
(c) that it is 'hypocritical' to ask poor countries to reduce their trade barriers when the rich countries have their own.

Bhagwati points out that average industrial tariffs are considerably higher in developing countries than developed countries and that developing countries have become as adept as developed countries in using anti-dumping actions to protect domestic firms. One significant cost of this lingering structure of protection in developing countries is that it hurts a substantial number of other developing countries, since trade among poor countries has risen significantly in recent years.

Therefore developing countries have an important role to play in further liberalising trade. In the past, recourse to the exemptions allowed by S&D provisions has allowed them to escape from making significant trade liberalization commitments of their own during the periodic rounds of multilateral trade negotiations. However, this has come at a price. The rich countries, denied reciprocal concessions from the poor countries, concentrated on liberalizing trade in products of interest largely to one another. Furthermore, high levels of protection have the effect of an export tax, which has inhibited the growth of many developing countries' exports.

Bhagwati has a cautionary word, too, on the trade preferences accorded by some developed countries to poor countries, such as the GSP and new initiatives like the Africa Growth and Opportunity Act and the 'everything but arms' initiative. He argues that they tend to pit poor nations against one another, depreciate in value over time with Most Favoured Nation (MFN) tariff reductions and, given their non-binding character, can be readily withdrawn. These factors make preferences unstable and a poor basis on which to take long-term investment decisions. There is no substitute for the MFN reduction of trade barriers in the rich countries.

In contrast to Bhagwati, Oyejide is largely agnostic about the ability of the multilateral trading system to address the requirements of developing counties, in particular economic development and the reduction of poverty. He believes that enhanced market access for developing countries will not be enough unless basic differences in economic conditions between developed and developing countries are recognized and addressed. These differences arise from several factors, including imperfect or absent markets, inadequate infrastructure and institutions, imperfect information and technological backwardness. The existence of such differences require that supply and production constraints be alleviated and that greater care be taken to ensure that new trade rules, more suitable for developed countries, are not extended indiscriminately to developing countries. LeRoy Trotman makes a somewhat similar point on WTO rules and developing countries, referring to the WTO's large number of rules and their increased complexity. He argues that this leaves small and poor countries at a disadvantage, since only the rich countries will have the capacity and know-how to navigate the sea of rules.

Oyejide believes that special and differential treatment (SDT) of developing countries in the WTO has an important role to play in providing enhanced market access for developing countries on a non-reciprocal basis, and affording them greater flexibility to manage their trade policies. On the whole, he judges that existing SDT provisions, while not entirely adequate, have benefited poor countries. Over time, GSP privileges have generated preferences on billions of dollars' worth of exports from developing countries. Greater discretion over their trade policies has allowed developing countries to pursue measures more conducive to the development of infant industries.

However, Oyejide acknowledges that SDT provisions may distort incentives faced by developing countries. He acknowledges differences in the industrial development experiences of many poor countries, with some such as the Asian Newly Industrializing Countries (NICs) successfully creating globally competitive industries, while other poor countries have languished with inefficient high-cost local industries. His conclusion is that continued support of infant industries by developing countries must be contingent upon adoption of objective performance standards. The current review of SDT provisions in WTO agreements must strengthen them although, where necessary, the provisions should be suitably reformed by a tighter reformulation of the rules and enhanced surveillance of their implementation.

There is more agreement among the members of the panel on what role developed countries should play in giving a development dimension to the current trade negotiations. They ought to allow more market access in the areas of agriculture and labour-intensive manufactures, such as textiles, and contribute resources to technical assistance and capacity building for poor countries. Robert E. Baldwin points out that the key to addressing the dissatisfaction of developing countries in the WTO is providing significant improvements in the access of these countries to the markets of the developed nations. This will require deep average cuts in import duties of developed countries, reducing tariff peaks and correcting the current pattern of tariff escalation that retards industrial growth in developing countries, as well as a reduction in the high levels of domestic support for farm products in the richest countries.

The panel members generally agree on the importance of technical assistance and capacity building for improving the prospects of developing countries. Bhagwati believes that enhanced technical and financial assistance will need to go hand-in-hand with trade liberalization by poor countries. By focusing this assistance more on the poor nations, the poor should be able to exploit trade opportunities that are opened up. Oyejide believes too that many low-income countries need and can use technical assistance and capacity building, especially if these are targeted at relieving their supply response capacity constraints. But he is unsure whether this would be enough for poor countries to be able to negotiate and implement some of the more complex and demanding areas proposed in the current negotiations.

The Doha Declaration made technical cooperation and capacity building core elements of the development dimension of the multilateral trading system. The WTO Secretariat is spearheading efforts to provide technical assistance to developing countries through the Coordinated WTO Secretariat Annual Technical Assistance Plan. This is just one part of a multi-pronged effort aimed at building capacity to developing and least developed countries. In other initiatives, the WTO is entering into strategic partnerships with regional development banks, multilateral institutions, relevant specialized UN agencies and bilateral donors so as to better mobilize resources and coordinate technical assistance and capacity building efforts.

3 Transparency

Increased transparency has been one of the main demands placed on the WTO. There are two aspects to this issue – external transparency and internal transparency. The former refers to the access available to non-WTO members, such as non-governmental organizations (NGOs) and other interested stakeholders, to information and the WTO's decision-making process. Internal transparency refers to transparency issues and working methods as these affect WTO member governments.

The principal complaint relating to external transparency is that since trade can have a significant impact on many non-trade areas such as the environment and employment conditions, the people who are affected should have the right to know what issues are being discussed in the WTO, to make their views known and to have their interests taken into account in the decision-making process. There have been demands, for example, that meetings of WTO dispute settlement panels and the Appellate Body be open to the public and that relevant civil society groups be given the right to submit *amicus* briefs in those cases of interest to them.

The members of the advisory panel agree on the need for external transparency, although a variety of views are expressed on how to go about achieving it. Sylvia Ostry is convinced that participatory processes

improve policy outcomes and enhance the legitimacy of policy. She believes that there will be systemic costs to the WTO, as an institution, if it
does not embark on an initiative for enhanced external transparency.
Konrad von Moltke laments the fact that external transparency does
not appear anywhere in the Doha Declaration. He feels that the lack
of contact with representatives of civil society leaves the WTO vulnerable to suspicions of behind-the-scenes lobbying and corrodes its legitimacy. Robert E. Baldwin sees no sound reasons why the initial stage
at which governments present their positions before the dispute settlement panel should not be open to the public nor why the Appellate Body
should not accept *amicus* briefs if it decides that this will inform their
decision-making.

To improve external transparency, Sylvia Ostry proposes that the WTO
should initiate discussion of the national policy-making processes of
members. The discussion would be intended to inform other WTO members of a country's practices in this field. She suggests that the most appropriate venue for such discussions would be the Trade Policy Review
Mechanism, since it has been designed precisely to encourage and promote greater transparency on trade policy matters. To make the suggestion
more amenable to the WTO's membership, this discussion of the national
policy-making process would be on a voluntary basis and would be subject
to an assessment after an agreed period of time.

LeRoy Trotman notes that labour standards are not discussed in the
WTO as a result of the objection of many governments, and argues that
this could be remedied with the participation of relevant civil society
groups.

Recognizing that the WTO is a member-driven organization, Robert
E. Baldwin argues that civil society groups should pursue the objective
of greater external transparency of the WTO through domestic political
processes. He suggests that they should pressure the governments of WTO
members for greater access to the decision-making process on trade policy. They should also pressure governments to instruct their delegations
to work for greater openness and transparency in the decision-making
process at the WTO level.

The issue of internal transparency is raised by Peter Eigen in the context
of his discussion of corruption. He argues that it is developing countries
who should have a strong interest in battling corruption because it is the
poor who bear the greatest burden from it. However, developing countries
have not been supportive of WTO discussions of transparency in government procurement. He sees the explanation in the disappointment

of developing countries in the 'discrepancy between the claim of formal equality of all members and the habitual resort to non-transparent, informal negotiations and decision-making'. He therefore sees internal transparency and institutional reform of the WTO as prerequisites for successful initiatives in the future.

4 New issues: sustainable development, corruption and labour

A number of the demands placed on the WTO by civil society groups have tended to focus on non-traditional issues such as environment and labour. Certain members of the advisory panel offered thoughtful arguments as to why these issues rightly belong in the WTO, what the WTO should be doing about them and what immediate steps could be taken to make progress.

The Doha Ministerial Declaration mandates negotiations on the relationship between existing WTO rules and specific trade obligations set out in multilateral environmental agreements (MEAs), the reduction or elimination of tariff and non-tariff barriers (NTBs) to environmental goods and services and improvement of WTO disciplines on fisheries subsidies. But Konrad von Moltke feels that these issues are of less importance than others that were neglected. He considers that a number of areas under negotiation which are not ostensibly related to environmental issues could have important effects on the quality of the environment. These include negotiations on agriculture, services (particularly construction, transport and tourism), Trade-Related Aspects of Intellectual Property Rights (TRIPS) and investment.

Konrad von Moltke notes that references to environment and sustainable development are extensive in the Doha Ministerial Statement, showing the importance of the issues but also risking a dissipation of efforts to promote sustainable development. He suggests the use of the WTO's Committee on Trade and Environment (CTE), and in some instances the Committee on Trade and Development (CTD), as a venue to pull together all the different strands of sustainable development and environment. He feels that it is important for the CTE to act as a conduit for the many environmental stakeholders outside the WTO who will not be involved in the negotiating process but who need to be kept apprised of the progress of discussions. If the use of the CTE in this fashion is not possible, perhaps because of the objections of some WTO members, an alternative would be the creation of a high-level advisory group on sustainable development, which will be able to communicate freely with stakeholders who are not part of the negotiations. The advantage of such a mechanism is that it would make any kind of compromise that will be an inevitable part of the WTO negotiations on environment and sustainable development more acceptable and legitimate to stakeholders outside the WTO process.

While the WTO has been remarkably successful in promoting the growth of world trade, Peter Eigen argues that it has not paid sufficient attention to cross-border corruption. Cross-border corruption can undermine the WTO's efforts to expand world trade and investments because it has significant anti-competitive effects. And the poor tend to suffer the most from corruption through higher-priced public goods, misallocation of public funds and the subversion of the democratic process.

Eigen notes the increased awareness in the international community of the corrosive effect of corruption and the need for the international community to make collective efforts aimed at containment. Recent international efforts have included the OECD Convention on Combating Bribery of Foreign Public Officials in International Business Transactions, which came into force in 1999, the Inter-American Convention Against Corruption under the auspices of the Organization of American States (OAS) and the European Council's 1999 Criminal Law Convention on Corruption and 1999 Civil Law Convention on Corruption. However, he goes on to suggest that this patchwork of enforcement efforts needs to be complemented by preventive efforts at the international level. The WTO should have a strong interest in such a campaign. First, it ensures that trade liberalization will create a genuinely competitive environment and more effectively translate expansion in trade into economic development. Second, the fear that the WTO is a captive of powerful multinational corporations (MNCs) in an unholy alliance with corrupt government leaders can be effectively addressed by designing a high-profile anti-corruption strategy driven by the WTO. Third, the WTO can count on the support of a broad coalition of institutions in its anti-corruption agenda.

Eigen argues persuasively that there is probably no more straightforward way of reducing corruption in the multilateral trading system than by tackling government procurement. He proposes a number of elements for an approach to transparency. He recognizes that many developing countries have resisted efforts to improve transparency in government procurement, despite the fact that they are often the worst victims of corrupt government procurement practices. He attributes this to the distrust by the developing countries of what they regard as an opaque decision-making process in the WTO. In order to make headway with transparency in government procurement, there would have to be complementary efforts aimed at institutional reform to improve the WTO's internal transparency and to institutionalize equitable opportunities for all members to participate in decision-making.

LeRoy Trotman laments the fact that some governments proclaim their adherence and support for basic labour standards in the International Labour Organization (ILO) but the same governments reject its introduction in the WTO. He believes that discussion of the social clause in the WTO is one way that labour can benefit from trade discussions. He suggests that the gap in communication between trade policy-makers and labour could be addressed if the WTO were to involve trade union groups and other NGOs in its work programmes.

Robert E. Baldwin has a different perspective. He believes that at the present time greater international efforts to improve working conditions around the world should take place mainly within the framework of the ILO. This organization already has the expertise to provide the sound analysis needed in investigations of alleged unfair labour practices. There is also an active effort within the ILO to better understand the social implications of globalization and to ensure that workers benefit from this process. While this may eventually lead to the adoption of enforcement mechanisms by the ILO that affect WTO rules and require consideration by WTO members, Baldwin concludes that it is best to let the ILO take the lead on the labour issue at this stage.

5   Dispute settlement

At the conclusion of the Uruguay Round negotiations, it was felt that one of the major improvements made to the multilateral trading system was the creation of a binding, predictable and timely mechanism for settling disputes. In the GATT, panel decisions had to be adopted by consensus to become binding. This was turned on its head under the Dispute Settlement Understanding (DSU). Now, a panel report is automatically adopted unless it is overturned by consensus.

There seem to be two emerging concerns about the current dispute settlement mechanism. As a result of a number of controversial environment-related cases decided by WTO panels and the Appellate Body, it has been claimed that these bodies have exceeded their authority and are 'legislating' through their interpretations of WTO rules. The second concern is that the new arrangements are encouraging members to become less flexible in their disputes, as the party which is upheld by the panel now moves quickly to demand compliance from the other party. This generates a greater likelihood that disputes will end with retaliatory action that reduces profitable trading opportunities. In contrast, under the GATT, both parties had incentives to arrive at a compromise even after a panel decision, since it could always be challenged by the losing party.

Robert E. Baldwin, Patrick A. Messerlin and Koichi Hamada all support introducing more flexibility in the unanimity rule of the dispute settlement mechanism. Baldwin suggests that more guidance be given panels and the Appellate Body by greater use of the WTO rule permitting interpretations of any multilateral trade agreement to be adopted by a majority of three-quarters of WTO members. Along the same lines, Messerlin proposes that panels examining well-defined WTO issues (such as tariffs) could use the current unanimity rule. However, in areas where the rules are not as well defined (his candidates are GATS and TRIPS), a consensus 'minus x per cent' rule could be contemplated. Koichi Hamada proposes the use of more informal procedures, doing away with western legal formalities in some cases, to resolve conflicts (see further discussion in the following section).

6   Impact of China's accession on the WTO

No accession to an international organization has attracted as much attention as China's entry into the WTO. Quite apart from the length of time involved in the process, it was the likely impact of trade liberalization on China and on her trading partners that proved so absorbing. But while full of dramatic moment, China's accession to the WTO represents but one step in an impressive process of economic reform that is now more than two decades in the making. Koichi Hamada succeeds in giving us a sense of the historic importance and immense scale of the challenges involved in China's modernization.

Much has been written by economists about the likely economic impact of China's accession. The benefits of this accession accrue first of all to China. The world as a whole will also benefit from China's entry to the WTO. However, there will be challenges, particularly in the areas of agriculture, state-owned enterprises (SOEs) and the banking sector. Koichi Hamada gives a succinct account of this extensive literature in his chapter.

But what interests him more are the related questions of the impact China will have on the WTO and how the WTO will need to treat China so as to create the most favourable conditions for China's successful integration into the multilateral trading system and for benefiting the organization itself. One area where he suggests China can have a positive impact on the WTO is in dispute settlement. He notes that the Dispute Settlement Body (DSB) is overloaded with cases and suggests the possibility of lifting some of the burden by encouraging the use of more informal procedures. He believes that China can be instrumental in bringing the informal Asian way of settling conflicts into the WTO.

Hamada argues for giving greater flexibility to China in the implementation of its WTO commitments. There seem to be a number of reasons for his proposal. First, he questions the economic justification of some WTO rules, for example on anti-dumping. He seems to imply that it does not make economic sense to hold China (or any WTO member for that matter) too strictly to account under this agreement. Second, he suggests that the internal battle in China between economic reformers and their interlocutors is far from over. Hence, pressing China too hard during the stage when it is beginning to implement its WTO commitments will risk upsetting what may be a fragile consensus on economic liberalization. Therefore, he recommends that while the WTO should encourage China's restructuring, it should be flexibile when China encounters difficulties, and allow it space to make the necessary adjustments.

7   EU enlargement

The 1990s saw a dramatic increase in the number of preferential trading arrangements around the world. At present, only a handful of WTO members are not members of a preferential trading arrangement (PTA). While preferential arrangements can create more trade and build up momentum for further liberalization, they also undermine the non-discriminatory nature of the multilateral trading system and distort the pattern of production and specialization from what would have emerged purely on the basis of comparative advantage. EU enlargement, which as Patrick A. Messerlin reminds us will lead to the largest-ever consolidation of PTAs since the creation of the GATT, therefore poses important questions on where the balance will be tilted. More specifically, Messerlin asks how enlargement will affect the EU's negotiating position in the current Doha negotiations. He evaluates the likely impact on the EU position in agriculture, non-agricultural products, services, environment and other social issues and on future PTAs.

Messerlin finds that the average tariff rates and the level of domestic support for the agriculture sector are considerably lower in the prospective new members than in the current members of the EU. This divergence raises the question whether enlargement will lead to a greater willingness by the EU for deeper reforms in the agricultural negotiations in the WTO. Messerlin's cautious answer is that it is unlikely to do so. First, the EU Council has capped the amount of transfers to the acceding countries at 3.4 billion euros during the pre-accession period, of which 0.5 billion euros is specifically for farmers from the acceding countries. Second, in his assessment, the farm sector in the acceding countries is 'generally inefficient' and may reinforce the protectionist farm lobby in the existing fifteen states.

The structure of protection is different for non-agricultural products. The level of tariff protection in this sector is on average higher in the prospective members than in the EU. Messerlin concludes that the likely impact of enlargement will be to erode the willingness of the EU to make new commitments in manufactures, particularly in a number of sectors which are considered sensitive in the prospective members, e.g. steel and clothing. However, Messerlin recognizes that this is not a forgone conclusion and a lot of other issues have to be taken into account. In the case of clothing, for example, he notes that the prospective members were large beneficiaries of the relocation of clothing plants from the EU and the more generous quotas granted them than under the ATC. Thus their privileged position will gradually be eroded as the EU implements its ATC commitments. Hence, the prospective members may have strong incentives to slow down the pace at which this process takes place. But whether the EU actually adopts this stance may depend on China's situation. If China implements fully its accession commitments, this will represent such a large market opening for all kinds of goods and services from the existing EU members that it will outweigh the narrower interests of the clothing industry from the existing and prospective members.

On services, Messerlin finds that the policy regime in the prospective EU members is more restrictive than in the EU. He also notes that in the EU, the negotiating competence in services is shared between the Community and the member states. The services included in the Single Market (often called the infrastructure services) are where the Community has some pre-eminence but services left outside the Single Market (business and health services, construction, retail and wholesale trade, tourism, etc.) are where member states have pre-eminence. This raises substantial problems of coalition and coordination since some of the latter services have been explicitly excluded by the Nice Treaty from the majority rule. Messerlin thinks that this opens up all sorts of possible coalitions among the current

EU members or between some of them and the prospective members. It is possible to imagine prospective EU members aligning themselves with the least open EU members. This may make it difficult for a common EU position on services to emerge.

On social issues such as the environment, Messerlin notes that the new members will face large costs in acceding to the EU and meeting the *acquis communautaire* in these areas. He notes that this may make them more willing to impose similar costs on the rest of the WTO membership given the commitments they were forced to make with the EU membership.

The prospective EU members are not likely to be supportive of bilateral free-trade agreements (FTAs) between the EU and middle-income countries, whose trade structures may be more competitive with theirs. Given that the current EU members will be reluctant to engage other developed countries (the USA or Japan) in FTAs, then enlargement may slow down the EU drive to conclude more FTAs as the list of desirable bilateral partners is whittled down. Enlargement may also strengthen the shift in EU–ACP trade relations from the old non-reciprocal arrangement to one which requires a *quid pro quo* for duty free access to the European market.

The overall assessment from Messerlin seems to be that future enlargement may make the EU on balance less ambitious in the current negotiations. It is important to point out, though, that future enlargement is but one of a number of other factors that will influence the EU's stance in the Doha negotiations. The state of the global economy, the economic situation in the EU and the momentum of the negotiating process created by the demands of trading partners will perhaps be more important in shaping how the EU pushes through its Doha agenda.

8 Concluding thoughts

The contributions of the advisory panel should help to clarify our thoughts on how to respond to the challenges facing the WTO. They should be food for thought for member governments, for civil society groups and all those who have something at stake in the continuing success of this institution.

For my part, I am heartened by what I have learned from them. Greater transparency, flexibility, leadership by the WTO and the willingness by all stakeholders to work together are often all it takes to make headway on many of these issues. This is not to say that success is guaranteed, nor that all parties in the debate will ultimately get what they want. But the message that resounds from the contributions in this volume is that the challenges can be met successfully by the organization, and that in many instances the answers lie in more creatively and effectively utilizing existing WTO mechanisms and rules.

I hope I have whetted the appetite of thoughtful readers sufficiently for them to explore the volume in more detail.

Mike Moore

Trade and sustainable development in the Doha Round

KONRAD VON MOLTKE

1 The 'trade' agenda

The 'trade' agenda has grown inexorably since 1980. In an initial stage, trade negotiations moved from addressing border measures that represented obstacles to trade in goods to behind-the-border measures such as non-tariff barriers (NTBs) or technical barriers to trade. The Uruguay Round took this development one stage further by taking up issues such as trade in services and intellectual property rights (TRIPs) and opening the door on foreign direct investment (FDI). The Doha Declaration may extend this process even further to include competition.

In this expanded trade agenda, the linkages between trade and the environment are everywhere. Indeed, they are so obvious that they are invisible to many. The relationship is largely defined by two fundamental realities:

- Both trade – in the narrow sense of 'trade in goods' and in the broader sense of the expanded 'trade' agenda – and environmental policy are essentially *international* in character. Much of their interface requires international action, creating unique challenges for trade and international environmental regimes alike.
- Trade policy and environmental policy both impact on *economic development* in complex ways. Ultimately they both create structural economic change, favouring some economic actors over others.

In many instances, trade and environmental policy work in congruent ways that reinforce each other. That is an ideal condition that requires no policy intervention. When they work at cross-purposes, however, the resulting conflicts are particularly difficult to resolve because they strike at the heart of what each is trying to achieve. Policy intervention becomes essential, and must frequently occur at the international level.

Despite the overlap and symmetries between trade and environment, the international regimes that have emerged to deal with these issues are dramatically different. The institutional character of these regimes reflects the problem structure of the issues they are designed to address. The liberalization of trade in goods requires entirely different institutional mechanisms than protection of biodiversity, or the management of water resources, or the protection of the stratospheric ozone layer, or the avoidance of climate change. The trade regime is built around the principle of non-discrimination, which is achieved through Most Favoured Nation (MFN) treatment, national treatment, certain measures for transparency and dispute settlement. Environmental regimes are based on scientific research and use a wide range of institutions such as assessment, monitoring, information, transparency and public participation. The institutions of transparency and public participation play a central role in the implementation process, comparable in importance to dispute settlement in the trade regime. These differences render the relationship between trade and environment particularly intractable at the international level.

In addition, the trade regime has not expanded its institutional capabilities as decisively as its agenda. The original GATT focused on trade in goods. Its sparse institutional arsenal reflected the fundamental reality that under the principle of comparative advantage all that negotiators needed to be concerned about was a process of trading 'concessions' where the beneficiaries of such concessions were just as often those making them as those pressing for them. Participants in the regime were united against the common enemy of protectionism, which they were largely helping one another to combat.

Negotiations on 'trade-related' issues such as trade in services, intellectual property rights, or competition policy are entirely different. They reach into the very fabric of each member's society and can also raise difficult issues of rent creation and consequently of distribution. Where liberalization of trade in goods is concerned with increasing economic efficiency by eliminating the rents associated with protectionism, parts of the newer trade agenda actually legitimizes certain rents and consequently contributes in complex ways to their distribution. Yet the institutions of the trade regime are quite unsuited to such a task, exposing it to accusations of increasing inequality rather than just contributing to economic growth. The trade and sustainable development agenda has become the fulcrum for many of these debates.

2 The trade and environment interface

The Doha Ministerial Declaration has the virtue of recognizing the trade and environment interface both explicitly and implicitly. The challenge is now to structure negotiations to ensure that the ultimate outcome represents an appropriate balance between the numerous conflicting interests that are at stake in the trade and sustainable development debate.

Some observers have argued that economic growth alone will create the necessary impetus to deal with environment and sustainable development, and that the contribution of trade liberalization to growth represents the trading system's most important contribution to environmental management.[1] This argument is beguiling because it suggests that policy intervention is not needed to ensure that the environmental outcomes from trade liberalization are positive. Unfortunately, it does not hold up to scrutiny.

The empirical evidence to support this thesis draws on emissions data for a number of key industrial pollutants. It says nothing about issues such as conservation or biodiversity loss. With their focus on industrial pollution, the underlying data do not consider the impact of agriculture, forestry, fisheries, or mining, activities that occur in the environment itself while many forms of industrial production can be isolated from the environment to a significant degree. One of the reasons why industrial pollutants per unit of output may fall in concert with economic growth is that industry is a growing sector attracting the highest level of investment. Newer industrial facilities are almost always less polluting than older ones, at least in relative terms. The same cannot be said about the production of commodities. Moreover, the historical data used in these studies cover a period before environmental issues were adequately understood or technologies had become available that permitted pollution reduction, sometimes while increasing production efficiency so as to generate positive rates of return on 'environmental' investments. They tend to overstate the increase in environmental quality that is attributable to economic growth alone.

The notion that environmental quality is somehow a luxury that only the rich can afford is actually counter-intuitive. The poor live in close

---

[1] Theodore Panayotou, 'Environment and Growth', CID Working Papers, 56, Cambridge, MA, Harvard University, Center for International Development, 2000, at http://www.cid.harvard.edu/cidwp/056.htm.

proximity to the environment. They pay for environmental quality in different ways than the wealthy. They have an intimate understanding of the costs that are being imposed on them. They are likely to spend a larger proportion of their limited resources to deal with the degradation of environmental quality, for example through loss of resources such as fuel wood, through the difficulty of accessing clean water and through the health costs of pollution in all its forms.

Studies that look at the 'ecological footprint' of the world's wealthy minority show that their environmental impact is largely hidden and dispersed.[2] Mechanisms exist that hide environmental costs from those who consume the most. They also hide them from most economic analyses.

It is time to take globalization seriously and to raise expectations for its performance. It must deliver not just greater economic efficiency and economic growth but sustainable development, that is environmental protection and the promotion of greater equity. The simple premise is that markets need disciplines to avoid market failure and to promote public goods; international markets need international disciplines.

The emergence of international markets has created new opportunities. It has also changed the way in which governments can provide essential environmental disciplines and obtain the resources that are needed to ensure that economic growth promotes sustainable development. It is time to embark on the task of developing international market disciplines that properly balance private rights and the public interest in environment and sustainable development. That is a demanding task that will require effort and commitment from many parties with important interests at stake. The Doha Declaration may serve to initiate this process of engagement.

Few realize quite how large the Doha Agenda for environment and sustainable development is. It offers several opportunities and entails a number of risks. The ensuing negotiations are the first to have been defined to a significant extent by the EU, with support from other European countries and the USA. This is reflected in many ways in the text of the Ministerial Declaration. The EU called for a 'comprehensive' Round, that is one that includes investment and competition; both issues are scheduled to be integrated into the negotiations following the next Ministerial in 2003. The EU pressed hard to include the environment as an integral part of the negotiations and succeeded in bringing some of its environmental agenda into the final package.

---

[2] Matthis Wackernagel and William Reese, *Our Ecological Footprint. Reducing Human Impact on the Earth*, Philadelphia, PA, New Society Publishers, 2000.

The final Declaration depended on several EU positions. Acceptance of language that envisaged for the first time a complete phase-out of export subsidies for agricultural products was the key EU concession. In the run-up to Doha, the EU had negotiated the Cotonou Agreement, which provided the key to bringing many African countries on board. These were willing to agree to broad negotiations in exchange for formal recognition of the Cotonou Agreement by the WTO. The USA was certainly helpful in getting the Ministerial declaration to support most of the goals of the EU, and was determined to avoid a failure of the Ministerial following the events of 11 September. The EU engaged in a systematic preparatory process for Doha while the USA was preoccupied, first by a close-run election, then by its lack of fast-track authority, and finally by the events of 11 September. US interests were largely defensive: to avoid concessions on textiles; to keep discussion of its anti-dumping practices to a minimum; and to limit the concessions that had to be made on TRIPS and public health.

The vigorous support for inclusion of the environment in the negoti-ations has been interpreted as a concession to public opinion in the EU. In practice, it is likely that the peculiarities of the institutional structure of the EU also played a role, in particular the complex relations between the Article 133 Committee (which oversees trade negotiations) and the Council (which is the ultimate legislative authority, and the institution where environmental decisions are taken). The central dilemma is that trade is within the exclusive competence of the EU, whereas environment (and for that matter investment and competition) are areas of shared competence. Negotiations that did not include the environment entailed significant risk for institutional conflict within the EU, a risk that the trade negotiators could minimize by pushing hard for the environment.

The role of developing countries in gaining acceptance of the environ-mental provisions of the Doha Declaration is less well known. Not only was the 'friend of the chair' responsible for crafting agreement on the environment from Chile but by all accounts Brazil played an important role in the final stages of the process. This reflects the fact that many major developing countries have by now fully understood that environmental management is not a rich-country luxury. They face particularly difficult choices in this regard because, unlike wealthy countries, they cannot sim-ply pay their way out of trouble.[3] As a result a 'Southern agenda' for trade

---

[3] 'Fiscal Deficit', in International Institute for Environment and Development (IIED), *Financ-ing for Sustainable Development*, London, IIED, 2002, pp. 37–42, at http://www.iied.org/wssd/pubs.html#fin.

and environment is beginning to emerge, one much closer to sustainable development than the one pursued thus far by developed countries.

In light of the exceptional role played by the EU in shaping the Ministerial declaration, and its environmental aspects in particular, the EU will presumably also play a key role in the further process. It carries a heavy burden of responsibility for ensuring the success of what it has worked so hard to initiate. Further development of the environmental agenda will pass through Brussels.

By the same token, the unprecedented strength of the developing countries in Doha will also continue to be a feature of the ongoing negotiations. It is therefore likely that the dynamics of this Round will differ markedly from previous ones, which were largely shaped by US priorities.

The Declaration does not fully recognize the progress that had been made on the environmental agenda prior to Doha, primarily through the dispute settlement process and in the area of transparency. The errors of the tuna/dolphin panel report have largely been rectified and first steps have been taken on the highly contentious issue of transparency – which is, however, not slated for further negotiations, leaving the job half-finished.

The absence of significant environmental expertise in all delegations is recognizable in the final text of the Ministerial Declaration, It gives more emphasis to issues that are of lesser importance (such as the relationship between WTO rules and MEAs). It gives less emphasis to some that are more significant from an environmental perspective (such as cost internalization in traded products, investment, services, TRIPS and external transparency). It is critical to ensure an adequate balance of environmental and trade expertise in the actual negotiations. This can be achieved only if those responsible for the environment at the highest levels make it clear to their counterparts in trade policy that they will personally supervise the environmental aspects of the negotiations.

It is possible to divide the environmental aspects of the negotiations into four categories: issues slated for negotiation; issues to be considered for negotiation; environmental issues likely to arise in the process of negotiating other matters slated for negotiation; and issues not included in the Declaration.

3   Environmental issues slated for negotiation (paragraph 31)

Multilateral environmental agreements

This is one of the issues on which significant progress had been made in the WTO prior to Doha through the dispute settlement process. The major risk is that the negotiations do not confirm the interpretation that underlies recent Appellate Body reports, notably on the shrimp/turtle dispute and the asbestos dispute.[4] From these reports it would appear that trade measures agreed by the parties to an MEA will be viewed as acceptable, provided they are not arbitrary or more trade-distorting than necessary. Even certain unilateral trade measures may be acceptable if serious efforts have been undertaken to negotiate or to otherwise achieve an amicable result.

The WTO negotiations will not address the difficult issue of trade measures that affect WTO members not a party to a multilateral environmental agreement, in practice the USA. It is paradoxical that the country with the greatest enthusiasm for unilateral environmental measures is now most at risk from measures that may be adopted against it by countries that are part of the multilateral consensus. The USA has a long history of being unable to participate fully in international environmental negotiations. This includes several major MEAs, notably the Basel Convention on the Transboundary Transport of Hazardous Wastes, the Convention on Biological Diversity (with the Biosafety Protocol) and the Kyoto Protocol to the UN Framework Convention on Climate Change. In addition the Western Hemisphere Convention is largely a dead letter and there is no regional agreement on long-range transboundary air pollution and none to protect migratory species, despite the obvious need for such arrangements. It is important to ensure that WTO rules do not create an incentive for states to stay outside of environmental negotiations and agreements. On the other hand, it remains true that a dispute initiated in the WTO against a member of a widely accepted MEA represents a hazard to the future of the organization and is therefore unlikely to occur.

Information exchange between MEA Secretariats and relevant WTO Committees

This item suggests that the relevant Committees may be permitted to develop special procedures to manage their relationship with the MEA Secretariats. It represents a pragmatic way of dealing with some of the differences in operating procedures of the MEA Secretariats, which are subject to quite broad rules concerning access to information and rights of

---

[4] 'United States – Import Prohibition of Certain Shrimp Products; European Community – Measures Affecting Asbestos and Asbestos-Containing Products', at http://www.wto.org/english/tratop_e/dispu_e/distabase_wto_members2_e.htm.

participation, and the WTO, which is generally very resistant to innovative forms of interaction with outside constituencies. This is one issue where it may be possible to address the fundamental institutional differences between the trade regime and international environmental regimes, but it will require a certain degree of innovation within the WTO context.

Reduction or elimination of tariff and non-tariff barriers to environmental goods and services

This could provide a welcome reduction in the costs of environmental goods and services while promoting their more efficient production in domestic markets. The key to this negotiation will be the definition of 'environmental goods and services'. There are numerous chemicals that are used in wastewater treatment that also have other commercial uses. Many modern environmental technologies are highly integrated with the productive facilities they relate to, so that the more recent and less polluting facilities are also economically more efficient. It remains to be seen how the 'environmental component' of such products or technologies is to be calculated. A similar problem was faced in the Agreement on Subsidies and Countervailing Measures, Article 8.2(c), which is no longer in effect, that dealt with subsidies to promote the adaptation of existing facilities to new environmental requirements.

Fisheries

The Declaration explicitly notes that fisheries is a matter of concern from an environmental perspective, even though it is likely to be negotiated as part of the interpretation of WTO Rules.[5]

4   Environmental issues to be considered for negotiation or other action (paragraph 32)

The effect of environmental measures on market access

This is one of the most contentious issues, since there are persistent questions whether environmental measures adopted by developed countries are protectionist. It is an issue that requires careful analysis. Some measures result in the internalization of environmental costs at the point of

---

[5]   See below for a further discussion of the fisheries issue.

production (in a developing country). That is desirable, provided it is possible to pass the increased costs to the ultimate consumer (in a developed country). Under these circumstances, environmental measures may act to limit market access to those producers who can meet the standards – but they provide these producers with the financial means to address environmental problems in the country of production and actually increase producer revenues from these products.

The impact of environmental measures on developing countries depends on the markets in which goods are traded, and whether they properly reflect environmental costs along the entire product chain. For most developing countries effective measures to ensure the proper cost attribution along the product chain are likely to be more advantageous than attempts to circumvent environmental requirements. The effect of such measures would be to provide the necessary resources to address the environmental consequences at the point of production, effectively increasing the share of total resources that accrue to the developing country. In markets that do not ensure proper cost attribution, the opposite is true: environmental conditions impose additional costs on producers who are for the most part price-takers in the first place. It will be a welcome departure if the WTO begins to address this aspect of the issue.

Relevant provisions of the Agreement on Trade-Related Aspects of Intellectual Property Rights (TRIPS).

Negotiations have been agreed on TRIPS, Article 27.3(b). This item suggests there may be other matters that will arise in relation to TRIPS and the environment. No pressing issues have been raised thus far, although the negotiations on geographic designations may ultimately lead to an environmental agenda. On account of its distributional impacts, however, TRIPS is of great concern from the perspective of sustainable development.

Labelling requirements for environmental purposes

The draft Ministerial Declaration referred only to 'eco-labelling'. By extending the issue to cover all forms of environmental labelling it has become more appropriate and much more difficult to handle. Labelling is a tool to attach information on processing and production methods to a product as it moves through its various stages of production, trade, transformation, use and disposal. It is also the line of first defence in controlling impacts from chemicals, namely by providing hazard information to those who handle or use a product.

The issue of 'processing and production methods' is the most important of all issues of relevance to environment and sustainable development that may arise in relation to trade in goods. It is closely related to the issue of market access, and like that issue responses are likely to vary depending on the nature of the market for certain goods. Identification of processing and production methods is desirable if proper attribution of the environmental costs of production and processing can be ensured. Where this is not the case, such identification is likely to act as a barrier to market access.

Over the past years there have been some notable advances in developing certification and labelling schemes that reflect the environment and sustainable development agenda. In some product chains, notably forest and fishery products, producers, traders, and environmental groups have begun to cooperate in the development of certification schemes. This should open new options for the WTO negotiators in an area that is particularly difficult.

Other issues

The Ministerial Declaration instructs the Committee on Trade and Environment (CTE) to work on 'all items' on its agenda but then goes on to list the three identified above. While this theoretically leaves open the possibility of raising other issues, it would need to be justified in a very convincing manner, given the extraordinary dimensions of the environmental agenda in the Round and likely resistance to its further enlargement.

The entire mandate on trade and environment (both paragraphs 31 and 32) is carefully hedged to limit its possible impact. Apart from the discussion concerning WTO members not party to certain MEAs, the Declaration states that action on environmental issues 'shall not add to or diminish the rights and obligations of Members under existing WTO agreements, in particular the Agreement on the Application of Sanitary and Phytosanitary Measures (SPS), nor alter the balance of these rights and obligations, and will take into account the needs of developing and least-developed countries'. The reference to the SPS Agreement has the effect of excluding negotiations on the precautionary principle This is appropriate insofar as the discussion about the precautionary principle has not matured to the point where it can usefully become the object of negotiations. It is inappropriate if the drafters assume that the question of the precautionary principle has been settled by the existing text of the SPS Agreement. It clearly has not, and the need to negotiate in this regard can arise so quickly that the issue may yet force itself onto the Doha agenda. The remainder of the passage is hortatory rather than binding since it must be recognized that the very act of negotiation changes the balance of rights and obligations.

5   Environmental issues likely to arise in the process of negotiating other matters slated for negotiation

Environmental issues cannot be easily confined to a discrete domain within the negotiations because they are liable to arise in almost every area that is slated for negotiation. In some instances the environmental consequences of other proposed negotiations may be much more substantial than those explicitly labeled 'environmental'. There is a distinct possibility that the results of negotiations on the issues that have explicitly been labeled as 'environmental' will appear as less important from an environmental perspective than the outcome of negotiations on other issues, agriculture and investment in particular.

Agriculture

The environment will be central to the agriculture negotiations. As tariff barriers are reduced and subsidies fall, the importance of 'non-trade concerns' in agriculture increases. The environment is a key non-trade issue, arguably the most important of all since it is a concern that is common to all countries, even though different countries employ different strategies to deal with it. The stability of rural communities, an issue of transcendent importance to China, is also likely to emerge as one of the critical 'non-trade' issues in the agriculture negotiations. These will revolve around definitions of the 'Green Box', which includes subsidies that are acceptable and the proposed 'Development Box', which would include policy measures of specific concern to developing countries. The Green Box is already part of the Agreement on Agriculture. No agreement has yet been reached on inclusion of a Development Box.

It is important to recognize that WTO negotiations do not aim at solving specific policy problems, such as the protection of the rural environment. They revolve around issues raised by member states and ultimately involve a process of bargaining that tends to exclude any item not represented at the table. Consequently the process of agenda-setting, initiated in Doha and likely to continue until 2005, is of critical importance. Issues that have not been raised in this time will prove very difficult to introduce later – and only at considerable cost in terms of bargaining leverage.

The ambiguity of the Doha text – in relation to 'non-trade issues' and many other matters is intentional. It transfers many of the hard decisions to the continuing process in Geneva.

Fisheries

The issue of fisheries – and fishery subsidies – is new within the WTO. The Doha Declaration views it as both an environmental issue and as a clarification of WTO Rules (paragraph 28). The commitment to negotiate fisheries subsidies ('clarify and improve WTO disciplines on fisheries subsidies' is the precise language) raises one of the more complex issues of contemporary environmental management – namely how to avoid incentives to overproduce and overexploit environmentally sensitive resources. The outcome of this negotiation could have broad implications for subsidies in other areas that impact on both the environment and commodity markets, notably forestry and mining. It is also worth noting that the pressure to include fisheries in the Doha Declaration represents a joint effort of certain governments and environmental organizations, not unlike the coalition that brought about the interpretation of the public health aspects of the TRIPS Agreement.

Negotiating an effective agreement to protect fisheries from the impact of excessive subsidies is a major challenge. The conflicts that this involves have frequently hindered agreement within national jurisdictions or within the EU. In that sense, the WTO negotiation would once again be aimed at helping countries to do what is politically painful but is actually good for themselves, something the GATT/WTO has proven adept in. The particular challenge of fisheries negotiations derives from the fact that their results will be tested not only against the political will of countries to take action but also against the harsh reality of the environment. An agreement on fisheries that does not protect fish stocks will be seen as ineffective. In this area the WTO faces the central dilemma of all environmental regimes. It is impossible to change the environment by legislative fiat, yet the standard by which measures are judged is precisely whether they change the environment.

Services

The Doha Ministerial Declaration added nothing to the continuing services negotiation, begun as part of the 'built-in' agenda from the Uruguay

Round. The Declaration effectively terminates the 'built-in agenda' in both agriculture and services, incorporating it into the single undertaking and making results in one area dependent on results in all other areas under negotiation. The lack of specific discussion of the services negotiation should not obscure the fact that this is of great environmental significance. After all, the Basel Convention on the Transboundary Movement of Hazardous Wastes is specifically designed to regulate – and to limit – one type of service.

The services negotiations focus on two areas: the extension of commitments and the development of rules on domestic regulation. Under the 'opt-in' system of the General Agreement on Trade in Services (GATS) countries are bound only for service sectors and delivery 'modes' on which they have specifically made commitments. The underlying assumption is that countries will continuously enlarge the commitments they have undertaken. Several service areas are particularly sensitive from an environmental perspective, in particular transport, tourism and energy services. Both banking and insurance have emerged as potential tools in the maintenance of environmental disciplines in international markets and play a growing role in the climate debate. Thus negotiations on such services, seemingly remote from any environmental impact, can turn out to have unexpected environmental implications.

In all of these areas the negotiation of a framework for domestic regulations involves potential restraints on the ability of governments to regulate. In the WTO, the explicit reaffirmation of 'the right of Members under the [GATS] to regulate, and to introduce new regulations on, the supply of services' signals that some members feel that there is a significant likelihood that this will actually not be the case.

Investment

There has been much discussion about the question whether the Doha Ministerial Declaration involves a commitment to negotiate on investment (and other Singapore issues) after the next Ministerial Conference, in 2003. Some observers believe that a statement by the Chair at the closing session effectively negates the strong language of the Declaration itself in this regard ('we agree that negotiations will take place after the Fifth Session of the Ministerial Conference on the basis of a decision to be taken, by explicit consensus, at the Session on modalities of negotiations'). This text suggests that voting will take place on this matter with unanimity required, rather than the traditional declaration of the Chair that assumes consensus. In practice, the process outlined in the Declaration for the coming two years is not that different from the initial phases of any negotiation, so that the burden of proof is likely to shift to those who wish to oppose formal negotiations.

This issue is as significant for environment and sustainable development as any other item on the WTO agenda.[6] Most international actions in favour of sustainable development involve investment, whether private or public. Indeed, the climate regime is almost entirely about promoting investment in projects that are desirable from the perspective of greenhouse gas emissions. An agreement that establishes a 'multilateral framework to secure transparent, stable and predictable conditions for long-term cross-border investment' can create a framework for future promotion of sustainable development, or it can create serious obstacles to the attainment of this goal. The reference to 'long-term' limits it to productive investments that are the most important from the perspective of environment and sustainable development.

The text of the Doha Declaration suggests that the investment negotiations in the WTO are to be different than those that failed to produce a Multilateral Agreement on Investment (MAI) in the OECD. Nevertheless the ultimate course of negotiations remains unpredictable. Foreign direct investment (FDI) involves complex relationships between foreign investors and host governments. No negotiation can long ignore this fundamental reality and even the most anodyne text must impact this relationship if it is to have any meaning. Indeed, the stated goal of securing transparent, stable and predictable conditions for FDI inevitably implies that actions by governments that investors may view as arbitrary or as changing essential conditions for an investment become a matter for negotiation, even when such actions are taken in furtherance of legitimate purposes of public policy. Thus negotiators may find themselves inexorably drawn into the areas of conflict that have been marked out by the MAI process. The difficulties that have arisen in relation to the investment provisions of the North American Free Trade Agreement (NAFTA) are an indication of the risks of unforeseen consequences that exist.[7]

---

[6] Konrad von Moltke, *An International Investment Regime? Implications for Sustainable Development*, Winnipeg, International Institute for Sustainable Development, 2000, at http://www.iisdl.iisd.ca/trade/pubs.html.

[7] Konrad von Moltke and Howard Mann, 'Misappropriation of Institutions: Some Lessons from the Environmental Dimension of the NAFTA Investor–State Dispute Settlement Process', *International Environmental Agreements*, 1(1) January 2001, pp. 103–23, at http://www.iisdl.iisd.ca/trade/pubs.html.

The bargaining process towards the end of most trade negotiations can lead to dramatic changes that are adopted with little discussion. In the Doha Declaration, differences between the penultimate text and the final version are difficult to explain, except that they reflect thirty-six hours of intense bargaining. The experience with intellectual property rights (IPRs) also provides a hortatory example. The Uruguay Round negotiations began with a limited focus on piracy, a matter of great concern for holders of rights but of lesser impact on development potential than the comprehensive structure of IPRs that emerged in the final version of the TRIPS Agreement. A similar transition through the process of negotiations on investment cannot be excluded.

Government procurement

The environmental dimension of this negotiation has not received any attention thus far. Governments have rarely imposed stringent environmental requirements on the goods that they bought. In practice government agencies have not been environmentally conscious consumers. Important areas of government procurement have historically been reserved to domestic suppliers, effectively closing that market to international trade. As the liberalization of government procurement progresses, even if it progresses but slowly as is currently the case, it is reasonable to expect that a range of technical barriers will be discovered that at least some countries will perceive as protectionist in character. Negotiations on government procurement will have to embrace whatever solutions emerge in other parts of the WTO for this dilemma – or they will have to develop *sui generis* approaches to the environmental dimension of government procurement.

Agreement on Trade-Related Intellectual Property Rights (TRIPS)

The TRIPS Agreement has given rise to numerous complaints. It is now evident that many countries were unaware of its implications when it was signed. It is also evident that studies undertaken by the World Bank and others predicting the likely impact of the Uruguay Round failed to take into account the powerful distributive effects of the TRIPS Agreement (or of the GATS, for that matter). This omission caused them to underestimate the benefits of the Uruguay Round for countries whose citizens held significant IPR and overestimate them for countries that did not, primarily developing countries.

The Declaration on TRIPS and Public Health that was adopted at the Doha Ministerial paved the way for an interpretation of that agreement that is less likely to require large transfer payments from poor to rich countries in regard to public health. It represented one of the most important results of the Ministerial Conference. It also represents a significant innovation in the process that led to its adoption, with developing countries and NGOs from developed countries working together to create an effective force within the WTO itself.

The Ministerial Declaration also opened negotiations on two aspects of TRIPS that are potentially significant from the perspective of environment and sustainable development: Article 23.4 dealing with geographic designations and Article 27.3(b) on the exclusion from patenting of plants and animals. There has been extensive debate about the relationship between Article 27.3(b) and the Convention on Biodiversity. The negotiations are bound to be difficult.

6   Sustainable development in the Round

The relationship of the WTO to sustainable development remains ambiguous. Sustainable development is the only qualitative criterion for the work of the WTO that is identified in the Preamble of the WTO Agreement. The preambular section of the Ministerial Declaration is even more effusive in its adherence to sustainable development as a principle for the WTO. However, the phrase does not occur once in the operative sections of the Declaration. The Declaration is full of statements concerning development, and repeatedly expresses concern for developing and least developed countries. Indeed, some observers have declared that this was a 'development' Round – presumably in contrast to the Uruguay Round, which dealt primarily with matters of concern to developed countries. But the principal measures to operationalize the development dimension involve capacity building, a difficult task whose impact on economic development is largely unproven. Achieving a proper balance between environment, development and the economic policies that will be negotiated is a task that remains to be tackled.

One possible approach to this task would be more effective cooperation between the Committee on Trade and Development (CTD) and the CTE, something that has not been possible in the past. Both organs are given a new role in the negotiations, 'each to act as a forum to identify and debate developmental and environmental aspects of the negotiations, in order to help achieve the objective of having sustainable development appropriately reflected'. This is a novel provision whose significance remains to be seen.

7 Issues not slated for further negotiation

Despite the fact that issues of concern from the perspective of environment and sustainable development are to be found all over the Doha Declaration, there are still some matters that are not addressed, indeed that appear to have been excluded by explicit decision. These include the precautionary principle and external transparency.

There has been extensive debate about the 'precautionary principle', primarily triggered by US concern that this may be used to exclude certain goods from European markets such as hormone-treated beef and genetically modified organisms (GMOs). The precautionary principle addresses a central dilemma of environmental policy that is faced by all countries. All environmental policy relies heavily on scientific research to understand what needs to be done to protect the environment yet there is rarely enough such information to provide clear guidance as to what actually must be done. Countries adopt different strategies to deal with this dilemma. Some countries emphasize formalized risk assessment procedures even though these can rarely be fully implemented in practice because they require substantial resources. Other countries recognize that administrative authorities must exercise some discretion and formulate the precautionary principle as a way to identify and circumscribe such activity. The international debate has not yet produced a common understanding of these issues so that WTO negotiations in this area appear premature. Nevertheless this remains a matter that overshadows many environmental issues in the Doha Declaration.

The Doha Declaration also does nothing to promote further 'external transparency'. One of the paradoxes of the WTO is that an organization that is devoted to liberalizing markets and creating economic opportunities for private actors remains deeply resistant to any direct contact with representatives of civil society. This leaves the organization vulnerable to the behind-the-scenes lobbying that has always been part of the process and even more vulnerable to suspicion of such lobbying.

Those interested in environment and sustainable development tend to press for greater transparency and participation. The fundamental reason for this interest is that transparency and participation are core implementation tools of environmental regimes at all levels, comparable in importance to the dispute settlement system of the trade regime. Even though the Ministerial Declaration said next to nothing about external transparency, this is an issue that is unlikely to go away.

8 Conclusion

The environment and sustainable development agenda in the new Round is surprisingly extensive. While other interests that are linked to trade, for example agriculture, IPRs, investment, competition and public health, are confined to a single paragraph or section of the Doha Declaration, environment and development are to be found all over it. This may dissipate efforts to promote sustainable development unless strong leadership is provided that ensures that the large environment and development agenda embedded in the Declaration is addressed in a coherent and systematic manner.

This challenge is characteristic of environmental management and a number of solutions have emerged in environmental regimes, even though they continue to struggle with the problem of balancing distinctiveness with cohesiveness of the international environmental governance system. One approach would involve using the CTE (and in some instances the CTD) creatively as a forum where the entire environmental agenda is pulled together and as a conduit to the many environmental stakeholders inside and outside government who will not be involved in the negotiation process. This would imply a conscious decision by the membership of the WTO to give the CTE some dispensation in its rules of procedure that permits creative solutions to the issue of communicating with outside constituencies.

Another solution, utilized with some success by the United Nations and the OECD, is the creation of a high-level Advisory Group on Sustainable Development. This has the advantage of avoiding the procedural problems that are liable to accompany efforts by the CTE to deal with outside constituencies. Such an Advisory Group can face inwards – and seek to pull together the dispersed environment agenda – and outwards – and communicate relatively freely with stakeholders who are not part of the negotiations. Its support could be decisive in achieving the kind of broad acceptance of the compromises that will be an inevitable part of any successful negotiation and that will certainly also involve the negotiation agenda on environment and sustainable development.

2

The WTO: the institutional contradictions

LEROY TROTMAN

1 The vision and the reality

There can be little doubt that when the various framers set out to establish international institutions, like the IMF, like the World Bank, like the WTO, they had a vision that their creations would serve to make the global community a better place. One has merely to note some of the stated objectives which drove their action:

- To fight poverty with passion and professionalism for lasting results
- To help people help themselves and their environment by providing resources, sharing knowledge, building capacity, and forging partnerships in the public and private sectors. (World Bank Mission Statement)
- To facilitate the expansion and balanced growth of international trade and to contribute thereby to the promotion and maintenance of high levels of employment and real income and to the development of the productive resources of all members as primary objectives of economic policy.
- To give confidence to members by making the general resources of the Fund temporarily available to them under adequate safeguards, thus providing them with opportunity to correct maladjustments in their balance of payments without resorting to measures destructive of national or international prosperity. (IMF, Article 1)
- The goal is to improve the welfare of the peoples of the member countries. (Goal of the WTO)

And yet, when these organizations meet, their debates are fraught with expressions of suspicion, are punctuated with examples of bad faith, are undermined by drifts into polarized sectors and end by seeming to create even more problems than those they set out to solve. And while these differences struggle for centre stage within the many well-appointed conference rooms, outside the corridors and in the surrounding streets there are significant public expressions of the disenchantment of large segments of the affected communities, their banners express in quite unambiguous language increasing global certainty that the stated objectives are not serving, did not serve and were never intended to serve the broad mass of humanity, but were intended only to address and secure the wealth and well being of privileged interest groups within the industrialized world.

This chapter seeks to examine these conflicts between the stated vision and the reality of the demonstrable disaffection within and without the council chambers. It seeks to explore the institutional contradictions which exist to discover the extent to which these may be the determinants of the expressions of disaffection. It is limited by predetermined space and by the time by which it needs to be presented; it is further limited by the inability presented by these two considerations, and the third one of cost, to have conducted a survey of the expressions of a wide cross-section of civil society and of those countries whose delegates attend out of fear and leave equally frustrated.

The chapter will therefore claim at best to be an attempt to challenge the current wisdom determining the work of the WTO particularly and to urge a new look at some of the governing principles, as well as a re-examination of some of the rules, regulations and practices which underscore those principles.

Finally, it must be said that the chapter is written from the bias of a believer in the international trade union movement who, at the same time, has a strong experience of the difficulties, setbacks and challenges of small developing countries, emerging from centuries of European imperial exploitation and discovering problems, many unnatural, in entering the clubs built for the northern industrialized imperial powers.

2   WTO Rules

The first thing one is forced to notice about the WTO is the volume of rules which are set down to govern the relationship of country-to-country and country-to-WTO. Here are no simple Ten Commandments which can clearly determine how the club member has to relate to other members. Here, instead, are actually hundreds of rules, clauses, subclauses, curved brackets and square brackets which may be fully understood only after hours upon hours of careful study. The only parties which may be expected reasonably to understand what each commitment is under a rule, are those parties who in one way or the other were involved in the original conceptualization and the subsequent drafting and development of the enabling legislation. It is they, and sometimes only they, who know where the escape clauses are and how particular regulations may be waived or otherwise disregarded to achieve a specific objective for the country of that party, and who equally know from the first step of the novitiate where that new club member has gone wrong, where the maze of the regulations will take the member and how, if at all, the member may re-emerge with any of his/her country's sovereignty intact. The March 2002 US Initiative in the steel industry is a most timely example of one aspect of this matter of the rules, while the 2001 efforts of Ghana to re-visit its cocoa commitment is the other aspect – the new club member, relegated into having to seek permission to change the terms of the trade and to pay for the change.

It is fitting that the EU–US dispute is one involving the more powerful actors in the world trading community; for their legal debate may serve to clarify for the lesser players what pitfalls they should come to expect. For those who stood in line in rose-tinted spectacles, it should serve to underscore the fact that no exaggeration was being attempted in the earlier references to original planning and designing. It should also raise the question of who else is able to compete with equal vigour and resource. The small island developing state of 70,000 adults, or the poverty-ravaged central African state, or the war-torn Eastern country – none of these will effectively be able to mount a challenge to such an interpretation of existing rules.

The reality is that the big players will have scores of attorneys and hundreds of staffers overall, specially dedicated to the business of international trade. The economists who specialize in WTO affairs are going in many instances to be significantly more than the economists in the total public service of other countries.

There ought not to be the need to spell out here the name or circumstances of any particular country. It ought to suffice to say that the major players, either as individuals or as regional bodies, were the vision and developers of the new Order; it was the smaller less powerful who sought association, in response to the offer of a better opportunity to participate for the benefit of their communities, and who entered an association where the rules, good or bad, were already prepared for others.

Here is no challenge to the original clarity of understanding of the framers. There is, however, every intention of suggesting that the club was not established for the general welfare of the world, in the same way that the 'World Series' was not intended for baseball players in China or Germany nor were the Rules of the International Cricket Council (ICC) originally intended to accommodate South Korea, or Mexico, or Bangladesh.

From the days preceding Marrakesh, therefore, the smaller countries of the world found themselves embarked on an exercise which seems to be one that is fraught with setbacks and contradictions. How, for example, can the African Caribbean and Pacific (ACP) countries which produced and sold bananas mainly in Europe view the rules and regulations of the WTO? Until the WTO was created they had a form of protection; they produced less than 3 per cent of world bananas, and could not be seen by any reasonable actor as constituting a threat to the three or so world producers who among them had swallowed up the rest of the market. And yet this was their introduction to the promise of a better life under the governance of a world trading system which replaced the preferential system they knew and relied upon, in some cases for as much as 75–80 per cent of their jobs and economic welfare. They were threatened with the withdrawal of that 3 per cent of trade which represented their lifeline.

3 Institutional difficulties

The distortions and disparities referred to so far are but a part of the institutional difficulties which may be said to be preventing international acceptance of yet another world institution developed by the great engineers of the post Second World War community. The framers were seeking to reduce the bases for further world wars; yet they were creating and instituting measures which could and would only result in creating enmity between and among nations.

The framers must not alone be blamed for the differences and disputes, which have served to alienate the vast masses of people worldwide and to make them sceptical of any declared initiatives being considered by global institutions. Each player who enters the club has sought to have the rules varied or reinterpreted to suit his/her special interests. Each has insisted that he/she must be in full agreement with any proposal for change before the WTO management is able to effect change; for when the crunch comes it is governed by the reality that states have no principles, only interests.

Smaller countries were no doubt reacting to the abuse of their veto powers by the major industrialized countries. They are understandably saying that in this latest club their size and/or their recentness of entry into the global league should not be allowed to reduce them to the status of non-playing members. Thus the Director General's office is relegated to that of a highly paid civil servant who, according to his own public complaints, cannot even proceed to shred obsolete or discarded documents unless each member of the club agrees to the action.

Reference has so far been made to the weakness and contradictions which were built into the structure and development agenda of the WTO. One has to note also the difficulties in the national operational structures which have limited smaller countries in their efforts. Indeed, this may be similarly applicable to larger countries. The WTO, although it was to become the largest single institution governing the economic – and, hopefully, the social and environmental – development of the world, did not manage to attract the national bureaucratic structures properly to manage the international dimension or the domestic organization.

There can hardly be many states with a suitable governmental machinery in place to deal with the core issues of the WTO. The work is instead covered under the objectives of Ministries of Trade, of Agriculture, of Economic Affairs, of Education, of Foreign Affairs – all in the same country. One does not have to be an authority in political science to be aware that such fragmentation is likely to be a recipe for disaster. Many countries have had their *bona fides* questioned as a consequence. It has been known to happen that some countries have, in conference *A*, committed to particular positions, which have in the following week been contradicted in conference *B* and then completely rejected in conference *C*. A very pertinent example of this is the position taken by various countries in relation to the place that human welfare is to take in the creation of global wealth.

The Social Clause debate, as it is called, is a classic example of the conflicting positions which countries assume, particularly where they perceive that their interests are being challenged. It ought to be true to say that most countries in the world are desirous of having some basic labour standards as well as standards for the sustainability of the environment. This may be heard expressed on the floor of every meeting of the ILO. Yet, in the halls of the WTO, the same governments can be heard vehemently opposing such basic human conditions. There may be many reasons for this; but the following two suggestions may serve to incorporate all the other theories. The one has to do with the parties which have been in the forefront of the crusade for standards. The 'Who' in such a question then brings countries into their positions of defensiveness, and elicits the view that the industrialized world is endeavouring to gain an advantage over other countries. This then leads on to the 'What' in the question, meaning what are the means by which the advantage is to be had? And many countries, though knowing better, still put out the propaganda that an effort is being made to impose on fragile economies conditions of democracy which are too costly for those countries.

Everyone knows that what is being sought is a body of rules which is consistent with that body governing TRIPS or TRIMS. The promoters of a social dimension in world trade have merely requested that workers within each member country of the WTO should be able to exercise the democratic freedom to associate, and with like-minded persons to bargain collectively for their welfare as workers; they demand an environment where all persons are treated equally; they require that children should be allowed sound education and training before entering the labour market; and they demand that prisoners be protected from exploitation of their labour.

4   The future

Surely it ought to be possible for each nation of the world to use these as governing principles, in the same way that they should all be committed to an environment which gives sustenance to today's generation while at the same time assures the well being of future ones. And no doubt this would happen if there were not the constant fear that the great opportunity which global trade offers all businesses might in fact become the occasion for the demise of the uncompetitive. George Soros is no doubt aware of what he is saying when he declaims 'business is motivated by profit; it is not designed to safeguard universal principles'.

What has been set down above have been some of these matters which are noted by civil society as examples of actions and stances taken by governments, not prompted by any altruistic plan for animals, plants or people, but rather driven by their fear that the offering they make to big business may one day be inadequate to prevent that business from exploiting a source of higher profit margins. Civic society is made to see governments as institutions working with big business rather than treating with business on the behalf of the broader masses. Clearly, such a picture does not properly reflect the massive effort that is made by most governments to be the protector of and provider for all sections of the society. The question then has to be: 'Where has it all gone wrong?' and 'How can it be redressed?'

Something has to be done to arrest the gap which continues to widen between the rich and the poor. The rhetoric that shows that the gross domestic product (GDP) of a country has increased must be re-examined in the light of the realities on the ground. The GDP, after all, is merely a means of camouflaging the truth; for the practice of adding the income of the wealthy with that of the poor and the marginalized to find the level of national wealth is a mere exercise for deception. The WTO and its colleagues within the global financial environment need to find a different formula for measuring a country's economic growth. They need to satisfy the disenchanted, the frustrated, the impatient and the opportunistic that they are to be relied upon.

In an effort to win this confidence international institutions like the WTO will have to re-visit their mandates. They have to build into their action programmes different operational activities, which will involve the trade union movement as well as other NGOs, rather than to continue to reflect the picture of being representatives of big business.

During the World Economic Forum held in New York in January–February 2002, many businessmen from this very elitist club were heard to express their concerns at the plight of the 'marginalized' and the 'excluded'; some went as far as a specific expression of the clear demand for democracy to become the underpinning of every society; and others were blunt enough to state that what is necessary is for a body of labour standards to become part of the rules of engagement. According to them, if there are no rules then the sprint for the competitive advantage will forever disregard the human factor.

The unbridled pursuit of self-interest leads most communities to plan for countervailing forces in parliaments; it leads to there being a legal requirement in many countries that an accused, however poor, must be given protection by the legal system even where the allegation is that a vicious crime has been committed against society. One could go on. The seekers after a better global society will not go away. Their protests will become greater and greater and will take on different forms. This will happen sooner rather than later unless some meaningful attempts are made to reach those who are genuinely seeking solutions.

3

China's entry into the WTO and its impact on the global economic system

KOICHI HAMADA

See the waters of the Yellow River leap down from Heaven,
Roll away to the deep sea and never turn again![1]

At the Yellow-Crane pagoda, where we stopped to bid adieu,
The mists and flowers of April seemed to wish good speed to you.
At the Emerald Isle, your lessening sail had vanished from my eye,
And left me with the River, rolling onward to the sky.[2]

1 Introduction

China was one of the cradles of human civilization; it has been the centre of Asian civilization for thousands of years. It is an immense country, as the two poems by Li Po (Li Bai) quoted above illustrate. The first poem refers to the Huang He (the Yellow River) and the second to the Chang Jiang (the Yangtze River). Chinese culture is ubiquitous in Asia, whether in terms of art, written characters, classical literature and, of course, food. The entrepreneurship of the overseas Chinese has made them successful

I am much indebted to Ambassador Koichi Haraguchi (Japanese Embassy in Geneva) and Ms Nozomi Sagara (Research Institute of Economy, Trade and Industry) for their careful reading and for many valuable comments. I thank also Mr Hidenori Murakami (Ministry of Agriculture), Ms Megumi Sagara (Keio University) and Mr Masakazu Sato (Japanese Embassy in Beijing) for their discussions, and to Mr Eric Gower, Ms Carolyn Beaudin and the editor of this volume for their advice on stylistic improvements. Also, I wish to thank many economists in Beijing who helped me draft this chapter by frankly answering my questions in interviews. The remaining errors are strictly mine, and the opinions expressed in this chapter are by no means those of the Japanese Government.

[1] Li Po, 'The Feast of Life', in *Gems of Chinese Verse*, trans. W. J. B. Fletcher, Shanghai, Commercial Press, 1918.
[2] Li Po, 'Gone', in *Select Chinese Verses*, trans. Herbert A. Giles and Arthur Waley, Shanghai, Commercial Press, 1935.

wherever they have settled. Thus as it enters the WTO, China must be viewed in the context of Heaven (time), Earth (space) and Man (human organization).

First, China's entry into the WTO marks a unique epoch. Until the nineteenth century, Asian history could be regarded as revolving around China. But the Second World War and the socialist revolution interrupted the full participation of China in the world trading system. In December 2001, more than fifty years after the end of the war, and following fifteen years of patient negotiations, China entered the WTO as a full-fledged member. Taiwan, too, as a separate custom territory, has entered the WTO after a lengthy wait. China's full return to the world economic community as an eminent member will mark a new era in world history.

Second, China's massive size makes it a force to reckon with. Its two great rivers flow through a vast landscape of about 9.6 million square kilometres. Its population of approximately 1.25 billion people is five times as large as that of the USA and about ten times that of Japan's. Its sheer size alone will have a significant impact on the WTO and its member nations.

On the one hand, this grand scale means that China's domestic development may take time and encounter various problems of regional coordination. On the other hand, the international implications are tremendous. If China were to attain a level of economic development similar to the level enjoyed today by developed countries, it would have a profound impact on global prices and terms of trade. It is possible to imagine factor prices in other countries being driven to levels that prevail in China. China is a rare example of a *large* country case in the theory of international trade.

As far as the temporal dimension is concerned, while China's growth is slowing, official statistics indicate that growth is still above 7 per cent.[3] If this pace continues, China's GDP may well surpass that of Japan within twenty years (Kwan, 2001).

Finally, the world must recognize the human aspect of China's entry into the community of trading nations. It is at this historical junction that China is expected to modernize its institutions, markets and legal system. The key questions are whether China has the time and the capacity to manage this profound change in its domestic institutions.

This chapter asks first how entry into the WTO will change China's economy and society. It then considers how the accession of China will

---

[3] Rawski (2001), however, casts doubt on the accuracy of China's GDP statistics.

affect the workings of the WTO. The chapter also attempts to describe the nature of China's entry into the WTO and to explore desirable roles for China and the WTO (and its members) that will enhance the synergy of China's entry.

Section 2 describes the events that led to China's entry into the WTO and the process of trade liberalization that is taking place with its entry. Section 3 briefly summarizes the recent literature on the implications of China's entry into the WTO. Section 4 considers the impact of accession on China itself. Can China overcome the impediments to liberalization? Can WTO membership hasten the structural adjustment of the Chinese economy? Section 5 discusses the effect of China's entry to the world economy, touching on issues such as the 'hollowing out' of neighbouring countries, impacts on the current account and the role of exchange rates. Finally, section 6 asks what impacts China's entry into the WTO will have on the WTO itself. Section 7 briefly concludes.

2   A historical sketch of the negotiation process

China started negotiations on membership in the GATT (the predecessor of the WTO) in 1986, aiming to be an important member of the international economic community. The negotiating process was coming to an end when it was interrupted by the Tiananmen Square incident in 1989.

After the GATT was reorganized as the WTO in 1995, China continued its attempts to enter. China was about to become a member when, in May 1999, the accidental bombing of the Chinese embassy by the USA delayed the process again. As Long Yong Tu[4] has described, the entire negotiation process was frustrating for the Chinese negotiators.

All of these efforts eventually led to China's entry into the WTO. Even prior to its accession, China's progress in reducing tariff rates had already been substantial and well documented.[5] The average tariff rate was 40 per cent during the early 1990s and this was reduced to about 15 per cent before entry into the WTO. Today (2002) it is 12 per cent, and China plans to reduce it further to 10 per cent by 2005. Existing NTBs as well as agricultural quotas will be lifted, and the legal system in China will be reformed to fulfil WTO requirements.

---

[4] In any case, it is astonishing that he expressed such a frank view on the internet. See Research Institute for Economics, Trade and Industry (RIETI) website (in Japanese), at www. rieti.go.jp/users/china-tr/jp/011217world.htm.

[5] For example, see OECD (2002).

Why is China so eager to enter the WTO, despite the many anticipated hurdles to transforming its domestic economy to fulfil WTO requirements? In a speech in 2002, Sun Zhenyu, China's Ambassador to the WTO, explained China's intention in acceding to the WTO:

> China's accession to WTO fully demonstrated the determination of the Chinese Government to further reform and opening up. China, as a responsible member, shall abide by the WTO rules. It has been doing its best to implement its commitment, made during its accession process.

> China takes its membership in the WTO very seriously, since it will in the long run further promote China's reform and opening process, attract more foreign investment and benefit its long-term economic growth.[6]

The Chinese Government thus recognizes that WTO entry is an indispensable step for China to become a full citizen in the world economy, and that, without the benefits of freer trade, China's future economic development will become increasingly difficult. China seems to be using WTO entry to overcome the resistance of domestic interest groups, emphasizing the transforming effects of its entry rather than the immediate loss of tariff revenues or the erosion of the protection extended to specific domestic industries.

3   A brief sketch of the literature

There is already an extensive literature on the implications of China's entry into the WTO. The main themes or ideas in this literature are summarized below.

Though he fully recognizes the potential difficulties arising from the accession to the WTO, Justin Yifu Lin (2001) presents a hopeful picture of the prospects of the Chinese economy after entry into the WTO. According to Lin, entry creates big hurdles for various sectors of China to overcome. But it is these very hurdles, Lin says, that will enable China to restructure its problematic sectors, especially agriculture, SOEs and banking.

Supachai Panitchpakdi and Mark Clifford (2002) take a measured view of the potential difficulties China faces as well as the potential benefits it may reap as the result of joining the WTO. Moreover, they emphasize the benefits that the WTO and the whole world will obtain when China successfully fulfils its WTO commitments.

---

[6] Zhenyu (2002).

Yamazawa and Imai (2001) shed some light on the impact of WTO accession on different sectors of China's economy. They predict that the pattern of China's trade will be more reflective of its comparative advantage. Some subsectors in agriculture will be net exporting sectors, but others will lose their competitiveness.

Though Alwyn Young (2000) does not directly address the problems that will face China as a result of WTO accession, his study casts doubt on the more optimistic assessments offered by other analysts. He is concerned with the lack of efficiency in the allocation of investment in the Chinese economy, which is governed less by market forces than by 'socialist' dictates. He is also concerned that regulation and the resulting rent-seeking activities may increase price differentials between regions rather than decrease them during the process of reform.

Thomas Rawski (2001) questions the remarkable growth of China's GDP. He notes some important inconsistencies in the Chinese data. For example, while the officially stated GDP grew by 24.7 per cent between 1997 and 2000, energy consumption actually *decreased* by 12.8 per cent. According to China's official statistics, output increased in all but one province, despite floods in 1997 and 1998. Rawski detects other discrepancies, and suggests much lower growth rates: a maximum of 4 per cent for 2001 and considerably less for preceding years. However, as many other suggest, this downward correction is at least partly offset by the fact that the 'underground' or 'informal' economy should be added to the national income accounts.

The OECD (2002) presents a well-organized and extensive study of China's various sectors, and of its many problems. Its view is that:

> [T]he accession of China to the World Trade Organization (WTO) marks an important milestone along the reform path China has been following for more than twenty years, rather than a new direction. China has been liberalizing its international trade and investment policies since the mid-1980s and is now as open as some present WTO members. Although China stands to gain significantly from opening its export markets under the terms of its accession, the depth and breadth of its commitments to liberalize access to its domestic economy are acknowledged to be more extensive than those agreed to by previous adherents to the WTO. This willingness reflects the fact that opening to international markets promotes market discipline, access to technology, and other qualities that have been important goals of domestic economic reforms. In this respect, WTO entry is a complementary aspect of the next phase of China's reforms.

4   How is China affected by its entry to the WTO?

Liberalization of trade will place a heavy burden on China's less-efficient sectors. Easier access into the Chinese market by foreign investors will also intensify competition. Many point out that agriculture, SOEs and banking will be affected critically by China's entry to the WTO and the resulting liberalization of trade and investment.

Agriculture

China's agriculture faces complex problems. One problem is to reorganize the structure of domestic production to cope with the inflow of agricultural imports; the other is to seek outlets in the world market for those products where China has a comparative advantage, although it will take time for Chinese agriculture to realize its genuine comparative advantage (Bhattasali and Kawai, 2002).[7]

Despite the large size of the agrarian sector, China is not necessarily an agricultural exporter. The shortage of water seems to be a major factor constraining agricultural production in the Northern area. China is self-sufficient in grain when the crop is good. Soybeans are, however, a major import item of China, and the amount imported is about to exceed the size of domestic production. Some in China are afraid that eventually a large proportion of soybean production may be displaced by imports, mainly coming from the USA.[8]

The agricultural problem is also an unemployment problem. China is a classic example of the unlimited supply of labour as modelled by Arthur Lewis. The economy has to find ways to accommodate the surplus labour from the rural sector as the potentially redundant labour is released from the agricultural sector. Moreover, income inequality between the rural and urban sectors may become more acute.

The incentive mechanism should be improved and unnecessary government intervention should be removed (Feng Lu, 2001). Excess production of grain should be adjusted. As it seeks to find its niche in agricultural

---

[7] For a Japanese observer, it may seem unfair to comment on a neighbour after Japan's half-century's slow progress in the liberalization of rice. Here, the degree of protection is high and very visible. Many advanced countries are, however, subject to a similar censure with respect to agriculture because they protect agriculture implicitly by various means, including direct and indirect subsidies.

[8] Vegetables like scallions, which were in fact introduced and produced by the Japanese, once triggered a safeguard measure by the Japanese government and attracted international attention.

export markets, China is concerned with the effects of subsidies in developed countries. Accordingly, as Sun Zhenyu argues:

> New measures should be taken to remove or reduce the vast amount of export subsidies and domestic support provided by the developed members. Only rich countries can afford such huge amount of supports and subsidies, which have greatly undermined the ability of developing countries to compete with them in the world market.

SOEs

While the development of China has been rapid, we should not forget that China is a transition economy. Most SOEs should be rationalized and transformed to market-oriented private enterprises. There will be political resistance to the transformation process because the status quo is beneficial to individuals who are collecting the rents generated by regulation.

China's entry into the WTO may create more difficulties for SOEs and make the transition harder. Liberalization will test the efficiency of Chinese enterprises. But the Chinese government seems intent on utilizing this shock to facilitate the necessary changes. 'Nothing ventured, nothing gained', seems to summarize their attitude. Or, as Lin (2001) puts it: 'the survivors are those who are forced to go all out fighting against the death-trap [Sunzi, *The Book of War*]'.

The banking sector

The banking sector is also a major source of problems. It is intended to channel funds to projects promoted by government planners rather than to the most profitable. Accordingly, a non-performing loan problem has emerged. To transform the system into one that channels funds by market signals, the OECD (2002) argues that the 'lead bank' or 'main bank' system may be useful.

In addition, monetary policy in China is difficult to separate from government expenditure policies, given the need to provide financing for various projects. A more independent monetary policy is necessary to cope with the deflationary pressures now occurring in China.

These sectors are only a few examples among many that may face potential problems. In many other sectors, China faces the challenge of capacity building. The WTO's Doha Declaration has emphasized capacity building and WTO members have set aside a substantial sum of money (CHF 30 million) for the Doha Global Trust Fund to help build capacity in developing countries. As Sun Zhenyu emphasizes, China is eager to accept offers of capacity building. Already, a large number of seminars and consultations have been conducted in China. This seems to be one of those areas where the interests of developed and developing countries coincide.

To put China's entry into the WTO in a historical perspective, it may be of interest to recall how Japan entered into the GATT provisionally in 1953. Japan was admitted as a provisional member (without voting rights) because it could not reduce its tariff rates to the rate required by the GATT.[9] It was not until 1955 that Japan became a full member of the GATT.[10] Japan gained its full citizenship in the international community in 1963 by changing its status to that of an Article VIII country in the IMF and to an Article XI country in the GATT.

During those ten years, Japanese industries developed with remarkable speed. Japan became a major exporter of industrial products such as electrical appliances and automobiles. Coincidentally, the Tokyo Olympics were held in 1964, and China will host the Olympics in 2008. Here again, we find an analogy between Japan in 1953 and China in 1992.

The similarity stops there, however. On the optimistic side, China has already developed many sophisticated and technologically advanced products and industries unimaginable in Japan during the 1960s. The fact that it is a transition country may facilitate the shift in industrial structure because the government plans the reform to a certain extent. On the more pessimistic side, as (former) Minister Taichi Sakaiya of the Japanese government argues, time is running out more rapidly for China now than it did for Japan in the 1950s. First, the need for environmental protection is keener for China than for Japan, whose pollution problems became serious after the middle of the 1960s. China also needs to moderate its population growth. The single-child policy may still be beneficial now because it limits the (otherwise) infinite supply of labour, but the Chinese economy will soon be confronted by a rapidly aging population and will need to support a very large 'greying' generation.

5 The impact of China's entry on neighbouring countries

Neighbouring nations are concerned with the effects of China's entry into the WTO and the resulting trade impacts. For example, the inflow of

---

[9] Japan's tariff reduction was technically difficult because its major partner, the USA, did not engage in tariff reduction negotiation owing to its internal political situation.

[10] Many countries, however, appealed to GATT, Article XXXV and gave unfavourable treatment to Japan for about ten years.

inexpensive textiles from China creates difficulties for Japanese farmers. (Ironically, some of them are made by Japanese producers with the aid of Japanese technological know-how, and accordingly not 'import' in its ordinary sense.) Japanese direct investment to China releases workers in Japan by utilizing inexpensive labour in China. Thus, many people argue, Japanese industries are being 'hollowed out' by the emergence of this huge trade competitor. A similar process also seems to be affecting the ASEAN members, Taiwan and South Korea.

What do various versions of trade theory tell us about the effect of a further liberalization of China on the rest of the world? By 'various versions' of trade theory I mean the Ricardian labour-value theory generalized by Dornbusch, Fisher and Samuelson (1977), the Heckscher–Ohlin theory of comparative advantage through differences in factor endowments, and the Lancaster–Dixit–Krugman theory in the framework of monopolistic competition. What are the consequences of trading with a very large country like China?

Seldom is a large country case studied. Most medium-sized countries are small countries relative to a developed China. In general, the expansion of production opportunities in China benefits surrounding countries as long as the terms of trade do not turn against those countries.

The first lesson, then – definitely according to the first two types of theory and most likely according to the last type as well – is the lesson on the levels of factor prices. Trade theory predicts that the differences in factor prices, such as real wages and the rate of return to capital, will tend to narrow among trading countries. If technology is identical between countries and transportation costs can be neglected, then there may be a complete equalization of factor prices. Thus, if China adopts free trade and if Chinese technology is similar to Japanese technology, then real wages and rates of returns on capital will be equated. Moreover, since China is a very large country, factor prices will be closer to the initial Chinese level than to the initial levels in Singapore or Japan.

The assumption of the same technology among countries is clearly unrealistic. But direct investment will work toward equalizing technological levels; it will just not do so completely. Accordingly, wage rates will not converge completely.[11]

---

[11] Consider a hypothetical world with identical technology brought on by a perfect dissemination of technological knowledge between countries. The resulting wages correspond to the new technology and will be similar to that of the advanced countries. But the wages of advanced countries workers may still go down, because factor proportions can remain different between these countries unless factor movements are completely free and costless.

Compare, for example, real wages in Hong Kong and China. In 1999, the *per capita* income of Hong Kong was US$23,200; that in China was $790. Even in terms of the purchasing power parity (PPP) base comparison, Hong Kong's *per capita* income was $20,900 while China's real income was about $3,300. China's *per capita* income, adjusted for price levels, then, was about one-sixth that of Hong Kong and a little more than one-eighth that of Japan ($24,000).

Hong Kong and China are, relatively speaking, most closely related in foreign trade, investment and possibly in migration. This shows that, even in Hong Kong, real wages and real *per capita* income are not equal to those in China. The fear that Japan's wages will fall to the level in China is thus not warranted in the short run; if it happens at all, it won't be for a very long time. We see, though, that the economic growth rates of Hong Kong, Japan and Taiwan are slowing down. Therefore, there is some tendency for international convergence in the levels of real income.

The problem is that factor price movements and the resulting movement of workers between sectors are not sufficiently smooth. The rigidity of nominal and real wages among China's trading partners create unemployment and the 'hollowing out' problem. In China, the rigidities will aggravate unemployment problems. A call for more flexible management of the exchange rate may come from both China and foreign countries. It will then be easier for countries to adjust macroeconomic policies to deal with inflationary as well as deflationary situations.

Thus, most of the 'hollowing out' problem which accompanies the adjustment process is short- and medium-term in nature. One long-run consequence of this is that a country may not be able to develop new technologies if a substantial part of production moves out of the country because direct investment is attracted by inexpensive labour abroad. If no externalities exist, this argument does not hold because firms are free to choose where they intend to develop new skills and technologies. Only when externalities exist due to agglomeration effects and network information facilities can one argue about the long-term effects of 'hollowing out'.

The second lesson concerns welfare gains or losses from trade to the rest of the world. When a new trading nation (say China) emerges, or when a new nation increases her ability to trade, or when technical progress occurs in the nation, will the rest of the world gain or lose? This is a separate question from the first question above. In general, the welfare of countries in the rest of the world depends on how the terms of trade for these countries are affected. Increased participation in trade and technical progress in China will typically improve the terms of trade of other countries. The basic exception is the case that Harry Johnson (1958) called 'anti-trade biased technical progress'. If a new entrant has a comparative advantage in the product that a neighbouring country used to export, then the terms of trade may turn against the neighbouring country. Suppose a country's main export is caviar and it imports all other things from abroad. If a newcomer to the system is also an exporter of caviar and it has comparative advantage relative to the incumbent country, then the incumbent will definitely lose. The existence of many countries may give rise to other cases of immiserized partners (cf. Bhagwati, 1958 and also Yano, 1983). But, in any case the possibility is rather limited. One can safely assume that China's entry into the WTO and accompanying expansion of its trade will definitely increase the welfare of the countries in the rest of the world unless the entry of China reduces the flow of trade compared to the time before its entry.

The calibration results by Abe and Urata (2002) indicate that gainers from the entry of China to the WTO include China itself, Hong Kong, Taiwan, South Korea, Singapore, Vietnam, Australia and Japan and that losers include Peru, Mexico, Thailand, Indonesia and the Philippines. Though one should be cautious about these numerical results, they are consistent with the theoretical prediction mentioned above.

Similarly, productivity increases in China as a result of technical progress and the mobilization of its labour will benefit the world community, as long as it is not anti-trade biased. The immiserizing effect on other countries will not occur because China's major export items are not completely identical with the major export items of surrounding countries. This is also consistent with the result in the generalized Ricardian trade model (Dornbusch, Fischer and Samuelson, 1977) that the technical progress of a trading partner in those goods that are competing most closely with the home country matters the most in determining the relative wages between the countries, which is equal to the relative income in this model with a single factor of production.

6   China's entry and the role of the WTO

Let us now consider the impact of China's entry to the WTO. Before going into the main topic, I would like to correct a possible misunderstanding: that the rules prevailing in the developed economies are always desirable for the world community. The mechanical extension of the existing rules may not only hurt the welfare of developing countries but also the welfare of the world as a whole (see also chapter 2 in this volume).

First, the economic logic used to justify anti-dumping and safeguard actions is often unjustified even from the point of view of mainstream economics.[12] The idea is that since competition generally achieves the Pareto optimum, one should make the most of the free market and correct it only whenever there are externalities or incomplete information.

The case for anti-dumping is generally justified only when dumping is predatory in the sense that it drives out existing international rivals so that high prices can be charged later. Otherwise, the partner of a country that practices dumping should be pleased rather than offended to be supplied with less-expensive imports than would otherwise be the case. The safeguard clause is justified only when the adjustment process is too costly for the nation that is suddenly flooded by inexpensive exports.[13] Thus, for these two issues, what is needed is to apply more precisely what neo-classical economics tells us. For the detailed economic analysis, see Willig (1998) and Deardorff (1993). See also Jackson (1997) for the legal implication of the economic analysis.

I now will develop in more detail two cases in which the straightforward application of market logic to the international situation may lead to some misleading results.

The first topic is intellectual property rights (IPRs). Standard theory tells us that one should protect IPRs to encourage innovation and creative activities. Protection of IPRs will achieve an efficient intertemporal allocation of resources. However, there are cases (such as in the case of HIV) where the public will lose if an already invented medication is not made widely available because of the strict observance of IPRs. It is necessary to take into account the public-good aspects of invention, in the sense that inventions that are good for society should be widely disseminated. This benefit from the dissemination of ideas and their products should be weighed against the loss of incentives for innovation.

The basic conflict between the long-term incentives for innovation and the benefits from the use of the product already invented is this: there

---

[12] One might call it the 'Washington Consensus'.

[13] One could argue that if the adjustment process is already anticipated, then firms will choose the optimal adjustment speed, and that there is no need to allow for safeguard measures by government action. In a broader perspective that encompasses the negotiation process to liberalize trade before actual trade takes place, it may be argued, though, that the presence of safeguard rescues may facilitate the successful completion of negotiations. For the insurance function of the safeguard arrangement, refer to Jackson (1997).

must be some balance between the strict enforcement of IPRs that the 'Washington Consensus' may prefer to emphasize and the need for public dissemination of the idea.

In fact, scholars find a rather uniform message. Too-strict protection of IPRs may be desirable for the developed countries (the North), but the unlimited use of IPRs should often be restricted, both for the welfare of the developing countries (the South) and for the benefit of the world. Chin and Grossman (1990) find that the developing world cannot enjoy the fruit of IPR protection until it passes a certain stage of development. Deardorff (1991) finds that the desirable length of patent protection differs for the North and the South. Grossman and Lai (2001) extend the analysis to a strategic game between the North and the South, obtaining similar results. Exhaustion of patents should be allowed and parallel imports should not be unduly restricted.[14]

Needless to say, I am not arguing that CDs and books should be sold without the payment of royalties or that the production of fake brand-name goods should be allowed. This is just to indicate that, in some cases, one has to strike a balance between incentive protection and dissemination of already invented knowledge. Fortunately, we can see some signs of reconciliation. Sun Zhenyu (2002) expresses his commitment to the rules of the TRIPs in the following way:

> [China] has adopted effective measures to strengthen further the protection of IPRs. It has amended and improved its trademark law, copyright law, [and] patent law, which provide high level of protection of IPRs. Since China joined WTO, it has put more emphasis on the enforcement of these laws. For example, last year China confiscated and destroyed 95 million pieces of pirated CDs and the courts punished those serious offenders by up to 7 years imprisonment.

In addition, the Doha Declaration on the TRIPs Agreement and public health announces that 'the TRIPs agreement should not prevent members from taking measures to protect public health', and 'the agreement should be implemented – in a manner supportive of WTO members' right to protect public health and to promote access to medicines for all'.

One can see in other areas the conflict between the standard neo-classical consensus view and a kind of developmentalism – the policy scheme that the Ministry of International Trade and Industry (MITI, now called the Ministry of Economy, Trade and Industry) used to pursue

---

[14] The WTO leaves the question of exhaustion outside its Agreement.

(Murakami, 1998). One example is the case of special economic zones (SEZs). In standard economics, any differentiation in tax rates in a country is seen to exert distorting effects on incentives. Export processing zones (EPZs) that give some favourable tax treatment are thus considered to conflict with the efficient working of a neutral tax system. Moreover, the reduction of tax revenues is undesirable for the tax authorities. This device can be welfare-deteriorating under a high rate of protective tariff (cf. Hamada, 1974), but the incentive effect of export processing may work for the benefit of the country. Where externalities exist, the gain from conglomeration effect is large, and the political pressure against trade liberalization is strong, the SEZ can be an extremely attractive idea to trigger growth in the country.

China indeed exploited this scheme for the development of its coastal area, starting with such forerunners as Shenzhen, Zhuhai, Shantou and Xiamen after 1979; many followed during the 1980s. Later, the specific economic zone became one of the basic themes of Deng Xiaoping's Nuxun 'Southern Tour' speech in 1992. To trigger growth in the presence of information externalities and when the total liberalization of trade is difficult to realize because of political resistance, he searched for a development strategy that would introduce foreign capital (and its tax advantages) into the zone and to make the zone a showcase of foreign technology.

SEZs are well known in Asia, particularly in China. The zones have been utilized very effectively to exploit the benefits of conglomeration, industrial externalities, information dissemination and the introduction of new technology. It is a delicate legal question whether the wide use of this scheme conform to the MFN principle, the principles of national treatment, the restriction of performance requirements under the Trade-Related Investment Measures (TRIMS), and finally the prohibition of export subsidies under the Agreement on Subsidies and Countervailing Measures (SCM).[15] Eventually, China's deregulation and liberalization must apply to all its citizens and territory; they must apply equally to foreign as well as domestic nationals.

There is concern about the special tax treatment of exports in special zones because SEZs may reduce tax revenues. Some people have suggested that, from now on, the building of infrastructure will probably become

---

[15] See also however, Article 27 for the waivers for developing nations. China is, however, treated as an advanced country member and has to abide by the rules in this respect. It is often announced that China is willing to keep open the existing specific zones that have contributed tremendously to the development of costal areas, but that she will build no new specific zones.

more important than favourable treatment of foreigners in terms of taxation. Infrastructure includes a comfortable living environment, schools, and community services that will make lives of the families of employees and employers more comfortable.

Here again we find some tension between a successful instrument for development – that is, the establishment of SEZs or EPZs – and the more traditional economic principle of avoiding tax distortions within a country. Uniform taxation is a desirable characteristic of a modern national economy, but one had better keep alive the golden goose that was instrumental in promoting development along the southeast coast.

Space does not permit a discussion of other issues such as environmental protection and labour standards, but it is important to enforce those standards that are needed to ensure a minimal level of human existence for the next generation and to take international action to combat transboundary pollution. There may be many cases, however, where imposing a uniform environmental or labour standard is counter-productive to the welfare of the world. In the case of labour standards, the WTO could explore an appropriate division of roles with the ILO.

Let us return from these somewhat academic discussions to the question of what the WTO can do. First, technical assistance will help. The International Monetary Fund (IMF), for example, is encouraging the Chinese government to go forward to budgetary reform. For that purpose, it provides such technical assistance as preparing uniform social security numbers to prevent tax evasion and to reduce corruption and announcing the budgetary status of the government. It is another matter whether these reforms will be carried out fully in both local governments and the central government. But this kind of technical help is very useful.

The OECD (2002) also conducted extensive studies on how different sectors in China will be affected by its entrance into the WTO. This will provide a good frame of reference for the administrators in China who will need to cope with the impacts. In sum, the WTO should not refrain from providing China with all kinds of technical information and guidance on tariffs, NTBs, IPRs and other matters related to trade and investment.

The WTO is expected to be a good vehicle of communication between developing and developed countries. The entry of China will add another perspective to the discussion in the WTO. Already, the Dispute Settlement Body (DSB) is overwhelmed with a large number of cases. Therefore, more informal (as opposed to formal) procedures should be used to improve the dispute settlement mechanism. Otherwise, the dispute settlement process may be overwhelmed. Western legal formalities could be combined or reconciled with more informal style of negotiation, which one may dare to call the 'Asian style'.

Some are concerned with the question of how much China or Chinese businesses honour promises.[16] We often hear of the concern that China will not honour its legal commitments. Until the transition to the market economy, the will of the government was practically the law in socialist China. Now, particularly after entry into the WTO, international disputes are to be resolved by international law, and legal statutes are to be prepared in conformity with international law.

Though there may be worries from abroad over China keeping its promises, China will be motivated to honour its commitments since its future reputation is at stake. Through this motivation, the WTO can be instrumental in introducing international standards to the domestic economy and in realizing the reform that is crucial to China's further development. This optimistic scenario will make self-fulfilling the initial intention of China to exploit its entry into the WTO as a device to restructure the economy. The downside risk is that China may have difficulty in fulfilling the commitments, and consequently political and social tensions may arise.

If China were to fail to keep its international promises, difficulties would emerge. Unemployment would rise and international investors would suffer. Even now, despite the official statistic that the unemployment rate is less than 4 per cent, actual urban unemployment is said to be above 7 per cent. In the agriculture sector, there could be as many as 150 million people who are in a state of underemployment. Disorder in China's economy would seriously affect both the WTO and the international community.

The idea of the two-level game is extremely useful in understanding the present situation of negotiations between China and other countries (Putnam, 1988; Barfield, 2001; see also Ostry, 2002). Putnam argues that international negotiations are almost always accompanied by some political conflicts inside each country. The premise for successful international negotiations is that each country ends up in a position better than the one it started from (the principle of individual (national) rationality, as a theorist would say). Putnam claims that, for national participation in an agreement, each involved group within each country should be happier than with the status quo in order to vote for the incumbent that is

---

[16] In the socialist regime, the will of the government or the will of administrators could have well been the law in practice.

represented in diplomatic negotiations; therefore, at least, the majority of group members should be happier. Otherwise, the negotiating government cannot win the next election. Such outcomes of negotiations to warrant re-election is sometimes called the 'win–win set', which is only a limited part of the contract curve.

In terms of this two-level game terminology, China courageously assumed that its entry to the WTO with a different grace period would satisfy her constituents and that the negotiation result would stay within the win–win set on the contract curve. If the negotiation results are already within the national consensus, all would benefit. If not, the Chinese government has a formidable task. The Chinese government is gambling on the possibility that each interest group will become more moderate because it may put the objective of honouring international obligations ahead of its own group objectives. Domestic group politics defines the negotiation results. Conversely, it is hoped that international negotiations and international commitments may in turn change the domestic political structure.

7   Concluding remarks

Since China understands the possible problems she faces in conforming to the requirements of the WTO, and since she is willing to take that risk, the WTO does not need to emphasize the possible difficulties in the process. Certainly, this is not the time to preach to China how to cope with these difficulties, the Chinese people know them all too well. And because of the political as well as technical obstacles to resolving these difficulties, they have appealed to this rather bold commitment to honour international promises. In this chapter I have not pursued the question of what China can do for the WTO. Rather, we should be asking what the WTO can do for the smooth integration of China into the multilateral trading system.

To achieve an orderly adjustment process in China, we must constructively push China into delivering on its promises, but not too strongly.[17] It may be summed up as follows: 'Put pressure on China and encourage restructuring so that it can deliver on its promises. Never give up on pressuring China to follow the basic tenets of international law, but be

---

[17] Again, Sunzi, *The Art of War*, says: 'Do not drive the enemy into a corner', because then the enemy becomes desperate and becomes recklessly strong. 'You should provide even an escape route for him'. By no means should China be compared to an enemy! But many agree that the above principle can equally be applied to collaboration between friends.

flexible in forcing China to honour the rules and allow it to make minor adjustments by considering its initial conditions and culture'.

Socialist measures may be useful in directly or indirectly enforcing the provisions of WTO Agreements. This is the positive side. On the other hand, inexperience with the market economy may make it difficult to persuade the Chinese people of the merits of adopting WTO-consistent laws that facilitate the working of the market. The international community must be flexible and forward-looking in dealing with China and view its progress with both care and sympathy.

Considering the nature of the international rules, such as IPRs and SEZs, discussed in the last section, the existing rules may not be perfect. I think that the WTO and member countries will be benefited by the entry of China because it will add a new perspective to existing trade rules and to the function of the WTO itself.

In my opinion, the entry of China will enrich multilateral interactions in the WTO. Other countries will have more voices to listen to. The world community may now regard the entry of China as if it were a tail of the dragon that is the WTO. When China grows to become one of the leading economies in the world, China will no longer be just the tail; it may well develop into the very heart of the dragon.

Bibliography

Abe, K. and S. Urata (eds.), 2002. *China's Entry to the WTO and the Future of Trade among Japan, China and Korea*, Tokyo, Nihon-Keizai-Hyoron-Sya

Barfield, C. E., 2001. *Free Trade, Sovereignty, Democracy: The Future of the World Trade Organization*, Washington, DC, AEI Press

Bhagwati, J., 1958. 'Immiserizing Growth: A Geometrical Note', *Review of Economic Studies*, 25, pp. 201–5

2002. *Free Trade Today*, Princeton, Princeton University Press

Bhagwati, J. and T. N. Srinivasan, 1983. *Lectures on International Trade*, Cambridge, MA, MIT Press

Bhattasali, D. and M. Kawai, 2002. 'Implications of China's Accession to the World Trade Organization', in H. G. Hilpert and R. Haak (eds.), *Japan and China*, New Yorks, Palgrave

Chin, J. and G. M. Grossman, 1990. 'Intellectual Property Rights and North–South Trade', in R. W. Jones and A. O. Krueger (eds.), *The Political Economy of International Trade*, Cambridge, MA, Basil Blackwell

Deardorff, A. V., 1991. 'Welfare Effects of Global Patent Protection', *Economica*, 59

1993. 'Economic Perspectives on Antidumping Law', Chapter 6 in R. M. Stern (ed.), *The Multilateral Trading System*, Michigan, University of Michigan Press

Dornbusch, R., S. Fischer and P. A. Samuelson, 1977. 'Comparative Advantage, Trade and Payments in a Ricardian Model with a Continuum of Goods', *American Economic Review*, 67, pp. 823–39

Grossman, G. M. and E. Lai, 2001. 'International Protection of Intellectual Property', Princeton University Working Paper

Hamada, K., 1974. 'An Economic Analysis of the Duty-Free Zone', *Journal of International Economics*, 4

Ichimura, S., 2002. 'On the Difficulties that China Faces', Tokyo

Jackson, J. H., 1997. *The World Trading System*, Cambridge, MA, MIT Press, rev. edn.

Johnson, H. G., 1958. *International Trade and Economic Growth, Studies in Pure Theory*, London, George Allen & Unwin

Krueger, A. O. (ed.), 1998. *The WTO as an International Organization*, Chicago, University of Chicago Press

Krugman, P. R. and M. Obstfeld, 1991. *International Economics*, New York, HarperCollins, 2nd edn.

Kwan, Chi Hung, 2001. 'Chugoku Kyoi Ron ni Igi ari' (The Objection to the "Chinese Threat" Argument)', *Ni-Chu Kei-Kyo Journal (Sino-Japanese Economic Relationship Journal)*,

Lin, Justin Yifu, 2001. 'WTO Accession and China's SOE Reform', Chapter 2 in K. T. Lee, J. Y. Lin and S. J. Kim (eds.), *China's Integration with the World Economy: Repercussions of China's Accession to the WTO*, Seoul, Korea Institute for International Economic Policy

Lu, Feng, 2001. 'China's WTO Accession: Impact on its Agricultural Sector and Grain Policy', Chapter 7 in Kyung Tae Lee, Justin Yifu Lin and Si Jung Kim (eds.), *China's Integration with the World Economy: Repercussions of China's Accession to the WTO*, Seoul, Korea Institute for International Economic Policy

Murakami, Y., 1998. 'Anticlassical Political-Economic Analysis', Stanford, Stanford University Press

OECD, 2002. 'China in the World Economy: The Domestic Policy Challenges', *Synthesis Report*, Paris, OECD

Ostry, S., 2002. *The Trade Policy-Making Process, Level One of the Two Level Game: Country Studies in the Western Hemisphere*, IDB-Intal Occasional Paper, 13, Buenos Aires, 2002

Panitchpakdi, S. and M. L. Clifford, 2002. *China and the WTO: Changing China, Changing World Trade*, New York, John Wiley

Putnam, R., 1988. 'Diplomacy and Domestic Politics: The Logic of Two-Level Games', *International Organization*, 42, pp. 427–60

Rawski, T. G., 2001. 'What's Happening to China's GDP Statistics?', *China Economic Review*,

Willig, R. D., 1998. 'Economic effects of Antidumping Policy', in Robert Z. Lawrence (ed.), *Brookings Trade Forum 1998*, Washington, DC, Brookings Institution Press

Yamazawa, I. and Ken-ichi Imai, 2001. *China Enters WTO: Pursuing Symbiosis with the Global Economy*, Institute of Developing Economies, Japan External Trade Organization

Yano, M., 1983. 'Welfare Aspects of the Transfer Problem', *Journal of International Economics*, 15

Young, A., 2000. 'The Razor's Edge: Distortions and Incremental Reform in the People's Republic of China', *Quarterly Journal of Economics*, November

Zhenyu, Sun, 2002. 'Statement by Ambassador, at WTO Symposium', 29 April

4

Key challenges facing the WTO

ROBERT E. BALDWIN

1 Introduction

As the broadening in the scope of its rules and recent rapid rise in membership demonstrate, the World Trade Organization (WTO) arguably has become the most successful international organization dealing with economic relations among nations. This success has, however, been accompanied by an increase in strains within the WTO and in outside pressures that challenge the long-run viability of the institution. This chapter briefly examines the nature of the major challenges that have arisen and discusses various proposals for successfully meeting them, including actions agreed upon at the November 2001 Ministerial Conference in Qatar launching the Doha Development Round.

The discussion focuses on six issues confronting the WTO that require attention by its members to ensure the continued effectiveness of the institution. They are:

1. The *work 'overload'* on WTO members and the WTO Secretariat brought about by the significant increase in recent years in the number and technical complexity of matters on which WTO rules have been negotiated and are currently being proposed
2. The deep dissatisfaction of the developing countries over the *balance of gains and adjustment costs* between developing and developed countries in recent rounds of multilateral negotiations, especially the Uruguay Round
3. The impact of recent WTO rules on *domestic economic and social conditions* that traditionally have been influenced mainly through domestic political decision-making processes
4. The claim that dispute settlement panels and the Appellate Body are *exceeding the authority granted them* under the new dispute settlement

rules adopted in the Uruguay Round and, in effect, are legislating through their interpretations of WTO rules

5. The strongly held differences in viewpoints, especially between some developed and most developing countries, concerning the desirability of *extending WTO Rules* to cover such topics as environmental issues, international investment, labour conditions and competition policy

6. *Pressures from NGOs* that range from increasing the transparency of the WTO decision-making process and providing a greater role for NGOs in this process to transforming the WTO from an organization primarily concerned with trade liberalization to one whose goals also include the promotion of various human rights, the protection of the environment and the alleviation of poverty.

Since a number of the issues cited above are interrelated and some of the actions planned or proposed for dealing with them are relevant to more than just one of the issues, the nature of each issue is first explained in more detail in sections 2–6. Section 7 discusses those parts of the work programme agreed upon at the Doha Ministerial Conference that are aimed at successfully dealing with the challenges associated with the various issues, while section 8 sets out the author's views concerning these and other proposals for achieving this goal.

2 The overload issue

Participating in periodic rounds of multilateral negotiations and han-dling day-to-day matters arising under the GATT were much simpler tasks for GATT members in the early days of the organization than is the case under the WTO. Far fewer countries were involved in the rounds of negotiations and in settling ongoing trade disputes than today. For example, the number of countries signing the original GATT that took effect on 1 January 1948 was twenty-three compared to 144 countries that were WTO members in early 2002. Moreover, the five multilateral negotiations from 1947 through the Dillon Round in 1960–1 focused only on reducing tariffs and, even in this area, a principle followed was that 'the developed countries cannot expect to receive reciprocity from the less-developed countries'.[1] Negotiations aimed at reducing non-tariff barriers to trade (NTBs) did take place in the Kennedy Round from 1962 to

---

[1] See Preeg (1970, p. 297).

1967, but the accomplishments in this area were very modest.[2] However, the successful negotiations on non-tariff measures in the Tokyo Round (1973–9) significantly raised the level and depth of expertise required to negotiate and monitor new GATT agreements successfully. Detailed 'codes of behaviour' were negotiated on such non-tariff issues as subsidies and countervailing measures, anti-dumping measures, government procurement policies, customs valuation procedures and technical barriers to trade. Various committees were established within the organization both to monitor compliance with the new rules and settle disputes arising among members on these matters.

The Uruguay Round (1986–92) resulted in an even greater increase in the scope and complexity of trading rules. The extensions were significant enough to change the name of the GATT to the WTO. Among the accomplishments of the Uruguay Round was the negotiation of a General Agreement on Trade in Services (GATS) establishing rules covering not just cross-border trade in services but services supplied by foreign firms within a country to consumers in that country. Another major extension of rules was an agreement on intellectual property rights (IPRs) requiring members to provide copyright, trademark and patent protection to foreign holders of these rights and to establish domestic civil and criminal procedures for enforcing this protection. Rules aimed at eliminating discriminatory trading requirements against foreign investors were also introduced. Other major changes were requiring members to accept all the agreements negotiated during this and earlier rounds (with the main exception of those covering government procurement policies), rather than pick and choose among the various agreements, and reforming the dispute settlement mechanism in a manner that greatly strengthened the enforcement process for WTO Rules.

The Tokyo and Uruguay Rounds transformed the WTO from an organization concerned mainly with reducing import duties and preventing these reductions from being offset by various non-tariff measures to an institution with the goal of reducing a broad variety of (mostly) governmental measures that distort trade among nations from the patterns

---

[2] For example, the USA agreed to abolish the American selling price system that protected benzenoid chemicals by valuing them for duty assessment purposes at the domestic value of comparable products rather than their imported value. The US Congress rejected a uniform anti-dumping code negotiated during this Round. Many countries also successfully used GATT, Article XII, which permits restrictions in the quantity or value of merchandise imports to safeguard their external financial positions and their balance of payments, to continue or increase quantitative restrictions on imports.

produced by free competitive markets. In doing so, it significantly increased the workload and level of expertise required by governments to promote and defend their economic interests in an effective manner. This has been particularly burdensome for small and less developed countries whose governments find that they do not possess sufficient resources to promote and protect their national interests adequately in the broadened WTO.

In most other international economic organizations, smaller nations can rely on the technical experts within the organization itself to supply useful information and relevant studies for making informed decisions about matters of concern. However, because the initial purpose of the GATT was simply to carry out temporarily the commercial policy role assigned to the much broader International Trade Organization (ITO) being negotiated at the time, it did not include a formal, well-designed organizational structure. Thus, when the ITO was not accepted by the United States Congress, the GATT began with a very small, low-budget Secretariat whose role was mainly to provide the housekeeping services required for the meetings associated with the organization's various ongoing committees and its periodic multilateral negotiations. The burden of providing the analysis needed to make informed judgements on substantive issues coming before the delegates fell very much on the countries themselves. Thus, the GATT began as very much of a 'member-driven' organization. Moreover, the remarkable success of the early members in transforming an organization designed to last only three years into an institution that was able not only to extend the tariff cuts made initially but to achieve significant further reductions in import duties among the major trading nations over the years strengthened the view of members that they did not need a large bureaucracy of support staff nor a chief executive with considerable decision-making powers. This view is still widely held today and exacerbates the problem of meeting the increased information needs of members as the scope of the WTO has expanded.[3]

3 The dissatisfaction of the developing countries with the current WTO system

Not only are the developing countries among those members who find it most difficult to handle the increased and more complex workload

[3] See Blackhurst (1998) for a more detailed discussion of the limited capacity of the WTO to carry out its various mandates.

associated with the extension of WTO Rules into new economic areas but, more fundamentally, many of these countries are questioning whether their benefits from the new WTO Rules introduced in the Tokyo and Uruguay Rounds exceed the economic and social costs involved in imple- menting these rule changes (see also chapter 2 and 3 in this volume).[4] They point, for example, to the substantial gains by the developed countries in the markets of developing countries from the new agreements on IPRs, trade in service and trade-related investment policies TRIPS, while not- ing that establishing facilities in developed countries to provide services in these countries or seeking the protection of newly created intellectual property are not major economic activities on their part. However, the trade in services and TRIPS Agreements have involved such consequences in their own countries as substantial governmental implementation costs, higher prices to consumers for such important products as medicines, a weakening of governments' abilities to preserve traditional cultural activ- ities and job displacements for substantial numbers of workers.

In signing the Uruguay Round Agreements, the developing countries contend that they were led to believe that the Agreements on Textiles and Clothing (ATC) and on agriculture would result in market access benefits for the developing countries comparable to the gains to the de- veloped countries from the TRIPS Agreements and on services. This has not been the outcome, in their view. For example, unlike the developing countries expected, the developed countries have tended to adhere only to the minimum phrase-out of import quotas required under the ATC over a ten-year period. The developing countries interpret this behaviour as making it likely that the removal of import quotas on 49 per cent of the total volume of imports of these goods will be delayed until the last day of the ten-year period. Even then, developing country exporters will face high tariffs on textiles and clothing. The limited extent that agricultural markets have been opened in markets such as the EU and Japan since the Uruguay Round Agreement on Agriculture has been another major source of disappointment to the developing countries, as well as to developed countries who are significant exporters of agricultural products. Further- more, despite new Uruguay Round Agreements covering anti-dumping and countervailing duty measures that they thought would reduce the use of these measures for purely protectionist purposes, the developing

---

[4] Excellent sources that indicate the various concerns of the developing countries over the WTO system are the Doha Ministerial Declaration itself and the Doha decision on implementation-related issues and concerns. These are available at the WTO website, www.wto.org.

countries find themselves facing an increased number of anti-dumping and countervailing duty actions on the part of the developed countries that they regard as being based on protectionism rather than unfair trading practices on their part.

If a significant number of developing countries conclude that the WTO system is not providing net benefits, the consequences could be very damaging to the achievement of the WTO's basic goals. One obvious outcome is the use by these countries of the consensus voting practice to block not only any actions on the so-called 'new issues' but liberalization efforts in traditional negotiating areas unless substantive provisions are included that aim at rectifying the imbalances in trading benefits and costs perceived by the developing countries. We also know from past experience that, in the absence of periodic trade liberalizing multilateral negotiations, the ever-present pressures from protectionists tend to erode the trade liberalizing gains already achieved.

In addition, an even greater increase in the use of regional trading agreements to achieve countries' trading goals than has taken place in recent years is likely to occur. Industrial nations, such as the USA and the members of the EU, have found that the attraction of trade-diverting market access gains can induce the smaller developing nations to accept provisions in regional agreements on such matters as labour standards and the environment that these countries reject in multilateral trade negotiations. Thus, the developed countries are very likely to move toward the greater use of regional agreements to achieve their trading objectives if gridlock takes place in the WTO. At the same time, the larger developing countries are likely to seek more regional agreements among themselves and with the smaller developing countries. The economic inefficiencies and political tensions resulting from the many different levels of trade barriers and trade-related rules among countries could seriously undermine the remarkable accomplishments under the GATT and the WTO in both eliminating discrimination among nations in trade practices and in continuing to liberalize world trade.[5]

4   Domestic economic and social consequences of new WTO rules

In successfully negotiating international rules aimed at reducing the trade-distorting effects of various non-tariff measures, the WTO has introduced

[5] See Bhagwati (2000) for a discussion of the dangers to the WTO system that are associated with regionalism, and also for insightful discussions of most of the other challenges to the WTO system covered in this chapter.

new rules and procedures that significantly affect economic and social matters of concern to various domestic interest groups who did not fully recognize their consequences and were not necessarily consulted in this international decision-making process.[6] In the view of these groups, a non-elective international organization composed largely of representatives from foreign countries is making decisions significantly affecting domestic economic and social conditions that should properly be handled through domestic political decision-making processes.

An early US example of this problem arose in obtaining the required congressional approval for the non-tariff results of the Tokyo Round of negotiations to take effect. In considering the set of negotiated agreements, members of the House Subcommittee on Small Business found that some minority citizens operating small businesses might lose their government procurement contracts as a consequence of the commitments made by the US government under the Tokyo Round code aimed at eliminating discrimination against foreign suppliers in government purchases of non-military goods. When expressions of concern about this possible outcome spread to other members of congress and threatened to derail approval of the entire sets of agreements, the Carter Administration quickly renegotiated the government procurement code so that it did not apply 'to set-asides on behalf of small and minority businesses'. The cost of this was an equivalent withdrawal of liberalizing procurement concessions by other countries.

It is significant that the charges of improper interference into countries' domestic affairs on the part of the WTO is coming not just from those directly affected economically or socially by the new rules but from broad groups of citizens deeply concerned about such matters as improving the welfare of lower-income and socially disadvantaged families within their countries, maintaining traditional ways of life, preserving national sovereignty and protecting the environment. In their view, the current structure of rule-making in the WTO unduly favours the economic interests of large corporations and foreign direct investors at the cost of weakening the traditional equity-oriented domestic economic and social programmes of their governments.

The new WTO Agreements on trade in services and Trade-Related Investment Measures (TRIMS) cover areas where such conflicts can easily arise. For example, permitting foreign-owned firms to supply services

---

[6] The best-known detailed study of the unfavourable domestic economic and social consequences of globalization is Rodrik (1997).

freely to domestic consumers from large-scale facilities within the country can displace many small local businesses, such as the US 'mom and pop' retail stores that many people think are important for maintaining socially stable local neighbourhoods. Or, opening up most sectors to foreign direct investment (FDI) can eliminate domestic programmes aimed at giving desirable preferential treatment to certain social groups.

5   Legislating through the new dispute settlement system

Charges of sovereignty-threatening influence over domestic economic and social conditions have also arisen as a consequence of the Uruguay Round modifications in the dispute settlement process.[7] To an important extent, these changes were a consequence of the expansion of WTO rule-making in the area of non-tariff trade measures that took place in the Tokyo Round and were being proposed in the Uruguay Round. New rules in new areas led to more disputes, as might be expected. Moreover, as is characteristic of bodies that establish their rules on the basis of consensus, the new rules were often somewhat vague and open to different interpretations.

Consensus among members was also required under the old system for approval of the findings by dispute settlement panels. This enabled a member who had been determined to be in violation of its GATT obligations by a dispute settlement panel to block adoption of the panel's report. This practice, together with the greater number of disputes being brought before such panels, caused a number of countries, especially the USA, to become increasingly dissatisfied with the nature of the then-existing dispute settlement system and to urge reform of the process as part of the Uruguay Round of negotiations. One of the outcomes of the changes implemented in that Round is that panel reports are now automatically adopted unless there is a consensus for *not* doing so. In addition, an Appellate Body was established that decides members' appeals from the panels' decisions.

These changes have significantly altered the manner in which disputes are settled. Under the old system, even if not formally adopted, the report of a panel still put considerable informal pressure on members to conform to the panel's findings. This encouraged negotiations among affected members to reach a mutually acceptable solution rather than following the route of seeking the imposition of sanctions against an offending

[7] An important study of this issue is Barfield (2001).

member. Now, however, the winner of a case typically demands that the loser fully comply with the findings of the panel and promptly proceeds to the sanctions-imposing stage if the country does not do so.

An awareness of their greater responsibilities for settling disputes also seems to have made panels, along with the Appellate Body, more willing to make clear-cut interpretations of the existing rules rather than saying that some are simply too vague to reach any definite judgements in a case. This has led to charges that they are, in effect, legislating rather than abiding by the language of the Dispute Settlement Understanding (DSU) that 'the panel and Appellate Body cannot add or diminish the rights and obligations provided in the covered agreement'. (Article 19.1, DSU).

In the well-known tuna/dolphin case, a dispute settlement panel upheld the contention by Mexico that US restrictions on the importation of tuna caught in nets that did not prevent dolphins from also being caught violated GATT, Article III, which required non-discrimination between domestic and foreign products. Mexico contended that the traditional interpretation of Article III should be upheld, namely that 'like products' (tuna, in this case) must not be distinguished because of the process by which they are produced. However, in a subsequent case concerning catching shrimp in nets that do not have a special device to protect sea turtles from also being caught, the Appellate Body implied that such restrictions were permissible under the exceptions to WTO Rules permitted under Article XX as being 'necessary to protect human, animal or plant life or health', provided they were not applied in an obviously discriminatory fashion among foreign suppliers.

The uproar from environmentalists that followed the tuna/dolphin decision led to widespread attacks on the WTO, not only from this group and various human and animal rights interest groups but from those concerned with the WTO assuming a legislative role that they believe should be the responsibility of domestic institutions directly responsible to the people through the voting process.

6   The 'new issues'

A number of countries have urged over the years that the WTO rule-making authority be extended to include trade-related investment, environmental, competition and labour rights issues. Several actions have already been taken on these matters. One of the agreements reached in the Uruguay Round, for example, deals with TRIMS and provides that no member shall apply any investment measure that is inconsistent with the national treatment provisions of GATT, Article III, nor with the provisions set out in Article XI prohibiting quantitative restrictions (QRs). An ongoing Committee on Trade-Related Investment Measures, open to all members, was also established under the Agreement. Article VIII of the GATS, which was also negotiated in the Uruguay Round and which extends WTO Rules from just trade in goods to trade in services, aims to prevent monopolistic behaviour on the part of service suppliers. However, the Ministerial Declaration launching the Doha Development Round in January 2002 stated that further negotiations on both investment and competition policies would take place after the Doha Round only 'on the basis of a decision to be taken, by explicit consensus, . . . on modalities of negotiations'.

There is currently no WTO Agreement dealing exclusively with trade and the environment. A Committee on Trade and Environment was established in 1994 at the Marrakesh Ministerial Meeting approving the various agreements reached during the Uruguay Round, but little progress has been made in the committee in recommending specific rules relating to the environment. However, at the Ministerial Meeting in November 2001, WTO members agreed to limited negotiations in the Doha Round on the relationship between existing WTO Rules and specific trade obligations set out in existing multilateral environmental agreements.

At the Marrakesh ministerial meeting the USA pressed for the creation of a committee on trade and labour standards, but this effort was rejected, with particularly strong opposition coming from the developing countries. A similar effort by the USA at the Singapore Ministerial Conference in 1996 also failed. In the Declaration emerging from this conference, ministers renewed their commitment 'to the observance of internationally recognized core labor standards' but also stated that 'the International Labor Organization (ILO) is the competent body to set and deal with these standards'. The Doha Ministerial Declaration explicitly reaffirmed this position.

Opposition to the negotiation of more detailed WTO Rules covering the 'new issues' is based on several concerns. One is simply the fear that the new rules will be used for market-protecting rather than market-opening purposes. The strong resistance on the part of the developing countries to the introduction of labour standards in the WTO is based on this concern. As the political leaders of these countries are fully aware, the relatively large (and thus relatively inexpensive) supplies of unskilled labour in developing countries is the basis of their comparative advantage in producing and exporting goods that for technological reasons intensively use relatively large numbers of unskilled workers, such as textile and apparel products. They believe that some developed countries, whose textile and apparel industries are currently facing stiff competition from textile and apparel products imported from the developing countries, seek to establish WTO labour standards more stringent than those already in place in the developing countries as a means of reducing imports of these products. The developing countries are similarly apprehensive about environmental rules that can be enforced by imposing sanctions against countries found to be in non-compliance. In their view, the developed countries were able to establish strong export positions in many industrial markets without having to adhere to strict environmental standards, and now these countries want to slow down the developing countries from doing the same by introducing costly environmental requirements.

Many groups within both developed and developing countries fear that additional WTO Rules in the 'new issues' area will undermine desirable domestic social and redistributive policies already in place. The further opening of domestic markets to foreigners by means of new rules on foreign investment or through an agreement covering competition policy may, for example, invalidate existing domestic laws providing special economic benefits to disadvantaged social groups or promoting other desirable social and environmental objectives. A third reason for the reluctance of many developing countries to negotiate in such areas as competition and environmental policies is their lack of the expertise required to evaluate carefully the implications of such policies on their own economies. They also point to the scarcity of such studies undertaken by the staffs of the various international economic organizations. Their experience in the Uruguay Round has been particularly important in shaping their views on this matter. They found that they had not appreciated fully either the implementation difficulties or the effects on their economic and social welfare of such agreements as that covering IPRs at the time they signed these agreements.

7   Pressures for change from NGOs

With recent agreements extending the reach of WTO rules into the domestic economy, tensions between the WTO and a wide range of NGOs have increased as a consequence of the very different agenda being pursued by the WTO and the NGOs. As the preamble to the text of the WTO (as well as the original GATT) states, the main activity of the parties to WTO is 'entering into mutually advantageous arrangements directed to the substantial reduction of tariffs and other barriers to trade and to the elimination of discriminatory treatment in international trade relations'. These arrangements are aimed at contributing to the objectives of raising living standards, ensuring full employment and expanding the production and trade in goods and services, 'while allowing for the optimal use of the world's resources in accordance with the objective of sustainable development and seeking both to protect and preserve the environment'. The WTO preamble also recognizes the 'need for positive efforts designed to ensure that developing countries, and especially the least developed among them, secure a share in the growth of international markets commensurate with the needs of their economic development'.

Most NGOs do not so much disagree with these general objectives as with the omission of certain other goals and with the relative efforts that in practice are devoted to the different goals set out. Many NGOs are, for example, very much concerned with the economic and social conditions faced by particular groups within both developed and developing countries – for example, the poor, women, children and minority ethnic groups. The reduction of tariffs and other trade barriers may, they argue, contribute to economic efficiency on a national level but, too often, ends up worsening economic and social conditions for the poorest and most disadvantaged domestic groups. The argument by economists and other free-market proponents that these conditions are best addressed through separate government redistribution measures is regarded as politically unrealistic, if not disingenuous. Thus, in the view of these NGOs, the WTO should ensure that trade liberalization does not harm these groups and should even support restrictive trade policies needed to help them. Many NGOs would also make the objective of sustainable development the key goal of the WTO and use trade policy as a tool to promote the protection and preservation of the environment.

An immediate concern of NGOs is a lack of transparency in the WTO decision-making process and its insufficient responsiveness to the views of important sectors of civil society. According to critics holding this view, international bureaucrats with little direct accountability to civil society are making decisions significantly affecting the economic and social well being of large parts of the population and sometimes arbitrarily overturning domestic policies that NGOs have worked for years to put in place. The 1993 tuna/dolphin case, discussed earlier, is the example most frequently cited by the NGOs of inappropriate interference by the WTO into countries' domestic affairs.

NGOs are demanding at a minimum that meetings of WTO dispute settlement panels and the Appellate Body be open to the public at the stage at which the various parties present their cases. In addition, they want the right to submit *amicus* briefs, even if they are not solicited by the panels or the Appellate Body. They are also critical of the manner by which decisions are reached during regular WTO meetings and during the periodic multilateral rounds of negotiations. Basically, they want to be much better informed on just what is being considered in these meetings and negotiations and have an opportunity to provide input into the rule-making process.

Since their protests at the Ministerial Meeting in Seattle in 1999, the NGOs have been very successful in getting the attention of the general public to what they regard as serious deficiencies in WTO Rules and decision-making processes. Initially, the protesters tended to be dismissed as anarchists or selfish protectionist groups more interested in destroying the WTO rather than reforming it and in advancing their own short-term economic interests. Gradually, however, environmentalists and various human rights groups, who approve of the basic objectives of the WTO but wish to modify these goals, have come to the forefront and garnered considerable public support for a WTO that is more transparent and gives greater consideration to the impact of trade and investment policies on the environment, the distribution of income and social and human rights conditions generally.

8 Meeting the challenges

The Doha Development Agenda

Ministers were well aware of the issues discussed in the preceding sections and their implications for the future viability of the WTO at the outset of the fourth WTO Ministerial Conference in Doha in November 2001. Fortunately, they were able to agree on a Work Program that addressed many aspects of the challenges raised by these issues. They focused, in particular, on addressing the concerns of the developing countries detailed earlier in the chapter; Ministers agreed to make technical cooperation and capacity building core elements of the development dimension of the multilateral trading system, for example. Moreover, this Declaration was followed within a month of the Doha Conference by the adoption of a new WTO budget that increased technical assistance funds by 80 per cent and established a Doha Development Agenda Global Trust fund with a proposed core budget of about 9 million dollars. Ministers also approved some fifty decisions clarifying the implementation obligations of the developing countries and agreed to make negotiations on other outstanding implementation issues an integral part of the work programmes.

Other parts of the Work Agenda directed at the particular concerns of the developing countries include: (a) agreeing to negotiate on the WTO's anti-dumping and subsidies rules with the aim of clarifying and improving disciplines under these rules and taking into account the needs of developing and least-developed participants; (b) establishing a Working Group to examine the relationship between trade and the transfer of technology and make possible recommendations to increase flows of technology to developing countries; (c) establishing a Working Group to examine the relationship between trade, debt and finance and enhance the capacity of the multilateral trading system to contribute to a solution to the problem of external indebtedness of developing and least-developed countries; (e) reviewing all special and differential treatment (SDT) provisions with a view to strengthening them; (f) committing to the objective of duty free, quota free market access for products originating in the least-developed countries; and (g) agreeing to negotiate to reduce tariffs, including the reduction or elimination of tariff peaks, high tariffs and tariffs escalation, as well as NTBs on products of export interest to developing countries. Another major accomplishment of interest to many developing as well as developed country exporters of agricultural products was committing to comprehensive negotiations in the agricultural sector aimed at 'substantial improvements in market access; reductions of, with a view to phasing out, all forms of export subsidies'; and substantial reductions in trade-distorting domestic support.

Establishing a deadline of May 2003 for the DSB to reach agreement on improvements and clarifications of the DSU reached in the Uruguay Round represents a positive response to the concerns of many governments and NGOs over the present dispute settlement system. Moreover, including the statement 'that under WTO Rules no country should be prevented from taking measures for the protection of human, animal or plant life or health, or of the environment at the levels it considers appropriate' and adopting a separate declaration on public health permitting countries the right to grant compulsory licences for medicines on the grounds they determine appropriate should be welcomed by those concerned both about panels and the Appellate Body in effect legislating in rendering their decisions, and about the unfavourable social effects of the Uruguay Round TRIPS Agreement. The views of those concerned in general about the domestic implications of expanding the scope of the WTO were also taken into consideration, with the decisions to delay negotiations on trade-related foreign investment, on the interaction between trade and competition policy, on transparency in government procurement and on trade facilitation until after the next Ministerial Conference in 2003 and, then, only on the basis of a decision taken by explicit consensus.

Implementing the Doha Agenda and more

The Doha Agenda consists for the most part of commitments either to undertake negotiations on various topics or conduct examinations and reviews of these topics with the possibility of recommending negotiations. While the breadth of the issues placed on the agenda represents a major accomplishment, especially for the developing countries, the crux of the negotiations involves reaching agreements that all members are willing to sign and that ensure the long-term viability of the WTO by successfully meeting the challenges raised in the introductory section. This part of the chapter discusses specific actions for achieving these goals.

The overload problem

The significant increase in funding for WTO technical assistance and training activities, together with the reorganization of the WTO Secretariat to better meet the Development Agenda of the new trade Round, are important steps in easing the overload problem faced by many developing countries. But, as WTO Director General Mike Moore and others have stressed, these steps alone are not enough. There must be much more substantial and coordinated efforts to provide technical assistance on the part of both the major international economic agencies and NGOs interested in promoting better economic and social conditions in the poor countries. The WTO will never be able by itself to raise sufficient funds to provide the types of training and research programmes necessary to make many developing countries fully informed and capable partners in the WTO system. Only the international financial organizations (IFIs) such as the World Bank, the regional development banks, and the IMF together with private foundations and various advocacy NGOs have the funds and expertise needed to accomplish this task. Moreover, the developing countries themselves must devote more resources toward providing educational and research opportunities for their nationals to gain the knowledge necessary for their countries to participate meaningfully in the globalization process.

Dissatisfaction of the developing countries with the WTO

Technical assistance and training efforts by the WTO and other institutions, together with the various other provisions in the Doha Declaration directed at promoting growth in the developing countries, will also be helpful in overcoming the deep dissatisfaction of the developing countries with certain aspects of the WTO system. However, the key for success in meeting this challenge is providing significant improvements in the access of these countries to the markets of the developed nations. Textiles and clothing are of special importance, since it is clear that many developing countries could quickly and significantly increase their exports of these products if the quantitative restrictions and high tariffs of the developed countries were appreciably reduced. While members reaffirmed their commitment 'to full and faithful implementation of the Agreement on Textiles' in adopting the Declaration on implementation-related issues and concerns at Doha, the likely removal of import quotas on about half of the total volume of imports of these goods only at the end of 2005, and the lack of serious planning in the developed countries for the adjustment problems the industry will face at that time, suggests that many developed countries will utilize the special 'transitional safeguard' provisions in the ATC. This could delay the elimination of import quotas for up to three more years. Even then, the misuse (as in the recent US action on steel imports) of the traditional safeguard measures of the WTO could continue to deprive the developing countries of meaningful access to the world textiles and clothing markets. The same concerns apply to the liberalization commitments made by the developed countries with regard to agricultural products. Domestic political pressures seem to be resulting in more, rather than less, subsidies in this sector.

Significant and comprehensive reductions in tariffs on the part of developed countries is another essential element for providing increased market access for the products of the developing countries. Besides seeking a deep average cut in import duties, negotiators must focus, in particular, on reducing tariff peaks (such as exit for textiles and clothing) and correcting the current pattern of tariff escalation that retards industrial growth in developing countries by imposing progressively higher tariffs as the production of goods proceeds from the raw material to final processing stage.

Market access is, of course, a two-way relationship. The political economy of the international bargaining process over trade policy is such that the developed countries expect greater access to the markets of the developing countries in return for greater openness of their own markets. A crucial issue members will face in undertaking the review called for in the Doha Agenda of all SDT provisions in WTO agreements is just how quickly developing countries should be expected to open their markets under existing and new agreements. Presumably, all countries support the view that every WTO Agreement should be in the long-run interests of every member. But we know that this need not hold in the short term. Some WTO Rules constrain members from gaining in the short term at the expense of other members, on the grounds that such actions are likely to lead to retaliatory actions that produce a long-run outcome in which all lose. However, owing to the lack of the appropriate economic and social institutional framework, there can also be some liberalizing agreements that result in significant adjustment burdens for some countries longer than the current five- or ten-year maximum adjustment periods given to developing and least-developed countries to adhere to WTO Agreements. The serious concerns raised by many developing and least-developing countries about the inadequacy of the time periods for implementing some of the Uruguay Round, e.g. the TRIPS Agreement and the GATS, are indications of the existence of such situations. Frustration and disillusionment with the WTO system on the part of both developing and developed countries has been the result.

One way of dealing with this problem is for members to refrain from trying to negotiate trade agreements that are likely to impose significant adjustment costs on some members for time periods than can turn into decades rather than just five or ten years. Alternatively, more precise SDT rules could be put in place that recognize the possibility of such long-term adjustment costs and exempt these members from the rules for longer time periods than are typical under current practices. The exemption for these countries would be contingent upon agreeing to take measures to put in place the adjustment measures and establish the institutional framework needed to produce net long-run benefits from the rules. It would seem necessary, however, to permit other members to bring actions under the dispute settlement process at periodic intervals to determine if the countries had indeed carried out their part of the exemption agreements.

The more extensive domestic impact of WTO agreements

WTO agreements have always significantly affected some domestic groups. When agreements mainly involved tariff reductions, these groups were mostly the employees and owners of firms in the industries in which domestic or foreign tariffs were reduced. The impact on the welfare of an individual consumer was generally not significant. To deal with the adjustment problems faced by employees and owners, WTO members have adopted such policies as gradually phasing-in duty cuts over a period of time, reducing tariffs in some industries less than the average or not at all, and providing various forms of financial and technical assistance to those in the import-competing or export-oriented sectors most affected.

As previously discussed, the agreements on non-tariff issues reached in the Tokyo and Uruguay Rounds considerably enlarged the domestic reach of WTO Rules. At the same time, environmentalists and human rights groups have been successful in obtaining domestic legislation that promote their goals but that also sometimes has important trade policy implications. Unfortunately, both trade negotiators and the private interest groups too often do not fully appreciate the conflicting nature of each other's policy actions. As a consequence, both groups are sometimes frustrated by each other's actions. This has led to sharp condemnations of the policies of some public-interest groups by trade policy officials and vigorous protests by various NGOs against the WTO and calls for radical changes in, or even the complete elimination of, the organization.

The solution to easing the tensions between these two groups would seem to be quite straightforward. Each group must become more fully aware of the implications on its own objectives of the policies that those in the other group are pursuing. Among the many ways this can be accomplished are by including NGOs on the various trade policy advisory boards consisting of individuals from the private sector that many governments establish to receive inputs and provide information about current government trade policy activities, making sure that the WTO, national governments and the NGOs have staff members who are knowledgeable about each other's policy positions, holding more conferences and briefings bringing together NGOs and government officials from different countries and working to make the entire WTO process more open and transparent. Domestic political processes must then be used by both NGOs newly concerned about trade policy and the more traditional private-sector groups affected by trade policy actions to influence the specific trade policies that governments pursue. In a member-driven organization such as the WTO, this will, in turn, enable those NGOs who have felt left out of the decision-making process to help shape the decisions reached in the WTO.

The dispute settlement process

Thus far, complaints by WTO members that dispute settlement panels and the Appellate Body are sometimes making new WTO Rules rather than simply interpreting existing ones have not been widespread but, instead, mostly confined to a relative small number of issues. Moreover, the instances where widespread concerns have been expressed seem to have been resolved fairly easily through normal WTO procedures. For example, the Doha Ministerial Declaration explicitly states that 'no country should be prevented from taking measures for the protection of human, animal or plant life or health, or of the environment at the levels it considers appropriate' subject to such measures not being applied in a discriminatory manner nor being disguised forms of protectionism. Similarly, the Declaration on the TRIPS Agreement and Public Health, adopted by consensus at Doha, should satisfy the those concerned about dispute settlement decisions infringing on 'WTO Members' right to protect public health and, in particular, to promote access to medicines for all'. However, we should expect and encourage more guidance being given to panels and the Appellate Body by greater use of the WTO Rule permitting interpretations of any multilateral trade agreement to be adopted by a majority of three-quarters of WTO members.

Labour standards and other 'new issues'

The reaffirmation in Doha of the decision taken in Singapore in 1996 that the ILO is the 'competent' body to deal with core labour standards was disappointing for some industrial countries.[8] As a minimum, they had wanted to establish a WTO Working Group to investigate the implications of including labour standards as a part of WTO Rules. However, the developing countries strongly opposed even this proposal. To better understand their position, it is important to recognize that rules about labour standards are largely about economic fairness rather than economic efficiency. This in itself does not rule out their introduction into the WTO, however, since there are already a number of WTO Rules mainly about fairness. For example, in the labour standards area itself, WTO Rules already permit countries to ban imported goods that are produced by prison labour. Existing rules dealing with trade policies that discriminate among countries or that are directed at dumping by foreign firms

---

[8] The four core labour standards of the ILO are: (i) Elimination of all forms of forced or compulsory labour; (ii) Effective abolition of child labour; (iii) Elimination of discrimination in employment; (iv) Freedom of association and the right to collective bargaining.

or government subsidization of economic activities are also motivated by fairness concerns as well as efficiency considerations.

A key feature of these rules is that all WTO members support the concepts of 'fairness' embodied in them. Consequently, disputes arising over them do not involve challenges to the 'fairness' principle in the Rules but rather to such matters as whether the imported goods were actually produced by prison labour or whether the WTO criteria for determining the existence of injurious dumping or subsidization were fully met. The situation is quite different in the case of core labour standards. Developing countries believe they are not yet at the development stage where it would be 'fair' to permit other members to ban imports produced under labour conditions where all four core labour standards were not met. In their view, a requirement that all these standards be met would not only slow down their economic growth by reducing their exports but also slow down their progress in meeting these standards in the future. They also suspect that the efforts of some industrial countries to bring core labour standards into the WTO are a disguised form of import protection on their part. Moreover, they believe the high costs of enforcing these standards would require the use of scarce domestic resources that could be better used to promote the economic and social welfare of their people in other ways.

Whatever the social or economic merits of the arguments over this issue, a key requirement for the success of an organization such as the WTO, whose rule-making process on issues significantly affecting economic and social conditions within member states does not include inputs from an international legislative body directly responsible to the citizens of the member nations, is that rules must be either reached by consensus or else can be accepted or rejected by individual members. Attempting to force members to accept rules with which they strongly disagree is not only fruitless but endangers the viability of such an organization.

At the present time, greater international efforts to improve working conditions around the world should take place mainly within the framework of the ILO. This organization already has the expertise to provide the sound analysis needed in investigations of alleged unfair labour practices and is widely respected by labour, business and government interests worldwide. There is also an active effort within the ILO to better understand the social implications of globalization and to ensure that workers benefit from this process. This may eventually lead to the adoption of enforcement mechanisms by the ILO that affect WTO Rules and require consideration by WTO members, but it seems best to let the ILO take the lead on the labour issue at this stage.

Other factors seemed to drive the opposition at Doha from the developing countries to immediate negotiations on such 'new' issues as competition and investment policies, or more traditional issues such as transparency in government procurement and trade facilitation, as well as broad negotiations on environmental matters. These countries did not contend that new rules in these areas would actually reduce their economic or social welfare in the short term, but that they were uncertain about these short-term effects and needed more time to study the issues and put in place the infrastructure necessary for them to be welfare-improving. As mentioned earlier, they greatly underestimated the institutional and social costs of implementing the TRIPS Agreement, and do not want to make this miscalculation again.

There is considerable merit to this position, in my view. We need many more in-depth studies of just what the economic and social costs have been on individual countries of the lack of common international rules on competition or investment policies, for example. Such studies were undertaken in advance of efforts to reduce tariffs or establish rules on government subsidies, and they are needed now on the 'new' issues. The type of technical assistance and training efforts by public and private organizations mentioned in discussing easing the 'overload' issue will be crucial for producing such studies and enabling the developing countries to develop negotiating positions that they feel confident will promote their self-interests.

Expanding the role of NGOs in the trade policy decision-making process

As the widening impact of WTO Rules tends to affect more domestic groups who traditionally had been little impacted by these rules, it is quite understandable and proper that these groups should have greater voice in decision-making in the trade policy field. As argued in earlier parts of this section, much of the responsibility for achieving this objective rests with these NGOs through their use of domestic political processes. Using a combination of well-reasoned arguments and political lobbying, they must pressure the governments of WTO members for greater access to the decision-making process on trade policy. Environmental and human rights groups should be able to provide inputs through governmental advisory panels and informal consultations just as business and labour groups are able to do in most countries. They should also pressure the governments of WTO members to instruct their delegates to press for greater openness and transparency in the decision-making process at the WTO level. There seem no sound reasons why the initial stage at which governments present their positions before dispute settlement panel should not be open to the public, for example, or why the Appellate Body should not accept *amicus* briefs if it decides that this will inform their decision-making. Other ways of increasing transparency in decision-making at the national and WTO levels without violating generally accepted legal and legislative standards should also be encouraged.

The bottom line

The WTO is indeed facing internal and external challenges that threaten its long-run viability. However, these challenges can be met successfully, in my view, by utilizing existing WTO mechanisms and Rules for making changes and do not merit the radical reforms advocated by some. The Doha Ministerial Declaration is a good example of how an agenda for making significant changes can be agreed on by members through traditional WTO processes. Carrying through on the promises in this agenda will be much more difficult than setting the agenda, but the record of past trade Rounds provides good reasons to be hopeful also in this regard. In other words, the WTO needs some important fixing, as has been described in this chapter, but this can be accomplished without abandoning the existing basic structure of the organization.

Bibliography

Barfield, C. E., 2001. *Free Trade, Sovereignty, Democracy: The Future of the World Trade Organization*, Washington, DC, AEI Press

Bhagwati, J., 2000. *The Wind of the Hundred Days: How Washington Mismanaged Globalization*, Cambridge, MA, MIT Press

Blackhurst, R., 1998. 'The Capacity of the WTO to Fulfill Its Mandate', in Anne O. Krueger (ed.), *The WTO as an International Organization*, Chicago, University of Chicago Press

Preeg, E. H., 1970. *Traders and Diplomats: An Analysis of the Kennedy Round of Negotiations under the General Agreement on Tariffs and Trade*, Washington, DC, Brookings Institution

Rodrik, D., 1997. *Has Globalization Gone Too Far?*, Washington, DC, Institute for International Economics

5

Development dimensions in multilateral trade negotiations

T. ADEMOLA OYEJIDE

1 Introduction

This chapter sets itself a fairly straightforward set of tasks – i.e. to identify the key development dimensions of multilateral trade negotiations, discuss how they have (or have not) been embedded in the framework of previous negotiations and suggest why and how they could be more effectively integrated into future negotiations. To start with, however, it may be useful to ask a related question: why is there a current concern with integrating development dimensions into the framework of multilateral trade negotiations?

This concern appears to be fuelled by several considerations. One of these reflects institutional ambition. The World Trade Organization (WTO), which is the primary institutional organ of the multilateral trading system, has sought greater inclusiveness and the globalization of its coverage, in terms of membership, as well as the widening of its mandate over an ever-increasing range of trade and trade-related issues. In seeking global membership and a comprehensive mandate, the system makes an implicit commitment that all member countries stand to benefit from the system's market access and rule-making agenda. Yet, in reality, wide gaps continue to exist among developed, developing and least-developed member countries of the system. Hence, it is becoming increasingly crucial that efforts be made to address and ameliorate the marginalization of low-income countries and redress the marked differences in the distribution of the benefits of multilateral trade negotiations.

This consideration is strengthened by the reality on the ground: around 70 per cent of the membership of WTO is made up of low-income countries (defined as those with *per capita* income of US$1,000 or less). This large majority of WTO members has articulated reasons why, in their perception, the multilateral trading system may be aspiring to globalism in name only while it is, in fact, becoming less fair and less relevant to their development concerns. In particular, the system is charged with the following:

- *Leaving intact trade barriers* whose removal could stimulate pro-poor growth in low-income countries
- Supporting a *continually expanding trade agenda* focusing primarily on issues of interest to high-income countries
- Engaging in negotiations on issues that have become *so complex* as to be beyond the capacity of low-income countries to fully understand
- Negotiating multilateral trade and trade-related rules which are, in reality, a mere *codification and harmonization of existing rules* and practices prevalent in high-income countries but which are not necessarily appropriate in low-income countries
- Imposing, through various WTO Agreements, specific trade and trade-related institutions and arrangements reflecting the prevailing environment in high-income countries but whose creation and maintenance involve *costs that are beyond the means of low-income countries.*

In recognition, perhaps, of this negative perception of the WTO, the Doha Ministerial Declaration explicitly recognized that the majority of WTO members are low-income countries and promised that their needs and interests would be placed at the heart of the Doha Work Program and that positive efforts would be made to ensure that they secure a share in the growth of world trade commensurate with the needs of their economic development.

For the low-income countries, poverty alleviation has become the central objective of development strategy. The international community has also embraced poverty reduction as a major policy challenge; it has established the international development target of reducing poverty by half by 2015. On both sides, there is clear recognition of increasing poverty in low-income countries. World Bank estimates (World Bank, 2002) suggest that more than half of the world's people live on less than US$2 per day and that even by 2005, as many as 36% of the population of low-income countries will remain at this level of poverty. The Doha Ministerial Declaration claims that by liberalizing trade, trade negotiations can play a major role in the promotion of economic development and the alleviation of poverty. What remains to be specified are the development dimensions which must be integrated into the framework of trade negotiations as a means of ensuring that these beneficial outcomes are fully realized.

The rest of this paper is structured as follows. Section 2 explores the theoretical and empirical links among trade policy, trade negotiations and economic development. It focuses specifically on the mechanisms through which trade negotiations influence economic growth, bearing in mind the institutional environment and policy complementarities in particular country settings. Section 3 examines the track record of the GATT/WTO framework in promoting development through multilateral trade negotiations. In the process, this section traces the evolution of efforts to integrate various development dimensions into the framework. In section 4, the chapter suggests key elements of development-centred multilateral trade negotiations in the context of the Doha Development Round and beyond. Section 5 concludes.

2 Trade policy, trade negotiations and development

As indicated earlier, sustainable development and poverty alleviation must be seen as the primary goals of economic policy in the low-income countries that are WTO members. Their trade policy initiatives, including their participation in trade negotiations are therefore means to an end which is the achievement of these goals. By extension, and to the extent that the WTO Work Program faithfully reflects the concerns and needs of the large majority of its members, it can be argued that the primary goal of multilateral trade negotiations is to promote sustainable development and poverty alleviation.

This raises several questions, such as whether or not trade negotiations can promote development and poverty alleviation, the channels and mechanisms through which trade negotiations influence development and how to enhance the effectiveness of the links between trade negotiations and development.

Typically, multilateral trade negotiations seek to widen market access by reducing or removing obstacles to trade; in addition, they articulate multilateral trade rules (some of which may also be associated with the creation of new institutions or strengthening of existing ones) aimed at facilitating trade flows. An old view of development suggests that it is focused on increasing the pace of capital accumulation and the efficiency of resource allocation. To the extent that trade negotiations succeed in removing obstacles to trade, they could contribute to the efficiency of resource allocation and thus promote development. But development is not just about greater accumulation of capital and increased efficiency in allocating resources. Stiglitz (2000) argues that while development embraces these two elements, it is a more comprehensive and multidimensional phenomenon: 'development is a transformation of society; a move from old ways of thinking, and old forms of social and economic organization, to new ones.' Within this broader view of development, there are at least two component parts. There is, first, the technical component which is involved with solving the technical economic problems of raising efficiency and resource mobilization. Then there is, second, the institutional component without which the technical problems cannot be efficiently solved. Because institutions are so critical in the development process, lack of appreciable progress in stimulating development in many low-income countries may be ascribable to their neglect.

To the extent that poverty reduction is viewed as the most fundamental of the development objectives of many low-income countries, the most appropriate ways of achieving it constitute the most important challenge to policy-making in these countries. In relation to this challenge, there are several areas of emerging consensus. For instance, it is generally agreed that economic growth is an important contributor to poverty reduction. The evidence in support of this consensus, both theoretical and empirical, appears to be quite robust and widespread. In addition, evidence suggests that when poverty and inequality are reduced, this provides an additional benefit in terms of stimulating stronger economic performance. Hence, poverty reduction is not only a desirable end in itself but also constitutes a means of achieving more growth. But while economic growth is generally associated with poverty alleviation, there is no guarantee that this desirable outcome will always be achieved. In other words, some growth strategies may be more pro-poor than others.

This suggests that the road to economic growth and poverty alleviation can take various forms and, hence, that the most effective strategy for the development of low-income countries is a question which continues to generate debate. Much of this debate implies that development strategies for accelerated growth and poverty alleviation must combine several additional elements with market-oriented policy reforms, including measures for building human capacity for effective participation in an increasingly competitive global economy, building and/or enhancing institutional capacity for reducing transactions costs so as to facilitate trade, investment and resource flows, as well as structural adjustment and export diversification (Sachs, 2001). Market-oriented policy reforms constitute the base of this development strategy. These reforms are typically aimed at generally deregulating markets so that market incentives can stimulate appropriate responses from private economic agents in favour of more efficient mobilization, allocation and utilization of resources.

A key component of economic policy reform focusing on market deregulation involves openness to trade which is, in general, achieved through trade liberalization. As this fosters greater openness to trade, it tends to promote trade. Trade derives its importance for economic growth and development from several sources. First, because it brings the people of a country into closer contact with those of other countries it promotes contacts that may eventually lead to changes in ways of thinking and doing things generally. Second, as a country exports, it begins to understand the nature of the international marketplace, its institutions and norms. The knowledge contributes to an enhancement of the skills required for more effective and profitable participation in the global economy. In addition, increasing exports are important as a means of financing imports. Third, trade is closely linked to growth in low-income countries which must rely on the importation of capital goods required for increasing their investment. Since imported capital goods tend to be significantly cheaper than those produced at home, liberal import policy in favour of these goods tends to reduce their costs and hence enhance investment and growth.

In spite of these theoretical mechanisms linking trade with economic growth, the relationship between trade policy and growth in practice remains a hotly debated question. An important reason for this debate relates to a question of public policy; i.e. how to design and implement trade policy in such a way that its benefits for economic growth and poverty alleviation can be maximized while the associated costs are minimized. One reason why the relationship between trade liberalization and economic growth may not be unambiguous is that the relationship may be dependent on several country and external characteristics; when these are conducive, trade liberalization promotes growth; when they are not the link becomes less effective and straightforward.

This contingent nature of the relationship is probably responsible for its conflicting empirical assessments in the literature. Hence, there are examples of cross-sectional studies showing that trade liberalization is positively associated with growth; while other assessments suggest that 'there is simply no credible evidence that across-the-board trade liberalization is systematically associated with higher growth rates' (Rodrik, 2000:102). But neither is trade protection systematically associated with more rapid growth rates. What history shows, however, is that virtually all high-income industrialized countries (whether one refers to the North American and European countries which achieved this status long ago or the Asian countries which have done it more recently) embarked on their growth process behind various forms of protection that were subsequently reduced. In other words, these countries liberalized their trade regimes partially and gradually over time contingent upon appropriate developments in their country institutional and structural characteristics and the external environment.

The debate about the link between trade openness (or trade liberalization) and economic growth has recently been converging on a broad consensus. This consensus includes the observation that while 'overall, the fairest assessment is that liberalized trade alone has not yet been unambiguously and universally linked to subsequent economic growth' (McCulloch, Winters and Cirera, 2001:24), it is not implied either that trade liberalization is, in general, a hinderance to growth or that trade protection should, as a general rule, be preferred to trade liberalization. This emerging consensus does imply, however, that reducing trade barriers in a country will not automatically lead it to the achievement of higher economic growth rates in the absence of other supportive conditions. In other words, while liberal trade policy constitutes an important component of the development strategy of a low-income country, the long-term benefits of such a policy may not be fully reaped unless it is combined with conducive external market access opportunities and domestic policies which enhance the supply response capacity of local firms and individuals required to take full advantage of the opportunities created by the opening up of both local and foreign markets.

In this context, low-income countries should view trade negotiations not only in terms of liberalizing their own trade policy, but also in terms of two other related perspectives. These are (a) the extent to which trade negotiations enhance their access to external markets with respect to goods and services of significant export interest to them and (b) the extent to which the trade rules established in these trade negotiations assist in enhancing (or at least do not unnecessarily constrain) the supply response capacity of their domestic economic agents. In general, multilateral trade negotiations have typically focused on enlarging market access through the reduction of various forms of trade barriers. Their basic premise is that liberal trade policies will generate increased trade flows and economic growth as market forces are unleashed. But in low-income countries, unleashing market forces may not generate economic growth unless they are associated with special policy measures, institutions and infrastructure. The appropriate institutions that enable markets to function tend to vary across countries and over time; they are thus not necessarily independent of a given country's history and its stage of development. Therefore, attempts by an increasing number of multilateral trade agreements to harmonize trade rules and institutional arrangements in low-income countries with the established norms and practices in the high-income industrialized countries tend to stifle rather than enhance the supply response capacity in the former. In particular, multilateral trade negotiations should permit low-income countries to pursue development-oriented trade, technology and industrial policies which enable them to diversify their economies and enhance their supply response capacity.

In addition, a recent study (World Bank, 2002) strongly suggests that the combination of trade liberalization, institution building and measures to enhance supply response capacity in low-income countries would have a greater chance of success if high-income countries provided a support-ive external environment. In particular, this support could take the form of the grant of special market access, in terms of duty free and quota free access, to all exports of low-income countries. This initiative would lead to significant export growth gains to the low-income countries with neg-ligible trade diversion, given that these countries account for only a small part of world trade. In addition, the initiative would help to remove some of the most significant drawbacks of existing trade preference schemes.

Beside special market access provisions which may be necessary for creating a supportive external environment for the growth of low-income countries, at least two other initiatives are probably required for enhancing the effectiveness of the links between trade negotiations and the develop-ment of this group of countries. These are (a) measures for eliminating their supply response capacity constraints and (b) measures to link their obligations under multilateral trade rules to their level of development. These trade rules essentially oblige low-income countries to accept in-stitutional arrangements for facilitating trade and investments that have evolved gradually in high-income countries. These may be good institu-tions, but they remain country and historically specific (Collier, 2000). Their transplantation into low-income countries is not without consid-erable (and, perhaps, unnecessary) costs. Implementing many of the in-stitutional reforms involves practical difficulties and does not necessarily reflect the institutional development priorities that can be reasonably as-sociated with the level of development of many low-income countries.

These difficulties have become more widely recognized since 1994 when the Uruguay Round was completed. The general response, in terms of offers of technical assistance and financial support, is not only inadequate but is also in some cases, quite inappropriate. In particular, the response has typically ignored the fact that development of institutions takes time and even where institutional adapation is appropriate, the process must be flexible and gradual to ensure success.

It is also widely recognized that for the long-term benefits of trade liberalization to be realized, adequate and timely supply response to the new domestic and external opportunities is essential. For instance, in a country whose dometic institutions and infrastructural services are weak supply response is likely to be weak, with the result that its economic agents may fail to exploit the opportunities offered by the changes in relative price incentives generated by trade liberalization. The critical importance of supply response is demonstrated by the experience of trade liberalization episodes in Africa, where policy reversals have been traced to the up-front costs of trade liberalization (increased competition and unemployment; import surges and balance of payments problems) which preceeded the benefits (Oyejide, Ndulu and Gunning, 1999).

This suggests the need for complementary policies aimed at enhancing supply response *prior to* trade liberalization, especially since these typically take a longer time to implement and yield results. But some aspects of the WTO Agreements appear to remove several complementary policies from the arsenal of low-income countries, although many of the high-income countries have exploited these measures in support of their own development in the past. To the extent that these Agreements have, in effect, imposed uniform standards of behaviour across countries which face markedly different problems and supply response capacity constraints, the trade negotiations that gave birth to them have sacrificed significant development dimensions that should have been an integral part of the process.

3 Promoting development through multilateral trade negotiations

Obviously, low-income countries can attempt to achieve their goals of sustainable economic growth and poverty alleviation by unilaterally liberalizating their trade regimes and strengthening their institutions and infrastructural services. Many of them have in fact embarked on this type of policy reform effort since the early 1980s, usually in the context of Structural Adjustment Programmes (SAPs) supported by the World Bank and the IMF. But trade liberalization through multilateral negotiations has, at least, three special features which make this approach particularly appealing. The most important of these is, perhaps, the fact that it offers the best way for prising open external markets and thus enhancing the access of low-income country exports to the markets of high-income countries. In addition, the multilateral approach may also help to overcome domestic opposition to liberal trade regimes and, when bound, multilaterally agreed tariff reductions endow the trade regime with greater credibility.

But trade liberalization through multilateral negotiations is also a two-edged sword. In addition to its advantage as a means of gaining external market access it may also end up imposing additional obligations (especially in the area of multilateral trade rules) which could prove burdensome to low-income countries. The implicit assumption in the GATT/WTO framework of multilateral trade negotiations is that its effective operation as a body of multilateral rules designed to guide international trade relations would automatically lead to economic growth in all participating countries, whatever their initial level of development. In essence, it was assumed that the multilateral rules would provide an environment in which the most efficient industries of low-income countries would expand by finding markets all over the world and thus help to achieve their development goals.

The observed realities of the 1950s and 1960s failed to validate these assumptions. Many low-income countries did not derive much benefit from various GATT Rounds; very few of them actually participated in the multilateral trade negotiations. The Haberler Report (GATT, 1985) identified several factors that could explain this outcome. First, some of the domestic policies of high-income countries contributed significantly to the decline in exports of low-income countries. Principal among these were the high tariffs that faced exports of low-income countries on a wide range of products in which they had comparative advantage. Second, low-income countries faced special difficulties in the context of multilateral trade negotiations. They were often not 'principal suppliers' of many products that formed the focus of these negotiations. They also had little or nothing to offer in return for requesting high-income countries to lower the tariffs on products of particular export interest to them. Finally, as countries with relatively small economies and markets with exports concentrated on a limited number of primary commodities, they could exercise only limited leverage in the framework of multilateral negotiations.

These and related reasons appear to have convinced developed country GATT contracting parties that the trade and development problems of low-income countries were, in certain ways, quite different from their own. In, these circumstance, it was thought that some flexibilities should be built into the GATT negotiating framework if low-income countries and their development needs were to be accommodated. This appears to be the background against which the concept of 'special and differential treatment' (SDT) of low-income countries in the multilateral trading system evolved. In broad terms, SDT covers the set of rights and privileges provided in the GATT/WTO framework for its developing and least-developed country members. Through its various provisions, SDT had the effect of (a) granting to low-income countries more favourable access to the markets of developed countries and (b) giving them substantial policy discretion in their own domestic markets. The first category of special privileges was operationalized through trade preferences granted to low-income countries by a set of developed countries. The second has been implemented by permitting low-income countries to maintain trade barriers. In particular, this category has included the use of trade barriers to protect domestic industries and the use of quantitative import restrictions for infant industry protection and for dealing with balance of payments problems. In addition, this set has also enabled low-income countries to establish preferential regional trading arrangements among themselves without extending such preferences to non-members and to benefit from multilaterally negotiated reductions in trade barriers, in accordance with the MFN principle without being obliged to offer reciprocity.

These SDT provisions evolved and have been modified over time. It is clear, however, that they were intended from the beginning to serve as a response by the multilateral trading system to the demand from low-income countries for multilateral trade negotiations which take into account their trade and development needs. In this context Article XVIII was the first concrete expression of this response. The 1954–5 review of GATT Articles provided three parts for Article (XVIII). Part A permits low-income countries to modify previously negotiated tariff bindings to assist them in establishing a new industry; but this modification is subject to compensation if the trading partners are adversely affected. Part B permits the use of quantitative trade restrictions for combating balance of payment problems of low-income countries. Finally, Part C permits the same set of countries to use quantitative restrictions (QRs) for infant industry protection, subject (as for Part A) to compensation or retaliation. Thus, the first response was to permit low-income countries substantial trade policy autonomy and discretion as far as their own domestic trade barriers were concerned.

The 1963 GATT Ministerial Conference took a step further in the direction of articulating the second type of response. It recognized the need for a *formal* institutional framework for dealing more effectively with the trade and development problems of low-income member countries. In particular, it approved a declaration accepting the objective of duty free access for tropical products without expecting reciprocity from low-income countries. Part of the institutional formalization was implemented in 1965 through the addition of Part IV to the GATT Articles. But Part IV is devoid of any operational significance. All it did, in essence, was to recognize the development needs of low-income countries, suggest that trade negotiations should give priority attention to products of special interest to low-income countries, restate the SDT provision of non-reciprocity and provide for joint action in studying export potentials of low-income countries.

In 1968, however, during UNCTAD II, the principle and objectives of a generalized and non-reciprocal system of trade preferences (GSP) for low-income countries were approved. The aim of this initiative was to increase the export earnings of these countries, promote their industrialization and accelerate their rates of economic growth. But it was not until 1971 that GATT finally provided legal backing for the GSP through its decision to waive the provisions of GATT, Article I, for a period of ten years. This made it legally possible for developed countries to offer trade preferences to low-income countries. The decisions of the Tokyo Round in 1979 summarized in the Framework Agreement (or Enabling Clause) took this issue a little further. It provided permanent legal cover for GSPs and identified the 'least-developed countries' as a separate category of members deserving more favourable treatment. But, in addition, it also articulated, in broad terms, the 'graduation' principle, under which low-income countries would be expected to take on more and more of the obligations associated with GATT membership as their economies grew stronger. Furthermore, the Tokyo Round Codes included three categories of SDT provisions aimed at making the Codes more acceptable to low-income countries. These are (a) offer of technical assistance to help them comply with the requirements of the new trade rules, (b) imposition of weaker discipline for low-income countries under some rules (including standards, customs valuation, and subsidies) and (c) exemptions from some of the new obligations based on the perceived limitations of administrative capacity of low-income countries. SDT appears to have reached its full development in the Tokyo Round. It was subsequently scaled back during the Uruguay Round. The broad result of the Uruguay Round is that low-income countries were called upon to meet virtually the same standard on a broad range of market access issues and trade rules as their high-income counterparts. More specifically, instead of exemptions from certain obligations various SDT provisions were reduced, essentially, to extended transition periods over which the same levels and scope of obligations as those demanded of developed countries would be assumed.

The rise and fall of SDT in the GATT/WTO framework raises a number of issues, i.e whether low-income countries need to be accorded SDT in the global trading system as a means of integrating key development dimensions into the framework of multilateral trade negotiations, and whether SDT provides appropriate incentives (and disciplines) for low-income countries to pursue trade policies that promote their development. A discussion of these issues requires a cost-benefit analysis of the key SDT provisions (Oyejide, 1998) which is briefly summarized below.

A key element of SDT for low-income countries recognized the need to nurture their infant industries. GATT Articles XVIII, Section C, enabled them to take appropriate measures for the protection of infant industries. It is not uncommon to view industrialization as a major indicator of economic development; hence rapid industrialization has been a goal of economic policy in many low-income countries. Active economic policy to speed up the development process has also involved efforts to develop a country's technological capabilities, build up its domestic capacity to manufacture a range of products and promote exports.

Active policy aimed at altering the speed and character of industrialization is justified by the existence of specific market failures and externalities which could cause a suboptimal share of the economy's resources to be allocated to the industrial sector, in the absence of corrective measures (Rodrik, 1992). The pervasiveness in low-income countries of pronounced market failures, as well as such phenomena as learning-by-doing, economies of scale and other externalities that are inherently tied up with modern manufacturing and service activities provides strong support for interventionist and non-neutral policies, including the use of various measures to protect and promote infant industries.

The market failures that are likely to be of special significance in developing countries enamate from various sources (Rodrik, 1992; Stiglitz, 1996). In the early stages of development, markets may be absent or not sufficiently well developed to provide good signals for resource allocation. The existing private markets typically have inadequate incentives for investing in the production and acquisition of information and expertise needed to boost the level of technology at which the low-income economy operates. In addition, when the increasing returns and learning-by-doing associated with modern manufacturing are combined with shortage of capital, the small firms in the typical developing country may be stunted. In these circumstance, infant industry protection and support are important means of ensuring that the young firms can gain the experience required to lower their cost of production and eventually become fully competitive. The backwardness of developing countries (broadly measured by their distance from the international technology frontier), the market handicaps that characterize their economies at the start of the development process and the time required to establish and nurture markets and marketing institutions and to acquire and build up the capacities to compete with advanced country firms, all point in the direction of a necessary period of infant industry protection as a prelude to rapid industrialization and overall economic growth.

It is widely recognized, in this context, that subsidies may play an important role in the development programmes of low-income countries. In particular, subsidies granted contingent upon export performance or use of domestic in preference to imported inputs in the production process could be valuable instruments of trade and industrial policy. Such performance-based incentive systems are associated with important benefits. Stiglitz (1996:157) argues that 'government intervention through a performance-based reward system . . . provides strong growth-oriented incentives'. When such a system is based on exports, it could serve as an objective and efficient selection mechanism for the award of subsidies. Since export markets are more likely to be competitive and firms competing in international markets gain from spillovers in marketing and production know-how, a firm that succeeds in the export market is more likely to be economically efficient. Thus, a performance-based subsidy award system is likely to promote efficiency and ensure that only industries with real long-term growth prospects are provided with infant industry protection and support.

The benefits to developing countries of the S&D provision for infant industry protection go well beyond theoretical arguments. The mechanism through which local firms are protected in a captive home market subject to an export performance target – enabling them to make high profits which, in turn, finance higher rates of investment, learning by doing and improving the quality of their products – is one that has been aggressively, effectively and successfully used by the East Asian countries. Their experience suggests that trade and industrial policies that take advantage of the SDT provision on infant industry protection could not have been successful without the imposition of export performance standards. By the same token, it is reasonable to suggest that a significant part of the failure of protection and subsidy policies in Africa may be traceable to the virtual absence of objective performance targets.

GATT Article XVIII, Section B, provided developing countries with the flexibility to impose quantitative import restrictions to protect their balance of payments. This S&D provision is a recognition of the special difficulties that the developing countries have often had in maintaining balance of payments equilibrium as they pursue their development goals. Given the volatile terms of trade and the greater susceptibility of external shocks which characterize many developing countries, especially those that are heavily dependent on the export of primary commodities, these economies may suffer from undesirable 'stop–go' cycles associated with recurring balance of payments crises. The SDT provision under discussion enables low-income countries to use discretionary trade and payments controls for dealing with short-term balance of payments problems and hence permits them to commit themselves to a long-term development strategy without having to change direction abruptly at the onset of a balance of payments crisis.

A development strategy that includes some elements of infant industry protection and import substitution is not necessarily or inherently prone to external payments instability or 'stop–go' policy cycles. Macroeconomic stability and external balance are not incompatible with any degree of trade protection. Regardless of its trade orientation, appropriate fiscal and exchange rate policies should enable an economy to maintain external balance. However, the typically thin foreign exchange markets of low-income countries may impose serious constraints on the efficacy of exchange rate policy in dealing with abrupt and large external imbalances. Similarly, the other important objectives of fiscal policy often preclude its exclusive focus on balance of payments concerns. In these circumstances, many developing countries have found the flexibility provided by GATT Article XVIII, Section B, particularly useful in dealing with abrupt external imbalances.

Non-reciprocity is the SDT provision that confers on low-income countries the benefits of trade liberalization in developed countries without requiring them to similarly open up their own trade regime. The beneficiary developing countries would obviously gain, in terms of improved exports, from additional and enlarged access to the liberalized markets of developed countries. The liberalization of their own trade regimes would also bring welfare gains to the developing countries, but these can be associated with significant fiscal costs when a developing country is heavily dependent on trade taxes as a source of government revenue.

The acknowledged need of developing countries for special assistance in respect of access to the markets of developed countries is met through the SDT provision embodied in the GSP schemes. The GSP arrangement has often been cited as the one major element of SDT for developing countries in the GATT/WTO framework which produces concrete benefits (Whalley, 1989).

Various studies generally show that GSP schemes have yielded benefits to the preference-receiving countries. According to Laird and Sapir (1987), roughly 50 per cent of dutiable imports in OECD countries up to the early 1980s was GSP-eligible; while of this, another 50 per cent actually received GSP treatment. Hence, only 26 per cent of the dutiable imports of the OECD countries from beneficiaries of their schemes actually enjoyed GSP treatment. In its review of the first decade of GSP schemes, UNCTAD (1985) broadly confirms this general result for 1982. A decade later, UNCTAD (1995) shows that in 1993, total imports of preference-giving countries from GSP beneficiary schemes amounted to about $439 billion, of which approximately $305 billion (or 69.5 per cent) were dutiable. But only $172 billion (or 56.3 per cent) were GSP-eligible and, of this, only $82 billion (or 47.9 per cent) actually received GSP treatment. In other words, only 27 per cent of all dutiable imports were granted preferential access. Over the 1976–93 period, the total value of preferential imports under various OECD GSP schemes increased at an average annual growth rate of 12.7 per cent, from $10.4 billion to $79 billion (UNCTAD, 1995:6).

Since the GSP schemes cover mostly manufactured products, developing countries with a wider industrial base and more diversified manufactured exports have gained more than those relying on exports of agricultural products and raw materials. Hence, up to the early 1980s, there was a remarkable concentration of GSP benefits among a few developing countries, with the top three (Hong Kong, South Korea and Taiwan) accounting for as much as 45 per cent of total GSP gains. The concentrated nature of GSP benefits remained largely unchanged through the early 1990s. UNCTAD (1995) reports that in 1992 between six and twelve largest beneficiaries accounted for 71–80 per cent of the preferential imports of Japan, the USA and the EU.

A critique of SDT provisions in the GATT/WTO framework comes from several directions. Sometimes, the critique reflects the belief that there is a nothing special about developing or low-income countries that could set them apart for any SDT, particularly in the area of trade policy. At other times, the critique is based on the idea that trade-restricting development strategies impose an unnecessary cost on low-income countries instead of assisting to speed up their development process. Whether specific SDT provisions give low-income countries an undeserved 'free ride' in the global trading system or permit them to suffer from the self-inflicted pain of wrong-headed policies, various criticisms of these provisions imply that they are associated with certain costs that are borne either by the 'beneficiary' developing countries themselves and/or by the global trading system as a whole.

Focusing specifically on SDT provisions relating to infant industry and balance of payments protection, Hudec (1987) considers them harmful on at least two counts; first, they permit developing countries to take 'market-distorting' measures, and second they amount to the abandonment of any real effort to limit or control the use of such measures by developing countries. To the extent that the use of such 'market-distorting' measures are, indeed, counter-productive, they could impose a cost on the developing countries themselves. Thus basic criticism can be (and has been – see Whalley, 1989) taken further. The continued justification for the S&D provision on balance of payments protection is questioned in the belief that, in the current economic environment, exchange rate changes supported by appropriate macroeconomic policies should be adequate for balance of payments adjustments. Thus, the continued use of quantitative import control measures to deal with external imbalances when more effective price-based and non-market-distorting alternatives are available would impose a resource-allocation inefficiency cost on the economy.

Both strands of this basic criticism ignore or assume away those special features of developing and low-income countries whose explicit recognition gave birth to the SDT provisions in the first place. When appropriate markets are missing or underdeveloped for various reasons, price-based measures are unlikely to provide correct signals for efficient resource-allocation decisions. Notions of inefficiency costs associated with inappropriate policies in the context of well-functioning markets with full information do not typically carry over into situations where these assumptions are patently violated.

Less fundamental objections to these SDT provisions have also been raised. Balance of payments justification for quantitative import restrictions may have a hidden sectoral protection intent. Thus, because of more stringent procedural requirements of GATT Article XVIII, Section C, compared to those of Section B, some developing countries appear to have found it relatively easier to obtain GATT 'cover' for infant industry protection under the guise of balance of payments protection. In making this supposition, Anjaria (1987) argues that in a large majority of developing countries that declared Article XVIII B restrictions, the measures covered less than half of import categories; and that if these restrictions are truly for balance of payments purposes, they would cover all import categories. This argument misses an important rationale of balance of payments protection in developing countries. Typically, the goal is to maintain current account balance at a rate of economic growth which is as high as possible. In this context, imports of capital and intermediate goods are treated as 'essential' and are thus protected from import control measures. As a result, quantitative import restriction measures taken for balance of payments purposes tend to cover primarily 'non-essential' consumer goods, not necessarily because there are any existing industries in this sector to be protected but simply because they constitute the 'discretionary' imports that can be curtailed without derailing the country's development programme.

The SDT provision that grants non-reciprocity rights to developing countries can, in principle, be associated with at least two different types of costs. First, lack of reciprocity may make it more difficult for developed countries to reduce trade barriers to exports from developing countries. Second, absence of obligatory and binding reciprocity may preclude the GATT/WTO from serving as an 'agency of restraint' for developing countries and thus make it more difficult to resist the claims of local protectionist interest groups.

The second type of cost may be particularly significant. As Wolf (1987:664) argues: 'a principal reason for participation in GATT negotiations is not just to obtain improved access abroad but to make it politically easier to liberalize at home.' A reciprocally bargained international agreement can, in this context, strengthen the hands of a developing country that wishes to resist undesirable protectionist measures championed by local producers. It is not necessarily the case, however, that the non-reciprocity S&D provision removes the right of any developing country to use the GATT/WTO institutional framework as an agency of restraint, since the provision does not prevent developing countries from reducing and binding their tariffs.

The first type of cost associated with non-reciprocity assumes that developed countries would treat exports from developing countries more liberally if a mutually reciprocal relationship was established (Hudec,

1987). There may be some substance to this assumption. It appears that certain restrictions on the coverage of various GSP schemes as well as pressures to 'graduate' certain product groups and developing countries out of the GSP may not be entirely unrelated to lack of reciprocity. For the majority of low-income countries, however, it does not seem clear that their commitments to reduce trade barriers against exports of developed countries play a significant role in determining the amount of market access they can expect in return.

Criticisms of various GSP schemes focus largely on their many limitations that preclude the realization of the full benefits that they could generate if they had been implemented, as originally conceived, as 'generalized and non-discriminatory' preferential systems. In effect, the costs associated with the GSPs emanate largely from these limitations.

First, since the GSPs are non-contractual and therefore subject to unilateral modification or withdrawal at the pleasure of preference-granting countries, they may not provide a reliable, and a stable basis of incentives provided by the GSP may be jeopardized by sudden changes and modifications to the system. Second, Wang and Winters (1997) argue that trade preferences impose significant costs that could ultimately subvert long-term development. It is suggested, in particular, that the desire to retain the privileges of GSP schemes open preference-receiving countries to immense pressures to accept various conditions imposed by preference-granting countries while the incentives generated by GSP schemes tend to create inefficiencies in production and trade, divert resources from critical sectors, and encourage rent-seeking instead of productive investment.

In spite of the severe limitations that rob it of its full potential, most studies of the GSP scheme confirm that it has yielded over time small but significant benefits, particularly to those developing countries which had acquired the appropriate supply-response capabilities. Interestingly enough, such major GSP beneficiaries have not, in fact, suffered from any of the 'costs' theoretically associated with the scheme. This suggests that the reform of the system should focus specifically on those limitations, such as product coverage, graduation criteria, rule of origin and safeguards, with regard to which multilaterally negotiated changes might further enhance the benefits derivable from the scheme.

The various SDT provisions that evolved in the GATT/WTO framework were established in response to the special problems of low-income countries. Many of these special problems, especially those emanating from underdeveloped and absent markets, imperfect information and economies of scale, continue to be relevant, particularly in the low-income countries of Africa. The underlying philosophical view regarding trade policy and its role in the development process has undergone more dramatic change. Common policy thrusts reflecting current thinking generally emphasize the opening of developing country economies to world markets and elimination of anti-export biases in domestic policies. Yet, in the light of significant market failures that remain in many developing countries, there continues to be an important role for trade and industrial policies aimed at building the domestic capacity to manufacture a range of products, developing technological capabilities to support this effort, and promoting exports. Both theoretical considerations and the practical experience of East Asian countries suggest that government intervention is often necessary and that a performance-based reward system can serve as an efficient subsidy allocation system.

Viewed from this perspective, the interests of low-income countries would be better served by an analytically based deliberative process in the context of which each of the various SDT provisions is reviewed – and, where necessary, suitably reformed. A dispassionate analysis of accumulated development experience would not support the total elimination of the SDT provisions; what it might suggest could be a tighter formulation of the Rules and enhanced surveillance of their implementation.

4   Development-centred trade negotiations: Doha and beyond

As suggested earlier, rapid economic growth and poverty alleviation are the primary development objectives of low-income countries who constitute the majority of WTO membership. Their trade policy and trade negotiation activities are an integral part of their development policy and strategy. Hence, it should not be surprising that they are insisting on changing the traditional market access focus of multilateral trade negotiations into one which is development-centred. In other words, they would like to see market access concessions as a means to an end (i.e. promoting growth and poverty alleviation) rather than as an end in itself. Key elements of this refocusing are the mainstreaming of measures for eliminating supply response capacity constraints and more closely relating obligations of low-income countries with respect to multilateral trade rules to objective indicators of their level of development. The major concern of low-income countries currently relates to how and the extent to which the Doha Development Agenda may be expected to help bring about these changes.

In launching the Agenda, the Doha Ministerial Declaration deliberately uses a substantial amount of 'development-friendly' language and suggests that the centrepiece of the Agenda is a 'development Round'. But one must make a distinction between what language promises and what the actual negotiations may eventually deliver. It is quite clearly the latter which will determine how much of the development dimension is taken into account and, hence, whether the Agenda ends up as a development Round.

To many low-income countries, reducing developed country barriers to imports of agricultural products, apparel, clothing, textiles and other labour-intensive manufactures is considered crucial as the market access component of the development dimension of multilateral trade negotiations. While average tariffs on industrial products are low in developed countries, they continue to penalize exports of low-income countries in several ways. First, the average tariff facing exports of low-income countries in developed countries is more than fourfold higher than that on imports from developed countries. Second, developed countries maintain peak tariffs (in excess of 12%) on many labour-intensive products in the production of which low-income countries have comparative advantage. These peak tariffs tend to reduce their exports and to divert their production from these products. Third, there is considerable escalation in the tariff schedules of developed countries. This discourages low-income countries from full exploitation of export-oriented processing activities with respect to both manufacturing and agriculture. As a result, the capacity of low-income countries to engage in higher value-added processing industries is constrained. In addition, because processing local raw materials offers the easiest way into manufacturing, the existence of tariff escalation in developed countries deprives the entrepreneurs and workers in low-income countries of the advantages of productivity spillovers associated with learning-by-doing. For these reasons, the commitment of developed countries to reduce peak tariffs and eliminate tariff escalation on products of export interest to low-income countries ranks quite high among the market access component of a development-centred Doha Development Agenda.

The Agenda appears to respond positively to this expectation of low-income countries. The Ministerial Declaration indicates that the negotiations shall aim to reduce or 'as appropriate' to eliminate not only tariffs but also tariff peaks and escalation, as well as NTBs 'in particular on products of export interest to developing countries'. There is a problem, however, since this component of the negotiations will be included in the single undertaking package and this creates problems for many low-income countries who are, apparently, not prepared to take on further liberalization in trade on goods, based on their past experience.

For many low-income countries, trade liberalization has typically been unilateral rather than through multilateral negotiations. It has also generally not been gradual. Hence, reductions in import barriers have occurred without giving domestic agricultural and industrial producers adequate time to adjust themselves to competition from imports. In addition, unilateral trade liberalization (induced by support of the World Bank and the IMF in the context of SAPs) occurred in many low-income countries without the prior conditions and complementary policies for enhancing supply response. In these circumstances, the long-run benefits of trade liberalization have generally not been achieved, while the previously protected industries have experienced contraction.

There is, therefore, a basis for the apparent reluctance of low-income countries to engage in negotiations aimed at reducing their own trade barriers with respect to agricultural and industrial products. But there are several considerations that may moderate this position. First, low-income countries stand to gain not only by increasing the access of their exports to the markets of developed countries but also through reductions in their own protection levels. Second, active participation in the market access negotiations will not only increase their chances of receiving concessions from the developed countries. It will also enhance their ability to resist their own domestic protectionist interest groups. Finally, the Ministerial Declaration indicates that the market access negotiations 'shall take fully into account the special needs and interests of developing and least-developed country participants, including through less than full reciprocity in reduction commitments'. This provides an assurance that market access offers from low-income countries in the context of the negotiations may reflect their 'special needs' in terms of the depth of reduction commitments and the speed of liberalization.

Preferences have been and continue to be important means through which low-income countries can obtain enhanced market access for their exports to developed countries. Two elements of the Doha Development Agenda suggest that developed countries may be finally ready to eliminate the defects which rendered the GSPs less than fully useful to the low-income countries. The Ministerial Declaration indicates a commitment 'to the objective of duty-free, quota-free market access for products originating from the least developed countries'. In addition, in the Implementation Decision, WTO members 'reaffirm that preferences granted to developing countries . . . should be generalized, non-reciprocal and non-discriminatory'. Taken together, these statements may lead to the acceptance of the EU's Everything But Arms (EBA) initiative by the WTO and its broadening, in terms of country coverage, beyond the least-developed countries. Achieving this in the market access negotiations will give low-income countries security of market access and reduce their negotiating costs. But it should be complemented by low-income countries in, at least, two ways. One is to implement measures for enhancing their own supply response, without which they may be unable to take full advantage of the improved market access. Second is to rationalize and bind their own tariffs at modest rates so as to take advantage of the gains associated with reductions in their own trade barriers.

With respect to trade in services, the most significant market access demand of low-income countries probably relates to the movement of natural persons. This is, coincidentally, an area in which there exists the greatest resistance from developed countries. Clearly, it has an analogy in the goods trade, i.e. the existence of peak tariffs and tariff escalation on the products in which low-income countries have comparative advantage. Just as in this case, improved access of low-income countries to the markets of developed countries in terms of freer movement of natural persons will make a significant contribution to their economic growth. The resistance of developed countries is probably traceable to the confusion of temporary movement of skilled and unskilled workers from low-income countries with permanent migration as well as concerns regarding the social impact of the latter. The resolution of this problem is a technical issue, i.e. the design of an effective system for managing temporary mobility of workers and professional service providers which ensures that they do not transform into permanent migrants.

Historically, the multilateral trading system has used the 'trade rules' component of SDT provisions to limit its intrusion into the domestic policy space of low-income countries. The Uruguay Round not only reversed this direction but also introduced additional trade rules agreements. The implementation of these agreements has imposed high up-front costs on low-income countries combined with little prospects, if any, of long-term benefits. It appears unlikely that the Doha Development Agenda will significantly improve matters in this respect since, like the Uruguay Round, it proposes to have negotiations on new trade rules which are likely to worsen the situation of low-income countries.

For instance, the Ministerial Declaration states that 'all [SDT] provisions shall be reviewed with a view to strenghtening them and making them more precise, effective and operational'. The associated Implementation Decision calls for the identification of those provisions that Members consider should be made mandatory. These Agenda 'intentions' do not respond to the demands of low-income countries with respect to a whole range of trade rules issues, including:

- The need to tailor the *implementation* of existing and new trade-rules agreements to the local capabilities of low-income countries
- Ensuring that trade rules allow for greater flexibility and provide for *transition periods* linked to development capacities
- Refraining from the use of *anti-dumping measures and stringent product standards* against exports of low-income countries.

In fact, the proposed Framework Agreement on SDT gets only a passing mention in the Agenda, which also only takes note of a proposal to treat as non-actionable subsidy measures implemented by developing countries with a view to achieving legitimate development goals.

While it thus remains uncertain that the Agenda will effectively address the outstanding implementation problems associated with Uruguay Round's SDT changes and trade rules agreements, it actually proposes to 'add insult to injury' by negotiating new trade rules agreements on investment, competition policy, government procurement and trade facilitation as part of 'single undertaking' – meaning that the new agreements will apply to all members without exception. Given the limited time provided in the Agenda (only three years) to think through, negotiate and sign binding agreements on these issues, it is clear that most low-income countries will have neither the time nor the expertise to take rational and well-informed decisions. In addition, agreements on these issues will impose the same kind of implementation burden on low-income countries as did the trade rules agreements of the Uruguay Round, i.e. high up-front costs with negligible future benefits. Given that these issues are already in the Agenda, the best strategy of low-income countries is probably to move them out of 'single undertaking' and into plurilateral agreements among developed countries.

During the Uruguay Round developed countries offered to provide technical and financial assistance to enable low-income countries to implement the agreements on new trade rules. These offers have mostly not been operationalized. Hence, an enduring demand of low-income countries is bind to bind the prior commitments in this respect. While this demand remains unsatisfied, the Agenda contains frequent references to technical assistance and capacity building initiatives in roughly the same context. There is no doubt that many low-income countries need and can use technical assistance and capacity building, especially if these are targeted at relieving their supply response capacity constraints. But technical assistance is generally inadequate for negotiating and implementing such complex and demanding trade rules agreements as those proposed in the Doha Development Agenda. In addition, capacity building, by its very nature, takes considerable time. Hence, it is unlikely to yield results in time that are adequate for enabling low-income countries to internalize and take full advantage of the proposed trade rules agreements.

5 Conclusion

The primary development goals of low-income countries are rapid sustainable economic goals and poverty alleviation. Trade and trade policy can make significant contributions to their achievement, provided that trade policy derives from each country's overall national development strategy that focuses on these goals. Multilateral trade negotiations are, in turn, part of the means for giving effect to a country's trade policy and development strategy.

In the context of multilateral trade negotiations, low-income countries may be expected to seek and offer 'concessions' that enable them to achieve their development goals. As these countries have become more active participants in the multilateral trading system, their demands have tended to focus on securing enhanced market access for their exports in developed countries, ensuring that multilateral trade rules support rather than prohibit a range of domestic policy measures designed for eliminating their supply response capacity constraints, ensuring that their obligations under multilateral trade rules are related to objective measures of their development and implementation capacity, as well as capacity building for more effective participation in trade negotiations.

The Uruguay Round results left many of these demands unmet and created additional problems, especially as they further intruded into the domestic policy space of low-income countries and established multilateral agreements on a range of new trade rules whose implementation has been burdensome without adequate compensating benefits. The Agenda may be viewed as an opportunity for low-income countries to ensure that multilateral trade negotiations take full account of their development goals. But the Agenda may, in the end, be a mixed blessing in this regard. If the low-income countries are fully and aggressively engaged in the process, it is not unlikely that substantial progress will be made in the area of enhanced market access in trade in goods and services. But they are likely to have an uphill task in the trade rules area where they are obliged to struggle not only to undo the damage of the Uruguay Round but also to prevent or stall any further move down the same slippery slope in the form of the proposed new trade rules. Low-income countries are better served by multilateral trade negotiations dealing with pure market access issues while minimizing 'behind-the-border' intrusive rules which require institutional development components that are generally neither affordable nor strictly appropriate given the current level of development of low-income countries.

Bibliography

Anjaria, S. J., 1987. 'Balance of Payments and Related Issues in the Uruguay Round of Trade Negotiations', *World Bank Economic Review*, 1(4), pp. 669–88

Collier, P., 2000. 'Consensus Building, Knowledge, and Conditionality', in B. Pleskovic and N. Stern (eds.), *Annual World Bank Conference in Development Economics 2000*, Washington, DC, World Bank

GATT, 1985. *Trends in International Trade: Haberler Report*, Geneva, GATT

Hudec, R. E., 1987. 'Developing Countries in the GATT Legal System', *Thames Essay*, 50, London, Gower

Laird, S. and A. Sapir, 1987. 'Tariff Preferences', in J. M. Finger and A. Olechowski (eds.), *The Uruguay Round: A Handbook on the Multilateral Trade Negotiations*, Washington, DC, World Bank

McCulloch, N., L. A. Winters and X. Cirera, 2001. *Trade Liberalization and Poverty: A Handbook*, London, CEPR

Oyejide, T. A., 1998. 'Costs and Benefits of "Special and Differential" Treatment for Developing Countries in GATT/WTO: An African Perspective', Nairobi, AERC, mimeo

Oyejide, T. A, B. Ndulu and J. W. Gunning (eds.), 1999. *Regional Integration and Trade Liberalization in Sub-Saharan Africa, II – Country Case Studies*, London, Macmillan

Rodrik, D., 1992. 'Conceptual Issues in the Design of Trade Policy for Industrialization', *World Development*, 20(3), pp. 309–20

2000. 'Development Strategies for the 21st Century', in B. Pleskovic and N. Stern (eds.), *Annual World Bank Conference in Development Economics 2000*, Washington, DC, World Bank, pp. 85–108

Sachs, J., 2001. 'A New Global Consensus on Helping the Poorest of the Poor', in B. Pleskovic and N. Stern (eds.), *Annual World Bank Conference on Development Economics 2001*, Washington, DC, World Bank, pp. 39–47

Stiglitz, J., 1996. 'Some Lessons from the East Asian Miracle', *World Bank Research Observer*, 11(2), pp. 151–78

2000. 'Development Thinking at the Millennium', in B. Pleskovic and N. Stern (eds.), *Annual World Bank Conference in Development Economics 2000*, Washington, DC, World Bank, pp. 13–38

UNCTAD, 1985.

1995. *Policy Options and Proposals for the Revitalization of the Generalized System of Preferences*, Report, TD/B/SCP/13, Geneva, UN

Wang, Z. K. and L. A. Winters, 1997. 'Africa and the Global Economy', Nairobi, AERC, mimeo

Whalley, J., 1989. *The Uruguay Round and Beyond*, London, Macmillan

Wolf, M., 1987. 'Differential and More Favourable Treatment of Developing Countries in the International Trading System', *World Bank Economic Review*, 1(4), pp. 647–68

World Bank, 2002. *Global Economic Prospects and the Developing Countries 2001: Making Trade Work for the World's Poor*, Washington, DC, World Bank

6

External transparency: the policy process at the national level of the two-level game

1 Introduction

The word 'transparency', which could be described (only partly in jest) as the most opaque in the trade policy lexicon, has become so widespread that it could be described as *the* buzzword of 'diplolingo'.[1] In the lingo of the WTO, 'internal transparency' refers to the nature of the decision-making processes of the institution while 'external transparency' deals with the relationship between the WTO and non-governmental institutions such as business, unions, farmers, academics and non-governmental organizations (NGOs). While there is no agreed definition of the term, it includes access to information as well as the nature of participation in the policy-making process.

The policy process of trade is usefully conceived as a 'two-level game' involving negotations among interest groups – or stakeholders – at the national level and negotiations among country representatives at the international level. The idea of the two-level game was formulated by Robert Putnam, as a theoretical approach to the interweaving of domestic and international policies, in a seminal article in 1988.[2] The concept stemmed from an analysis of the 1978 Bonn Summit[3] which involved coordination producing a complex outcome linking domestic policies in the Summit countries to support jointly determined international economic strategies.

---

[1] William Safire, 'On Language: Transparency, Totally', *New York Times*, 4 January 1998, Section 6, p. 4.

[2] Robert Putnam, 'Diplomacy and Domestic Politics: The Logic of Two-Level Games', *International Organization*, 42, 1988, pp. 427–60.

[3] Robert D. Putnam and Nicholas Bayne, *Hanging Together: Cooperation and Conflict in the Seven-Power Summits*, London, Sage, 1987.

In trade policy, especially for the big players (the USA and the EU), one could plausibly argue that the negotiating strategies are largely determined by domestic constituents. Yet there has been almost no empirical research on the subject of the national process and its interrelationship with the process in Geneva. Henry Nau's study of the Uruguay Round[4] and my own analysis of the international role of the American multinationals in catalysing the launch of the Round were both written well before the negotiations were concluded.[5] The profound transformation of the multilateral trading system and other definitive changes in the political economy of trade policy make the concept of the two-level game today far more complex than it was at the end of the 1980s. Indeed, given the spread of regional trade agreements (RTAs) the game often involves three levels, which also greatly increases the complexity of the process.

But this chapter is not intended to tackle the conceptual and theoretical problems (game theory is not my comparative advantage!). Rather, I will focus on the policy-making process at the national level and link that process not to the wily strategies of the Putnam 'statesman' seeking his optimal 'win set' but rather to the systemic issue of the future of the WTO. That's quite a different game and the statesman must deal with quite different players.

The chapter will begin with a brief review of the changes in the trading system stemming from the Uruguay Round and their unintended consequences. The changing political economy of trade policy will then be highlighted, including the prominence of new transnational actors who consistently and insistently demand more WTO transparency. We will then turn to the issue of the domestic policy-making process and explore a proposal for enhancing WTO external transparency.

2   The Uruguay Round and its aftermath

After twenty-five years in government I have learned a great deal, but one lesson has proved most resilient – in all significant government policies the unintended consequences overwhelm the original policy objectives. The Uruguay Round is a particularly striking example of this dictum.

---

[4] Henry Nau, *Domestic Trade Politics and the Uruguay Round*, New York, Columbia University Press, 1989.

[5] Sylvia Ostry, *Governments and Corporations in a Shrinking World: Trade and Innovation Policies in the United States, Europe and Japan*, New York, Council on Foreign Relations, 1990.

The Uruguay Round was the eighth negotiation under the auspices of the General Agreement on Tariffs and Trade (GATT), created in 1948 as part of the post-war international economic architecture. The primary mission of GATT was to reduce or eliminate the border barriers which had been erected in the 1930s and contributed to the Great Depression and its disastrous consequences. The GATT reflected its origins in the post-war world in that it provided rules to buffer or interface between the *international* objective of sustained liberalization and the objectives of *domestic policy*, primarily the Keynesian Consensus of full employment and the creation of the welfare state.

Before the Uruguay Round, GATT worked very well. Tariffs and non-tariff barriers (NTBs) were significantly reduced and trade grew faster than output as each fed the other. Most Rounds were essentially managed by the USA and the European Community. The developing countries were largely ignored as players. Agriculture was virtually excluded from negotiations so the transatlantic alliance, helped by the Cold War's constraint on trade frictions, was the effective manager of the international trading system.

The Uruguay Round was a watershed in the evolution of that system. For the first time agriculture was at the centre of the negotiations and the European effort to block the launch of the negotiations to avoid coming to grips with their heavily subsidized and protected Common Agricultural Policy (CAP) went on for half a decade. This foot-dragging also spawned a new single-interest coalition – the Australian-led Cairns Group, which included Southern countries from Latin America and Asia determined to ensure that liberalization of agricultural trade would not be relegated to the periphery by the Americans and the Europeans, as it always had been in the past.

But the role of a group of developing countries, tagged the G10 hard-liners and led by Brazil and India, was in many ways even more important in the Uruguay Round's transformation of the system. The G10 were bitterly opposed to the inclusion of the so-called 'new issues' – trade in services, intellectual property and investment – central to the American negotiating agenda.

Although the 'new issues' are *not* identical – obviously negotiations on telecommunications or financial services differ from intellectual property rights (IPRs) – they do have one common or generic characteristic. Thus, they involve not the border barriers of the original GATT but domestic regulatory and legal systems embedded in the institutional infrastructure of the economy. The degree of intrusiveness into domestic sovereignty bears little resemblance to the shallow integration of the GATT with its focus on border barriers and its buffers to safeguard domestic policy space. The WTO thus shifted from the GATT model of *negative* regulation – what governments must not do – to *positive* regulation – what governments must do.

The inclusion of the new issues in the Uruguay Round was an American initiative and this policy agenda was largely driven by American multi-national enterprises (MNEs), who were market leaders in the services and high-tech sectors. These corporations made it clear to the government that without a fundamental rebalancing of the GATT they would not continue to support a multilateral policy but would prefer a bilateral or regional track. But they didn't just talk the talk, they also walked the walk, organizing business coalitions in support of services and intellectual property in Europe and Japan as well as some smaller OECD countries. The activism paid off and it's fair to say that American MNEs played a key – perhaps even *the* key – role in establishing the new global trading system. I'll return to this shortly.

By the onset of the 1990s a major change in economic policy was underway. The debt crisis of the 1980s, and thus the role of the IMF and the World Bank, plus the fall of the Berlin Wall – a confluence of two unrelated events – ushered in a major transformation in the economic policy paradigm. Economic reforms – deregulation, privatization, liberalization – were seen as essential elements for launching and sustaining growth. Economic regulatory reform is at the heart of the concept of trade in services. Even without the thrust from the Uruguay Round, many developing countries began to see reform of key service sectors such as telecommunications as essential building blocks in the soft infrastructure underpinning growth and the GATT as a means to furthering domestic reform.

Thus, well before the end of the Round the hardline coalition had disappeared and coalitions of developing countries concentrated on liberalization of agriculture and textiles and clothing. Many undertook unilateral liberalization of tariffs and other trade barriers and by the conclusion in December 1993 were among the strongest supporters of the negotiations they so adamantly opposed in the 1980s. What I have called a 'North–South grand bargain' was completed and was quite different from old-time GATT reciprocity – 'I'll open my market if you'll open yours'. It was essentially an implicit deal: the opening of OECD markets to agriculture and labour-intensive manufactured goods, especially textiles and clothing, for the inclusion into the trading system of trade in services, intellectual property and (albeit to a lesser extent than originally demanded) investment. Also – as virtually a last-minute piece of the deal – the creation of a new institution, the WTO, with the strongest dispute settlement mechanism in the history of international law. Since the WTO consisted of a 'single undertaking' (in WTO legal-ese) the deal was pretty much take it or leave it for the Southern countries. So they took it but, it's safe to say, without a full comprehension of the profoundly transformative implication of this new trading system (an incomprehension shared by the Northern negotiators as well, I might add).

The Northern piece of the bargain consisted of some limited progress in agriculture, with a commitment to go further in new negotiations in 2000; limited progress in textiles and clothing with most of the restrictions to be eliminated later rather than sooner; and a rather significant reduction in tariffs in goods in exchange for deeper cuts by developing countries. On the whole not great, but not bad when compared with previous Rounds centred on traditional GATT-type market access negotiations. But this was not a GATT negotiation, as the Southern piece of the deal so amply demonstrates.

The essence of the South side of the deal – the inclusion of the new issues and the creation of the new institution – requires major upgrading and change in the institutional infrastructure of many or most Southern countries: governance. These changes will take time and cost money. Implementation thus involved considerable investment, often with uncertain medium-term results. Further, the transition periods for implementation for developing countries were arbitrary and not based on any analysis – or, indeed, on any awareness of this systemic problem. The technical assistance promised by the North was not followed up although this appears to have been rectified in Doha. *There has been an increase in agricultural subsidies and virtually no improvement in market access for textiles and clothing.* And even when the quotas of the infamous Multifibre Agreement (MFA) disappear, anti-dumping, the protectionist weapon of choice, is alive and well in the rich countries.

It is also important to note that the Uruguay Round Grand Bargain did not only include *economic* but also *social* regulation. In the OECD countries, but not the South, social regulation (environment, food safety, labour, etc.) started in the late 1960s, driven in large part by environmental and consumer NGOs, and has been accelerating since then. Since the establishment of the WTO the most high-profile and contentious disputes have concerned social regulatory issues (food safety and the environment) which are very sensitive in the OECD countries and has emboldened the NGOs in their attack on the WTO's lack of transparency.

There were two significant unintended consequences to this grand bargain (or bum deal). One is a serious North–South divide in the WTO. While the South is hardly homogeneous there is a broad consensus that the Quad (USA, EU, Japan and Canada) is no longer a 'directoire', that the asymmetry of the Uruguay Round must be ameliorated and must never be repeated and thus Southern countries must play a far more proactive role in all WTO activities. The symbolic importance of words should not be underestimated. The fact that the outcome of Doha was not a negotiation but a 'Development Agenda' is ample testimony of the new proactivist South. Many of the countries are far better organized and informed, in part because of the rise of democracy and the growing awareness of trade policy issues in the general public and political institutions and the business community, but also because of the role of a number of NGOs created in developing countries during the 1990s to provide information ranging from technical research to policy strategy papers. And since the mid-1990s the internet has accelerated the linkages of South NGOs with a number of Northern partners in both Europe and the USA. These NGOs together act, in effect, as a 'virtual secretariat'.

The other, and equally important, unintended consequence of the Uruguay Round has been the rise in profile of the MNEs, in part due to their role in the Round. Indeed, for the more paranoid the Round was simply a conspiratorial collusion between American corporations and the US government. In any case, the global current of deepening integration, accelerated by the Uruguay Round, has evoked a counter-current focused on both the MNEs and the WTO. Let me deal first with the MNEs.

The active role of the corporations in the Uruguay Round certainly raised their profile and made them a magnet for anti-trade advocates and made the WTO a magnet for what came to be called anti-corporate globalization. This is evident to anyone who watched on TV the battle of Seattle or the demonstrations at meetings in Washington, Prague, Genoa or Quebec City. It is also evident in the attack on biotechnology in agriculture first aimed at Monsanto. But the most significant recent example concerns the pharmaceutical industry and the Aids crisis in Africa.

As a result of a well-orchestrated campaign led by Oxfam and Médecins sans Frontières, pharmaceutical companies withdrew a law suit against South Africa; the USA abandoned a dispute against Brazil; and the Doha Declaration included a remarkable political statement concerning the TRIPS agreement and health emergencies. But the impact of NGOs on the WTO goes well beyond the mobilization of protests at meetings or the capture of the moral high ground on poverty and disease. Less visible, but over the longer run probably more significant, is their insistent demand for more transparency.

3   Transparency and participation

There are, broadly speaking, three main requests in the NGOs' demand for external transparency: more access to WTO documents; more participation in WTO activities such as Committee and Ministerial meetings; and the right to observer status and to present *amicus* briefs before dispute settlement panels and the Appellate Board. Of these three, the WTO has made considerable progress in providing information speedily and effectively on its website and through informal Secretariat briefings and has engaged civil society groups in symposia and, in the case of the Committee on Trade and the Environment, in discussions.[6] But even in these two areas, a North–South split is evident and other proposals – such as opening up the Trade Policy Review by webcast – have been opposed. And far more contentious has been the request to open up the dispute settlement mechanisms to *amicus* briefs. These demands have been strongly rejected by many Southern Governments and their NGOs who regard the evidentiary-intensive and increasingly legalistic system as already biased.[7]

Curiously, the issue of transparency and the participation at the national level has only recently been raised. The 'Open Letter on Institutional Reforms in the WTO' sent to members in October 2001 (just before Doha) includes the 'development of guidelines for national consultation with relevant stakeholders' among a number of other proposals.[8] Since reform issues were not on the table in Doha, there was no response. A similar silence greeted US efforts, after the Seattle débâcle, to discuss national policy processes in the WTO (of which more below).

Yet the WTO may be an outlier in its rejection of the relevance of this issue. It's useful to 'benchmark' other institutions in the rapidly evolving

---

[6] Gregory C. Shaffer, 'The World Trade Organization Under Challenge: Democracy and the Law and Politics of the WTO's Treatment of Trade and Environment Matters', *Harvard Environmental Law Review*, 25(1), 2001, pp. 2–97.

[7] For an account of the broader concerns with the dispute settlement mechanism, see Claude E. Barfield, *Free Trade, Sovereignty, Democracy: The Future of the World Trade Organization*, Washington, DC, American Enterprise Press, 2001, chapters 4 and 5.

[8] Open Letter on Institutional Reform, WTO Activist, October 2001, at wto-activist@iatp.org, posted 10 September 2001.

international policy environment because in a globalizing world 'policy spillover' has become increasingly significant. A review of developments in the OECD, and in international environmental and human rights law, will serve to illustrate this point.

OECD: transparency, trade, environment and development

In 1993, the OECD Joint Working Party on Trade and Environment proposed that Transparency and Consultation be established as a principle of policy-making in this domain. (That this innovation in governance involved environmental policies was hardly a coincidence – see below.) The proposal was adopted by Ministers as was the initiative to undertake case studies of member governments' consultative mechanisms and practices. These case studies were published in 1999 and 2000.[9] They revealed a wide diversity among the countries reflecting, *inter alia*, culture, history and legal systems, but also underscored the importance of 'capacity' – analytic and financial resources – as a factor in determining the nature of the process.

In July 2001, the OECD directorate responsible for research in public management (PUMA) published a Policy Brief outlining a number of principles for good governance.[10] The title of the brief was *Engaging Citizens in Policy-Making: Information, Consultation and Public Participation.* The lead paragraph provides the rationale for the initiative:

> Strengthening relations with citizens is a sound investment in better policy-making and a core element of good governance. It allows governments to tap new sources of policy-relevant ideas, information and resources when making decisions. Equally important, it contributes to building public trust in government, raising the quality of democracy and strengthening civic capacity. Such efforts help strengthen representative democracy in which parliaments play a central role.

The reference to building public trust and enhancing the credibility of governments is of key significance in catalysing the OECD initiative and

---

[9] OECD, *Transparency and Consultation on Trade and Environment, 1, National Case Studies,* COM/TD/ENV(99) 26/FINAL, Paris, October 1999 and Round 2, March 2000. See also in the same series, *NGO Consultation Summary Record,* August 2000 and *Transparency and Consultation on Trade and Environment in Five International Organizations,* August 2000, at http://www1.oecd.org/ech/trade&env/transparency.htm.

[10] OECD Public Management (PUMA) Policy Brief, 10, *Engaging Citizens in Policy-Making: Information, Consultation and Public Participation,* Paris, OECD, July 2001.

of particular relevance in the trade policy domain. The anti-globalization movement reflects a more pervasive secular change underway since the mid-1970s in all OECD countries: a clear, marked decline in confidence in government and all political institutions.[11] (While in the USA, the events of 11 September radically reversed this trend, it is not clear how this will affect, if at all, international economic policy). There are less data on this phenomenon in non-OECD countries, but anecdotal evidence suggests that an alienation from the elite is growing in many Southern countries and in Central and Eastern Europe.

There are many different views on the reasons for this worrisome phenomenon and no doubt different factors are operative in different countries. But one response – and not only by the OECD – has been to foster 'ownership' of the policy process by increasing information, consultation and active participation by a wider range of stakeholders. As the case studies and other OECD research demonstrated, while information access has increased over the past decade, there are large differences in consultation and 'active participation and efforts to engage citizens in policy-making' are rare, and confined to a very few OECD countries.[12]

What follows in the Brief are a number of policy suggestions and a set of ten guiding principles for OECD governments to engage citizens in policy-making.[13] While these principles are not binding on OECD governments – being a form of 'soft law' – their adoption by Ministers is not without significance. It should also be noted that the initiative by the Trade and Environment Joint Working Party was carried over to the Development Aid Committee (DAC) and resulted in proposals that 'participatory development and good governance' principle should be built into all country-based aid systems.[14] Again, this is not binding but is none the less highly significant in underlining the importance of 'ownership', as is now the practice in the World Bank.[15] Policy spillover is perhaps not surprising, except that it has not affected the WTO, at least not yet.

[11] Sylvia Ostry, *Global Integration: Currents and Counter-Currents*, Walter Gordon Lecture, Massey College, University of Toronto, 2002.

[12] PUMA, July 2001, p. 3.

[13] *Ibid*, p. 5.

[14] OECD, Development Assistance Committee, *Final Report of the Ad Hoc Group on Participatory Development and Good Governance*, part 1 and part 2, Paris, OECD, 1997.

[15] See Poverty Net, Poverty Reduction Strategies and PRSPs, at http://www.worldbank.org/poverty/strategies/sourctoc.htm for information. The Poverty Reduction Strategy approach was adopted in 1999 and involves countries preparing strategy papers (PRSPs) which, *inter alia*, would involve participatory consultations.

The Aarhus Convention

When we move from the OECD's soft law to the Aarhus Convention we move from soft to hard law. The United Nations Economic Commission for Europe (UNECE) Convention on Access to Information, Public Participation in Decision-Making and Access to Justice in Environmental Matters was adopted on 25 June 1998, in the Danish city of Aarhus at the Fourth Ministerial Conference of the 'Environment for Europe' process. It entered into force on 30 October 2001, with forty signatories including members of the Economic Commission for Europe (ECE) as well as states with consultative status with the ECE (mainly Central and Eastern European countries) and the European Community (EC).

Aarhus is built on Principle 10 of the Rio Conference on Environment and Development (UNCED) which underlined the importance of a participatory process in formulating and implementing environmental policy at the national level.[16] The idea of transparency and participation is deeply rooted in the environmental movement and policy domain both domestically and internationally because, as a number of international environmental law experts have pointed out, non-state actors frequently have more and better information than governments. These actors include private firms and various and diverse NGOs all of which have stakes (albeit often competing) in outcomes, either as objects or beneficiaries of regulation.[17]

But the Aarhus Convention is quite radical in both its content and, perhaps in its implications for international law. The Convention is built on three pillars – access to information, participation, access to domestic courts – and spells out in detail what each of these rights includes. It recognizes that forms of participation must be adapted to different legal and institutional systems and are dynamic in concept, i.e. should and will evolve over time. The intention of the Aarhus Convention however, is to identify basic or preliminary elements that would entail a participatory process. The Convention also includes the need for follow-up monitoring of implementation measures, which should be transparent. And to ensure transparency, the public is granted access to judicial review procedures when their rights to information and participation have been breached.

[16] See Jonas Ebbesson, 'The Notion of Public Participation in International Environmental Law', *Yearbook of International Environmental Law*, 8, 1997, pp. 51–3.
[17] Kal Raustiala, 'The "Participatory Revolution" in International Environmental Law', *Harvard Environmental Law Review*, 21, 1997, pp. 537–86.

Kofi Annan, the UN Secretary-General, described the Convention as 'the most ambitious venture in environmental democracy undertaken under the auspices of the United Nations' and 'a remarkable step forward in the development of international law'. He further stated (in an oblique reference to the North–South divide) that 'environmental rights are not a luxury reserved for rich countries' and called on the international community to use 'the World Summit on Sustainable Development to strengthen our commitment to environmental rights' not only in Europe but throughout the world.[18]

Whether or not Aarhus will catalyse the Rio plus 10 meeting in September 2002 in Johannesburg, the implications for international law are significant since there will no doubt be an effort by the proponents of transparency and participation to extend the Aarhus principles to customary international environmental law (see below). But while the Aarhus Convention concentrates on legal and administrative procedures (i.e. on procedural rights), it also includes a reference to human rights in the preamble and in some other provisions.[19] Many NGOs are pushing for a rights-based approach in the environmental domain and Aarhus may have opened up a small window of opportunity. But that aside, the human rights channel to greater transparency and participation looks very plausible, Aarhus or not.

Human rights and participatory democracy

The push for including human rights in the WTO is linked to the ongoing – and often heated – debate on customary international law. In international law, the status of a rule is determined by its source. Thus international conventions (such as the Aarhus Convention) are often described as 'hard law', with rules and enforcement agreed by and applicable only to members while customary law relates to obligations established from 'a general and consistent practice of states followed by them out of a sense of legal obligation' and binds all states.[20]

---

[18] See 'United Nations Environment Programme Welcomes Entry into Force of Arrhus Convention', Nairobi, 6 November 2001, at http://www.unece.org/env/pp.

[19] Ebbesson, 'The Notion of Public Participation', pp. 69–72.

[20] See Robert Howse and Makau Mutua, 'Protecting Human Rights in a Global Economy: Challenges for the World Trade Organization', Occasional Paper, International Centre for Human Rights and Democratic Development, Montreal, 2000, pp. 7–10.

There is considerable disagreement as to whether and which human rights have status as custom, and the proposal that human rights should prevail over international trade law (i.e. override those WTO rules which are alleged to violate basic human rights) has generated a storm of controversy.[21] The battle seems set to continue. Yet, as several experts have noted, recent rulings of the Appellate Board cite the Vienna Convention on the Law of Treaties which allows for the emergence of new laws in the future.[22] Thus, some legal experts have argued that the preamble of the WTO Agreement, which refers to sustainable development and the need for the poorest countries to develop and grow, states values that could be interpreted as basic human rights.[23] The ruling of the Appellate Body in an environment trade dispute (shrimp–turtle) cited the preamble in adopting its interpretation of the term 'exhaustible natural resources' to include endangered species because of the evolution of international environmental law in recent years.[24] Perhaps a dispute over services, especially in health or education or water, could provide the push that opens the door to human rights interpretations of the preamble. Certainly this aspect of the services debate is rallying a number of NGOs opposed to liberalization and privatization of public services in both rich and poor countries. A 'manifesto' entitled 'Stop the GATS ATTACK now!' has garnered support from a diverse mix of NGOs – including, not surprisingly, public-service unions – from over fifty countries around the world.[25]

The legal (as opposed to the legislative) route to inserting human rights into the WTO was given a leg up by another decision of a dispute settlement panel concerning American trade law Section 301. Included in the panel's decision was the statement that 'it would be entirely wrong to consider that the position of individuals is of no relevance to the GATT/WTO legal matrix. Many of the benefits to members which are meant to flow as a result of the acceptance of various disciplines under the GATT/WTO depend on the activity of individual economic operators in the national

[21] See Sylvia Ostry, 'Dissent.Com: How NGOs are Re-Making the WTO', *Policy Options*, Montreal, June 2001, pp. 11–13.

[22] Howse and Mutua, 'Protecting Human Rights', pp. 9–11.

[23] See Ernst-Ulrich Petersmann, 'Human Rights and International Economic Law in the 21st Century: The Need to Clarify their Interrelationships', *Journal of International Economic Law*, 4(1), 2001, pp. 24–8.

[24] Barfield, *Free Trade*, pp. 66–7.

[25] To 'sign on' (or see the manifesto and supporting NGOs), send an e-mail to polarisinstitute@on.aibn.com.

and global market places' and thus 'the multilateral trading system is, perforce, composed not only of the States but also, indeed mostly, of individual economic operators'.[26]

This astonishing conclusion of the panel has certainly attracted the attention of WTO-watchers in the legal community – though, evidently, not of member governments as one prominent legal expert noted: 'I would venture to guess that if this particular proposition were put to a vote in the General Council of the WTO, it would be rejected by governments who want to preserve the WTO as a cozy club of trade bureaucrats. In accordance with the WTO procedures, however, it was automatically adopted by the WTO Dispute Settlement Body. Thus, this cutting-edge decision will influence future WTO panellists and the *invisible college of international law* in the years ahead'.[27]

Among the individual rights of interest to the 'invisible college' are certainly the right of public participation in policy-making as, for example, specified in the Aarhus Convention. Indeed an entire school of international law based on 'interactional theory' points out that 'law is persuasive when it is perceived as legitimate by most actors' and 'legitimacy rests on inclusive processes [which] reinforce the commitments of participants in the system to the substantive outcomes achieved by implicating participants in their generation'.[28] This sounds very much like the OECD approach, that norms generated through inclusive processes of decision-making enhance governmental legitimacy and enjoy a greater degree of compliance. Part of the spreading climate of ideas – we could call it 'norm spillover'. The WTO is unlikely to be immune.

One of the strongest advocates of human rights as the basis for the WTO is Ernst-Ulrich Petersmann who, while welcoming the Report on Section 301, rejects the panel's reasoning 'that WTO law is based on a "principle of indirect effect" in the sense that the GATT/WTO did not create a new legal order, the subjects of which comprise both contracting parties or Members and their nationals as *premature*'. Why, he argues, should these individual rights be achieved 'indirectly' rather than – as human

---

[26] Sections 301–310 of the Trade Act of 1974, Report of the Panel, 22 December 1999, WT/DS/152/R, paragraph 7.72 and 7.76.

[27] Steve Charnovitz, 'The WTO and the Rights of the Individual', *Intereconomics*, March–April 2001, p. 108 (emphasis added).

[28] Jutta Brunnée and Stephen J. Toope, 'International Law and Constructivism: Elements of an Interactional Theory of International Law', *Columbia Journal of Transnational Law*, 39, 2000–2001, p. 53. See also Harold Hongju Koh, 'Why do Nations Obey International Law?', Review Essay, *Yale Law Journal*, 106(8), pp. 2599–2659.

rights law suggests – directly? Rather, WTO guarantees of 'freedom' and 'property rights' (also in TRIPS, most clearly) should be 'presumed to protect individual rights of citizens'.[29] Petersmann is not alone in his view. Raj Bhala, in his trade law textbook, asserts that: 'If the GATT/WTO regime is a just one in the sense [of] Kant or his modern-day disciples who defend liberal democratic theory, then the central focus of this regime must be on the protection and service of the individual'.[30]

So the 'invisible college' is active and also training a new cohort likely to be equally so. I would predict that if the *legal* route to inserting human rights law is chosen, the results will be profoundly traumatic for the WTO. Such a pervasive and open-ended transformation of the present system, determined by a panel or an Appellate Board, would be rejected by most if not all members and generate a furious backlash against the 'crown jewel' of the WTO – the dispute settlement mechanism. The issue of the WTO and human rights should be debated and decided by member governments, and thus any change to the rules should be legislated not litigated. But that debate on human rights (or indeed, other fundamental issues such as the definition of domestic policy space to be safeguarded by the multilateral system) has not taken place and, since there is no policy forum in which to launch it, is unlikely to do so any time soon. But that raises the question of internal reform and is not the subject of my article. Let's return to the main topic of external transparency and the participatory process at the national level.

4   WTO: 'legislate' don't litigate

I insert the word 'legislate' in inverted commas because my proposal need not involve a change in the formal rules of the WTO – a most difficult and lengthy proposition, as everyone would agree. Rather, I would propose an informal, voluntary initiative to incorporate discussion of the national trade policy-making processes into the WTO under the broad rubric of transparency, a pillar of the GATT/WTO system from its origins. As I have argued above, there is a growing consensus among not only legal and policy-analytic communities but also in a number of intergovernmental institutions that participatory processes improve policy outcomes and enhance the legitimacy of policy and compliance with norms and

---

[29] Petersmann, 'Human Rights', p. 33 (emphasis added).
[30] Raj Bhala, *International Trade Law: Theory and Practice*, New York, 2001, 2nd edition, p. 610, cited in Charnovitz, 'The WTO', p. 108.

laws. Most importantly, if the 'legislative' route is eschewed, the legalistic route remains the only game in town. One way or another human rights *per se* or customary international environmental law will seep into the system through the legalistic channel, with the serious repercussions I have described. But if the legalistic route is to be avoided how can the legislative route be achieved? Let's briefly review the state of play in the relationship between the WTO and the trade policy stakeholders, including the NGOs.

At the April 1994 Ministerial Meeting in Marrakesh which concluded the Uruguay Round Article V:2 of the Agreement stated:

> The General Council may make appropriate arrangements for consultation and co-operation with non-governmental organizations concerned with matters related to those of the WTO.[31]

In order to clarify the precise *legal* meaning of this broad directive the General Council, on 18 July 1996, spelled out a set of guidelines covering transparency including release of documents, ad hoc informal contracts with NGOs, etc. Guideline 6 is most pertinent in the context of this present discussion:

> Members have pointed to the special character of the WTO, which is both a legally binding inter-governmental treaty of rights and obligations among its Members and a forum for negotiation. As a result of extensive discussions, there is currently a broadly held view that it would not be possible for NGOs to be directly involved in the work of the WTO or its meetings. Closer consultation and co-operation with NGOs can also be met constructively through *appropriate processes at the national level where lies primary responsibility for taking into account the different elements of public interest which are brought to bear on trade policy-making.*[32]

Nothing happened with respect to the admonition to focus on the national level until after the Seattle débâcle. At a meeting of the General Council in July 2000, which included a discussion on external transparency (under the agenda item 'other business'), the Chairman suggested that members might make written contributions on the subject after making informal consultations in the autumn. This suggestion was criticized by several members, as was the Chairman's decision to propose discussion

---

[31] *The Results of the Uruguay Round of Multilateral Trade Negotiations: The Legal Texts*, p. 9.

[32] Cited in the appendix in Gabrielle Marceau and Peter N. Pederson, 'Is the WTO Open and Transparent? A Discussion of the Relationship of the WTO with Non-Governmental Organizations and Civil Society's Claim for more Transparency and Public Participation', *Journal of World Trade*, 33(1), 1999, p. 45 (emphasis added).

under the heading of 'other business'. The Chairman explained that since there was strong opposition to place this issue on a formal agenda he had decided to raise it under 'other business', but since some delegations did want to discuss external transparency 'he believed it would be difficult to continuously postpone even an informal discussion'.[33] After further discussion among the supporters and opponents of informal discussions, the meeting was adjourned.

On 13 October 2000 the USA made a submission to the General Council's Informal Consultations on External Transparency. After noting that the 1996 Guidelines suggested that the consultations should take place at the national level and a brief review of US processes in this respect, the American delegation proposed that since all members 'could benefit from an exchange of information on national experiences and approaches ... members be invited to provide information on this respective approaches to providing their public with information and opportunity for input on developments in the trading system'.[34] Seven other countries made submissions with suggestions to extend WTO information access and engage in more discussion with NGOs and other bodies, especially parliaments.

On 9 November 2000 an Informal General Council meeting was convened to discuss external transparency. Delegates were in favour of holding discussions on external transparency, and agreed that governments should inform their citizens about the WTO and its activities.[35]

The same countries (mostly developing) opposed to increasing transparency at the WTO level were also opposed to discussing the policy process at the national level. There has been criticism about the more powerful well-financed Northern NGOs demanding two bites of the apple. Fair enough – the issue merits discussion.[36] But how realistic, in the light of the current state of affairs in the multilateral trading system, is it to suggest *no* bite at the apple? For those countries who reject even an informal discussion of their domestic policy processes, it's useful to spell out the benefits of such a project.

---

[33] WTO, General Council, 17 and 19 July 2000, Minutes of Meeting, WT/GC/M/57, p. 60.

[34] General Council Informal Consultations on External Transparency, 13 October 2000, WT/GC/W/413/Rev.l, p. 3.

[35] External Transparency Informal General Council, 9 November 2000; sent to author in response to request for information to prepare this chapter.

[36] For an analysis of this and other aspects of the WTO and NGOs, see Steve Charnovitz, 'Opening the WTO to Nongovernmental Interests', *Fordham International Law Journal*, 24, November–December 2000, pp. 173–216.

First and foremost it is very important to emphasize that a discussion about the national policy processes would be simply that – a means for informing other countries about one's own practices and learning about theirs. There is clearly no one-size-fits-all model but rather considerable diversity related to history, culture, legal institutions, level of development and so on. A pilot project I have undertaken in cooperation with the Washington-based Inter-American Dialogue and the Inter-American Development Bank revealed very significant differences among the eight countries surveyed: Argentina, Brazil, Canada, Chile, Columbia, Mexico, the USA and Uruguay.[37] Of these, only Canada and the USA have established institutional arrangements involving both legislative bodies and a wide range of interested parties or stakeholders including business, farmers, unions, NGOs and academics. This is not surprising since the OECD studies showed that participatory processes were rare in member countries. And a 1996 study by the Swiss Coalition of Development Organizations showed that of thirty countries surveyed (both developed and developing) only three had formal mechanisms for consultation (Canada, the USA and Switzerland).[38]

None the less, given this North–South dichotomy (and there are significant differences between Canada and the USA because of differences in basic governance – i.e. a parliamentary versus a presidential system) the Latin countries were by no means homogeneous and, further, in some an evolutionary process was underway partly in response to changes in trade policy such as Mercosur. The discussion which these papers evoked at a meeting of authors and others in June 2001 provided ample evidence of how much can be learned about this important subject even by close neighbours. This pilot is intended to be a launch of a longer-term project to encourage governments to consider whether some set of preliminary basic norms could be agreed to enhance the legitimacy and sustainability of trade liberalization. The policy process should be evolutionary, reflecting systemic changes (such as the transformation from GATT to the WTO) and changes in the policy environment such as an increase in protectionist actions or an economic slowdown or a backlash against the 'failed' promise that trade liberalization would deliver Nirvana. A participatory consulting process permits governments to inform stakeholders

---

[37] *The Trade Policy-Making Process, Level One of the Two Level Game: Country Studies in the Western Hemisphere,* IDB-Intal Occasional Paper, 13, Buenos Aires, 2002.

[38] Christophe Bellemann and Richard Gerster, 'Accountability in the World Trade Organization', *Journal of World Trade,* 30(6), December 1996, pp. 31–74.

on a continuing basis, and while they may not always like what they hear (trade policy in the best of times involves change and change produces winners and losers) they will be less likely to reject the entire regime.

Moreover, by sharing information on national processes stakeholders in many countries without adequate technical or financial resources – like small and medium enterprises (SMEs) – gain useful information on market opportunities or other issues of interest. In a related point, it should be noted that lack of technical and financial resources for many stakeholders and also for some government ministries and parliaments was a major factor affecting the nature of the process in a number of countries.

While there are undoubtedly benefits accruing from a more partici-patory policy process there are also costs, which is certainly one reason many countries are wary of the project. There are costs for governments in terms of time, expertise and financial resources and there are significant differences in resources among the stakeholders. Since business lobbies are better equipped than other groups an insider–outsider mentality can develop and the media are always happy to highlight the battles. Or some stakeholders, simply by being engaged in the process, develop unrealistic expectations about outcome and are frustrated when all their demands are, inevitably, not delivered. For the wily statesman secrecy is considered essential, especially as the negotiations move to closure and the idea of a participatory process is an oxymoron – unless it provides an opportunity for cooption. All these issues arose in the Western Hemisphere country studies and the discussion repeatedly made clear that there were no magic bullets; the policy process was complex and messy; processes should be in a condition of continuing evolution; and, as in the case in all incremen-tal innovations, learning-by-doing and benchmarking, best practices are essential. And the bottom line in all this deserves, stressing: that it is the role of *government* to make policy; transparency and participation are *not* a replacement for *governmental responsibility*.

In the WTO context, weighing costs and benefits thus rests on the judge-ment of each member country. The arguments presented here suggest that there are likely to be significant systemic costs from doing nothing and that these should be considered by members when rejecting any WTO initiative. The erosion of the multilateral system will impact the weaker more than the stronger, because the alternative to a rules-based system is one based on power.

Having presented my case for a WTO external transparency initiative, let me conclude with a sketch of how it could be launched.

5   Transparency and the TPRM

As noted earlier, transparency was one of the founding principles of the postwar trading system.[39] Article 38 of the Havana Charter for the International Trade Organization (ITO) became Article 10 of the GATT, which survived the death of the trade organization. The Article was entitled 'Publication and Administration of Trade Regulations – Advance Notice of Restrictive Regulations' and was borrowed from the 1946 US Administrative Procedures Act (APA). The APA exemplified a new legal terrain connected with the expanding role of government initiated by the New Deal. Administrative law is not *substantive* but *procedural*, establishing norms to control what bureaucrats do and how they do it. While all western countries developed administrative law regimes because of the expanded role of governments, the APA was different from those in other common law or codified continental systems because of its greater emphasis on notice-and-comments for administrative rules, freedom of information laws and greater reliance on judicial review of the rule-making activities of agencies or departments, i.e. high levels of transparency. Embedded in the GATT, in Article X, transparency was greatly expanded in the WTO with the inclusion of services and TRIPS, and the word finally appears in the TRIPS Agreement as a heading in Article 63.

In the USA, the evolution of administrative law expanded the participatory role of stakeholders, partly in response to the increase in regulation beginning in the 1970s and to the growing literature on the dangers of 'regulatory capture'.[40] Many economists and legal scholars argued that the best antidote to the capture of regulatory agencies by those they regulate was to broaden the spectrum of interests whose voices should be heard before rules are laid down. This development is for the most part not reflected in the WTO, which focuses on the rights and responsibilities of governments not stakeholders. There are, however, some exceptions, such as the Subsidies and Countervailing Measures (SCM) Agreement, which includes the rights of 'interested parties' other than those of member governments. Consumer groups are named specifically as they are in the Dumping Agreement. In the Safeguard Agreement there is a specific obligation for the importing country to carry out an investigation

---

[39] The discussion on transparency is taken from Sylvia Ostry, 'China and the WTO: The Transparency Issue', *UCLA Journal of International Law and Foreign Affairs*, 3, 1998, pp. 1–22.

[40] See Raustiala, 'The "Participatory Revolution"', p. 577 and the references to George Stigler, Richard Posmer and Ralph Nader.

which includes 'public interest hearings' which could include any interest group. Similar provisions are in TRIPS and Article VI of the GATS on Domestic Regulation.[41] Although these examples do provide some procedural participatory rights, for the most part the WTO Rules situate the determination of the policy process in the domestic arena of the member governments. So WTO external transparency begins at home – with one major exception, the Trade Policy Review Mechanism (TPRM).

The TPRM was based on a recommendation of the Functioning of the GATT System (FOGS) negotiating group in the Uruguay Round. It was designed to enhance the effectiveness of the domestic policy-making process through informed public understanding, i.e. transparency.[42] Section B spells it out:

> Domestic Transparency
>
> Members recognize the inherent value of domestic transparency of government decision-making on trade policy matters for both Members' economies and the multilateral trading system, and agree to encourage and promote greater transparency within their own systems, acknowledging that the implementation of domestic transparency must be on a voluntary basis and take account of each Member's legal and political systems.[43]

In order to underline that the TPRM is voluntary and flexible in subject matter, the declaration of Objectives in Section A that 'it is not intended to serve as a basis for the enforcement of specific obligations under the Agreements or for dispute settlement procedures, or to impose new policy commitments on Members'.[44]

The TPRM's origins and objectives clearly embrace the policy-making process and thus seems the logical venue for launching this project – on a voluntary basis and as a pilot to be assessed after an agreed period. The WTO Secretariat is already seriously overburdened so it might be necessary for the volunteers to ante up some funding. If the pilot took off and a number of developing countries became involved the issue of more permanent funding would have to be faced, since there would be capacity building and technical assistance requirements. But these latter costs should clearly come under the arrangements agreed at Doha on capacity

---

[41] See Marceau and Pedersen, 'Is the WTO Open and Transparent?', pp. 37–40.

[42] See Sylvia Ostry, *The Post-Cold War Trading System: Who's on First?*, Chicago, University of Chicago Press, 1997, pp. 201–3.

[43] *The Results of the Uruguay Round of Multilateral Trade Negotiations: The Legal Texts*, p. 434.

[44] *Ibid.*

building. Enhancing capacity to improve and sustain a more transparent trade policy process sounds like a good investment. It's hardly a new idea. In the 1970s, during the Tokyo Round, an American official remarked to an academic researcher that the advisory committees established under the 1974 Trade Act were working extremely well because 'when you let a dog piss all over a fire hydrant he thinks he owns it'.[45] That's a rather less felicitous version of today's concept of ownership.

[45] Gilbert R. Winham, *International Trade and the Tokyo Round Negotiation*, Princeton, Princeton University Press, 1986, p. 316.

7

Trading for development: how to assist poor countries

JAGDISH BHAGWATI

1 Introduction

The launch of a new Round of multilateral trade negotiations (MTN) at Doha dealt a needed blow to the anti-globalizers who had triumphed at Seattle just two years before. But it was important for a different reason as well. The word 'Development' now unconventionally graces the name of the new Round, alongside Doha. Development of the poor countries will be the central objective of the new Round.

But pleasing rhetoric aside, we must ask: what *does* this mean? The question is not an idle one. For, if the current thinking in policy and NGO circles on what is the appropriate answer is any guide to what is in store for the poor countries, there is cause for alarm.

Of course, the proponents of trade have always considered that trade is the policy and development is the objective. The post-war experience only proves them right. The objections advanced by a handful of dissenting economists, claiming that free traders exaggerate the gains from trade or forget that good trade policy is best embedded within a package of reforms, mostly set up and knock down straw men, or aunt sallies, depending on your gender preference. Consider just the most insidious ones.

A currently fashionable argument is that trade is only a component of a package of good policies. Sure enough. But it requires either amnesia or ignorance, and focus on an occasional overenthusiast such as my Columbia University colleague Jeffrey Sachs, whose enthusiasm often strains credulity, to argue that the proponents of freer trade believe in monocausality in explaining good or bad economic outcomes. Indeed, a distinguished critic in this mode, Professor Dani Rodrik of Kennedy School at Harvard University, might profit from reading my Keynote

An abbreviated version of this chapter appeared as an Invited Article in *The Economist*, titled 'Trading for Development: The Poor's Best Hope', 22–28 June 2002, pp. 25–8.

speech at Cornell University, where I point to a virtuous circle of policies that defined why outward orientation – the Prince in *Hamlet* – led to such impressive economic outcomes. The outward orientation itself raised the marginal efficiency of capital and hence the investment incentive and therefore productive investment itself to 'miracle' levels (relative to inward-looking countries like India). In turn, this facilitated the import of embodied technology from abroad. Besides, the productivity of such equipment was enhanced thanks to near-universal literacy and to partly-induced policy of promotion of university education.[1]

Indeed, Rodrik has also contended that the proponents of freer trade forget that the cause of good economic performance is not outward orientation but the underlying 'fundamentals', especially good macroeconomics. Now, familiarity breeds contempt, but contempt does not breed familiarity. And unfamiliarity, in turn, breeds incompetent commentary and critique. In my synthesis volume on the mammoth multi-county project with Anne Krueger run under the auspices of the National Bureau of Economic Research, I argued that, since outward orientation required that there be macroeconomic stability, or else inflation would cut into export performance, the countries that chose outward orientation as their strategy would also enjoy the many advantages that follow from macroeconomic stability. In short, macroeconomic stability had to be considered endogenous to the trade strategy in this instance: and therefore the benefits of good macroeconomics could indeed be argued to be a result of the adoption of the outward-oriented strategy. Equally, I have noted often that the socialist countries behind the Iron Curtain (and India, too, as it happened) had excellent macroeconomic stability for decades: but they had an explicit anti-trade, inward-looking developmental strategy, with all the damage that we now know it to inflict. Indeed, anyone familiar with the developmental literature in depth knows that a common witticism was that Marx and Milton Friedman were bedfellows on macroeconomic stability.

But the latest form of the critique of freer trade is that directed more at the Bretton Woods institutions: that they have adopted a 'one-shoe-size-fits-all' strategy, a phrase that almost invites acceptance because it embodies and evokes the image of incontestable folly. Indeed, journalists have found this a fetching critique and often quote Rodrik, and sometimes

---

[1] This chapter is reprinted in my new collection of public policy essays, *The Wind of the Hundred Days: How Washington Mismanaged Globalization*, Cambridge, MA, MIT Press, 2000.

my new Columbia colleague, Joseph Stiglitz, to that effect. But this is a piece of plausible but nonetheless rank nonsense. The real choice is between wearing shoes and going barefoot. I would say that the latter practice is likely to produce a raft of pedestrians who are busy removing thorns from their feet instead of proceeding with due speed to their desired destinations! Post-war experience has shown that countries that adopted an outward-oriented strategy did better than those that went inwards; and there is no case in this period of a county that chose the inward-looking strategy and largely delinked itself from the benefits of international integration registering sustained growth. I might recall the famous joke – it is not apocryphal – where the 'neo-liberal' Gus Ranis of Yale and Joan Robinson, the famously radical economist who was one of my teachers at Cambridge, were agreeing for a change over Korea's phenomenal economic success. The riddle was soon resolved: he was talking about South Korea and she about North! We all know now which county did dramatically better on a sustained basis while the other went down the tubes; and outward orientation on trade was at the heart of this.

As for different sizes of the shoes (i.e. freer trade) that we must wear, again these critics get it wrong. The differences in political, historical and economic circumstance themselves lead, whether you like it or not, to *de facto* differences in the shoe size that you will wear. The speed at which trade liberalization has occurred has naturally varied, even though the prescription that freer trade is generally good for you, rather than bad for you, was properly disseminated in the 1970s through 1990s by economists and by international bureaucrats who also learned the lessons that emerged from post-war experience. In fact, it is impossible for a substantial straitjacket to be devised: reality always intrudes. Remember *The Bachelor's Cook Book* which had the recipe for scrambled eggs: 'start frying an egg'! I shall have some more to add on this later in this chapter.

2 Harmful misconceptions

But if trade is indeed good for the poor countries, what can be done to enhance its value for them? A great deal. But not until we confront and discard several misconceptions that make for bad prescriptions. Among them:

- The world trading system is 'unfair': the poor countries face protectionism that is more acute than their own

- The rich countries have wickedly held on to their trade barriers against poor countries while using the Bretton Woods institutions to force down the trade barriers of the poor countries
- It is 'hypocritical' to ask poor countries to reduce their trade barriers when the rich countries have their own.

3   Asymmetry of trade barriers goes the other way

Take industrial tariffs. As of today, the rich-country tariffs average 3 per cent but 13 per cent for the poor countries. Nor do peaks in tariffs, concentrated in textiles and garments, fisheries and footwear and clearly directed at the poor countries, change the picture much: UNCTAD has estimated that they apply to only a third of poor-country exports. Moreover, the trade barriers of the poor countries are among the significant restraints faced by the poor countries, even more than those imposed by the rich countries.

The situation is little different on the use of anti-dumping actions, the classic 'fair trade' instrument that has ironically been used 'unfairly' to undermine free trade. The 'new' users, among them Argentina, Brazil, India, South Korea, South Africa and Mexico, are now filing more anti-dumping complaints than the rich countries. Between July and December 2001 alone, India carried out the largest number anywhere of anti-dumping investigations.

(It is often thought that such spread of anti-dumping filings will make the USA and the EU, which have both resorted extensively to anti-dumping actions to protect their uncompetitive industries, become more malleable to reforming and sheathing this favoured protectionist sword as they themselves become victims abroad of anti-dumping actions by others. But this may be too optimistic. We thought that way about the spread of preferential trading agreements (PTAs); but, as I discuss below, with so many joining in, the bilaterals have turned into an epidemic with all countries now sinners so that none throws stones at others. As poor-country lawyers are increasingly trained at special seminars in Washington, DC on how to conduct anti-dumping actions, and a lucrative prospect is opened up for them to make the money that Washington law firms make from anti-dumping practice, it is much more likely that we will see the spawning of legal, not just industry, lobbies that are willing to put their money behind the politicians that support such practices: a good parallel being the massive investment that torts lawyers make in financing the politicians in the USA.)

These facts fly in the face of the populist myth that the rich countries, often acting through the conditionality imposed by the World Bank and the IMF, have demolished the trade barriers of the poor countries while holding on to their own trade barriers. Indeed, both the omnipotence of the Bretton Woods institutions, and the self-serving wickedness of the rich countries, have been grossly exaggerated, accounting for allegations that are the opposite of the true facts.

The World Bank's conditionality is so extensive and diffused, and its need to lend so compelling, that it can be bypassed: many client states typically satisfy some while ignoring other conditionalities. Besides, countries go to the IMF when there is a stabilization crisis. Since stabilization requires that the excess of expenditures over income be brought into line, the IMF has often been reluctant to suggest tariff reductions: they could reduce revenues, exacerbating the crisis.

Then again, since countries are free to return to their bad ways once the crisis is past, and the loans repaid, there can be reversals of the tariff reforms: unlike at the WTO, countries do not 'bind' their tariff reductions at Bretton Woods. Equally, reversals in tariff reductions can occur when a stabilization crisis has recurred and the tariffs are re-imposed for revenue purposes. My student Ravi Yatawara, who has studied what he calls 'commercial policy switches', documents several instances of such tariff reduction reversals by countries borrowing from the IMF. For instance, Uruguay in 1971 increased protection during an IMF programme which had begun the year before and even managed to get another credit tranche the year after. Kenya's 1977 liberalization was reversed in 1979, the year that another arrangement was negotiated with the IMF.

Moreover, the comparatively higher trade barriers against labour-intensive products are not the product of wickedness but are to be explained mostly by simple political economy. While unilateral reductions of trade barriers are not uncommon, and I document them for many countries and several sectors in the postwar period in my new book, *Going Alone: The Case for Relaxed Reciprocity in Freeing Trade* (Cambridge, MA, MIT Press, 2002), the fact remains that the developing countries were exempted by the economic ideology of the time, which embraced special and differential treatment (SDT) for them, from having to make trade concessions of their own at the successive MTNs that reduced trade barriers in the post-war period. The rich countries, denied reciprocal concessions from the poor countries, wound up concentrating on liberalizing trade in products of interest largely to one another, e.g. machinery, chemicals and manufactures other than textiles and garments.

If you want a free lunch, you do not get to eat at the Lord Mayor's banquet.

The situation changed when the poor countries became players. They then managed, in 1995 at Marrakesh where the Uruguay Round was concluded, to get at the infamous Multifibre Arrangement (MFA), which had grown from its birth in 1961 as the Short-term Cotton Textile Arrangement into a Frankenstein by 1974 when it brought under one umbrella several separate restrictive agreements restricting world trade in all textiles. MFA was put on the block, scheduled to terminate at the end of ten years.

But even if rich-country protectionism were asymmetrically higher, it would be dangerous to argue that it is then 'hypocritical' to suggest to the poor countries to reduce their own trade barriers. Except in the few cases (hardly applicable to the poor countries) where strategic tit-for-tat play is credible, the net effect of matching others' protection with one's own is to hurt oneself twice over.

There is ample evidence that many leaders of the poor countries have predictably made the wrong inference: that rich-country hypocrisy excuses, and justifies, going easy on relaxing their own trade barriers. We should instead be saying to the rich countries something quite different: if you hold on to your own protection no matter how much smaller, and in fact even raise it as the USA did with steel and the Farm Bill, you are going to undermine seriously the efforts of the leaders in the poor countries who have turned to freer trade in recent decades. For it is difficult to reduce protection if others, more prosperous and more fierce supporters of free trade, are breaking ranks.

4   Exports from the poor countries

In fact, the protectionism of the poor and the rich countries must be viewed together symbiotically to ensure effective exports by the poor countries. Thus, even if the doors to the markets of the rich countries were fully open to imports, the exports from the poor countries would have to get past their own doors.

We know from numerous case studies, dating back to the 1970s, that only corroborated elementary economic logic, that one's own protection is often the cause of dismal export, and hence economic, performance. It creates a 'bias against exports' by sheltering domestic markets that become then more lucrative. Just ask yourself why, even though India and the Far Eastern countries faced virtually the same external trade barriers, the inward-looking India registered a miserable export performance for a quarter of a century after the 1960s while the outward-looking South Korea, Taiwan, Singapore and Hong Kong chalked up spectacular exports. Charity begins at home; so do exports begin with a good *domestic* policy. In the near-exclusive focus on rich-country protectionism, this dramatic lesson has been perilously lost from view.

5 Effectively assaulting rich-country protectionism

Yet, rich-country protectionism matters, too; and it must be effectively assaulted. And we should be able to lend a strong helping hand, by countervailing the lobbying that makes it hard to make a dent, reinforcing the good work that reciprocal bargaining does. But here, too, we witness folly.

The current fashion is to shame the rich countries by arguing that their protection hurts the poor countries whose poverty is the focus of renewed international efforts. And where action is actually undertaken, the preference is for granting preferences to the poorer countries, with yet deeper preferences to the poorest among them (the 'least-developed countries' as they are now called) instead of giving MFN tariff reductions, and reducing subsidies in non-discriminatory fashion, in products of export interest to the poor countries. But the former solution is woefully inadequate; the latter is downright wrong.

If shame was sufficient, there would be no rich-country protectionism left: trade economists and international institutions such as the GATT and UNCTAD have denounced the rich countries on this count over three decades! Added support, such as that by today's 'charities' such as Oxfam, could nonetheless help in principle. But these charities need both informed expertise and a talent for strategy and not just a conscience with a voice to do so. They fall short.

Regrettably, by subscribing to the counter-productive language of hypocrisy and the ill-advised resort to the rhetoric of 'unfair trade' to attack protection by the rich when the phrase is a code word for protectionism today in the rich countries, a charity such as Oxfam, splendid at fighting plagues and famines, even does more harm than good in *our* good fight.[2] One must remark that mission creep, even by non-creeps, can be an added problem rather than part of the solution.

---

[2] Joseph Stiglitz, and his successors at the World Bank, are also guilty of thinking crudely (and also without awareness of the fact that 'unfair' trade is the favoured tool of the protectionists in the rich countries), of condemning the world trading system as 'unfair': a word that Stiglitz uses liberally in his book, *Globalization and Its Discontents*, New York, Norton, 2002.

An effective strategy requires that we handle the labour-intensive goods such as textiles separately from agriculture. The differences between them dwarf the commonalities. The labour-intensive goods in the rich countries typically employ their own poor, the unskilled. To argue that we should eliminate protection, harming them simply because it helps yet poorer folks abroad, runs into evident ethical (and hence political) difficulties. The answer must be a gradual but certain, phase-out of the protection coupled with a *simultaneous* and substantial adjustment and retraining programme. That way, we address the problems of the poor *both* at home and abroad.

Once this is done, one can ask the church groups and the charities to endorse this balanced and just programme. It is morally more compelling than either marching against free trade to protect the workers in the labour-intensive industries of the rich nations while forgetting the needs of the poor workers in the poor countries, or asking for these trade restrictions to be abolished without providing for the workers in such industries in the rich countries.

The removal of agricultural protection does not raise similar ethical problems as those when you hurt your poor workers: the production and export subsidies in the USA and the EU go mainly to the *large* farmers. That should make it easier to assault them on grounds of helping the poor countries. At the same time, however, unlike textiles *et al.*, agricultural protectionism is energetically defended on grounds of 'multifunctionality': that agriculture has to do not just with production and trade but also with preservation of greenery and the environment. The greens are therefore in play and make protectionism more difficult to remove. But, just as income support can be de-linked from increasing production and exports, measures to support greenery also can be and such new measures, and other environmental protections added as sweeteners, must be part of the strategic assault on agricultural protection.

Drawing on the way that a target date such as Jubilee 2000 focused efforts on the objective of debt relief, I (with Arvind Panagariya) suggested, with a nod in its direction by UN Secretary General Kofi Annan, a Jubilee 2010 movement to eliminate protection on labour-intensive products by 2010. Since agricultural protection is politically a harder nut to crack, and will surely take more time, 2010 cannot be a realistic target date for its demise: 2020 is more realistic if we are serious. Both rich and poor nations' leaders therefore need to endorse Jubilee 2010 to terminate protection of labour-intensive goods and Jubilee 2020 for eliminating protection of agriculture.

As it happens, a campaign launching Jubilee 2010 and 2020 was launched at the Johannesburg Summit of the United Nations on Sustainable Development on 28 August 2002 by the most influential Indian NGO, the Consume Unity and Trust Society (CUTS), which enjoys a worldwide reputation as the leading Third-World NGO on issues relating to the world trading system. I have little doubt that it will snowball, even though CUTS remains, in comparison with rich-country-based charities, a shoe-string operation.

6   Preferences: the wrong way

A final word is necessary on the efforts to open rich-country doors. This is often done not by dismantling barriers on a MFN basis, which reduces them in a non-discriminatory manner, but through grants of preferences to the poor countries. This approach goes back to the GSP, introduced in 1971 through a waiver and then granted legal status in 1979 with an enabling clause at the GATT. Under this, the eligible poor countries were granted entry at preferentially lower tariff rates.

GSP did little for the poor countries. The eligible products often excluded those on which poor countries had pinned their hopes of increasing exports. Thus the US GSP scheme excluded textiles, clothing and footwear. Upper caps were also introduced. The USA imposed a $100 million limit on exports per tariff line, per year, per country; beyond this limit, the preferential rate vanished. Even the benefits granted were not 'bound', and could be varied at the rich country's displeasure. Thus, when India was put on the Special 301 list in 1991 and the US Trade Representative determined unilaterally that India's IPR was 'unreasonable', President George Bush senior suspended duty free privileges under GSP for $60 million in trade from India in April 1992.

Preferences were also often dropped for commodities when they began to be successfully exported, a fact documented in a study by Caglar Ozden and Eric Reinhardt of Emory University. Rules of origin served to curb exports, too. Exported items had to satisfy local-content specifications (for example, shoes had to have uppers, soles and laces made locally) to qualify for GSP benefits.

The rich countries are still going down this preferential route today. The USA has introduced the Africa Growth and Opportunity Act (AGOA), while the EU has brought in the Everything But Arms' (EBA) initiative, to eliminate trade barriers for the forty–nine least developed countries. Yet virtually every drawback of the GSP applies to these schemes as well. If anything, they are worse. Under the AGOA, for example, preferences for African garments are tightly linked to reverse preferences for American fabrics.

Since preferences typically divert trade away from non-preferred countries, they tend to pitch poor nations against each other. They are also a wasting asset, since they are relative to an MFN tariff that will probably decline with further multilateral liberalization. And since they are non-binding and can be readily withdrawn for political reasons, investors are not likely to be impressed by them.

Preferences sound attractive and generous, and the poor countries have accepted them as such. But this has been a mistake. There is no good substitute for the MFN reduction of trade barriers in the rich countries. It should go hand-in-hand with enhanced technical and financial assistance. By focusing this assistance preferentially, directing it far more to the poor nations, the poor should be enabled to exploit the trade opportunities that are opened up non-preferentially.

This was the case with the remarkable Far Eastern countries that experienced the 'miracle' growth rates since the 1960s through mid-1990s. To think instead that the forty-nine least developed countries, including those in Africa, cannot compete as well as, say, the South Koreans who were more behind when they embarked successfully on their outward-oriented strategy, is to be patronizing and condescending to these nations and to deny the lessons of historical experience.[3]

---

[3] I have not dealt in this chapters with the dangers posed to the developing countries by Sanitary and Phytosanitary (SPS) and Technical barriers to trade (TBT) standards, and by environmental labelling, etc., all of which can pose obstacles to successful market access to the rich countries even though the rich-country doors have opened. In thinking about this, it is useful to keep in mind the distinction that I have made between 'openness' and 'penetrability'. I have also omitted the very different but equally important problem that the poor countries face: namely, the many 'non-trade' agendas that rich-country lobbies are pushing onto the WTO, starting with the TRIPS for intellectual property (IP) protection, and now with labour standards. This is a whole new threat to the poor countries and I have addressed this in diverse fora, including my contribution to the Symposium on Linkage in the Spring 2002 issue of *the American Journal of International Law*.

8

Controlling corruption: a key to development-oriented trade

PETER EIGEN

1 Introduction

The mission of the World Trade Organization (WTO) rests on the credo that barriers to trade are barriers to development. I share this belief. And yet, like other civil society organizations worldwide, Transparency International (TI) is intensely concerned about the WTO's single-minded concentration on the removal of trade barriers and its lack of attention to the development-obstructing phenomena that can accompany trade liberalization.

Unchecked global market forces can lead to exploitation, deepen poverty and fuel conflict. Strong, responsive governments, able to play an effective role in preventing or at least correcting such undesired globalization outcomes, are essential if trade liberalization is to foster sustainable development. For this reason, TI is particularly concerned about the unrestrained spread of cross-border trade corruption. Its corrosive effects on the integrity of governments vastly weaken the correlation between global trade expansion and societal well being. TI therefore strongly urges the WTO to recognize the fight against cross-border corruption as one of its major and immediate responsibilities.

The explicit purpose for which the WTO was founded was to liberalize trade worldwide, but the maximizing of global trade is not an end in itself. Even the most staunch proponent of neo-liberal economics would be loath to quarrel with the claim that the goal of trade liberalization is to contribute towards economic and concomitant human development. Yet while the WTO has certainly succeeded in stimulating the volume

A special acknowledgement is due to Shirley van Buiren, senior advisor to Transparency International, for her valuable contribution to this chapter. Transparency International is the leading non-profit organization engaged in the fight against corruption worldwide, www.transparency.org.

of international trade, the promise of increased, equitably distributed welfare gains for all world trade participants remains distressingly unfulfilled. Instead, the rapid expansion of transnational trade has extended the opportunities for, and the negative effects of, unfettered competitive practices while substantially increasing the damages of trade-related corruption. If the WTO is to help ensure that global trade fosters development, or at the very least that grand corruption does not seriously impede it, then it must part with the mistaken assumption that trade liberalization automatically bolsters development.

This chapter documents how global corruption counteracts the WTO's efforts to expand world trade and enhance worldwide development. It presents anti-corruption tools developed by coalitions of government, business and civil society, and their relevance and usefulness to the WTO system. Last but most certainly not least, it propounds transparency as the most effective single instrument against corruption, and urges the WTO to introduce institutional reforms ensuring greater internal and external transparency.

2   Corruption distorts competition, impedes trade and undermines development

From an ecological point of view, competition may be defined as the struggle between individuals of the same or different species for food, space, light, etc., when these are inadequate to supply the needs of all.[1] Behind the WTO's worldwide drive for the removal of trade barriers lies the basic assumption that free trade fosters competition and through it a more efficient production and distribution of goods and services for the benefit of *all*. It is well beyond the scope of this chapter to discuss the potentials and limitations of competition policies to achieve the purported effects. Suffice it to say that a well-designed competition policy and corresponding institutions are essential for competition to function in the mode described. Where the political will and the appropriate institutions for promoting competition are weak, corruption can flourish.[2]

Corruption engenders wrong choices. It encourages competition in bribery rather than competition in quality and in the price of goods and

---

[1] Collins English Dictionary, Millennium Edition, London, Collins, 1999.
[2] For a full discussion of corruption and competition policy, see Jeremy Pope, *TI Source Book 2000. Confronting Corruption: The Elements of a National Integrity System*, Berlin, Transparency International, 2000, chapter 26, pp. 259–68.

services. By inhibiting the development of a healthy marketplace and the optimal allocation of scarce resources, and by instigating mismanagement in public institutions, corruption distorts and endangers both economic and social life and undermines development. Ultimately, it denies an increased quality of life to the most vulnerable members of society.[3]

In the context of international trade, corruption too often means that the world's poorest, who are least able to bear the costs, must pay not only for the corruption of their own officials, but also for that of export companies from industrial countries. Once a pattern of bribery is institutionalized, it invariably breeds a 'culture' of illegality, engenders massive market inefficiencies and in the extreme the destruction of development opportunities. If corruption is not contained, it will grow. Most importantly, the heaviest cost is in the underlying economic distortions triggered by bribery and in the undermining of institutions of administration and governance.

Although corruption is as old as it is widespread, it is neither a natural phenomenon nor may it be considered an unavoidable evil. While hard evidence on the incidence and magnitude of corruption is difficult to find, reliable surveys do indicate that the problem varies widely across countries and business sectors and that even within countries some public agencies, e.g. customs and tax collection, are more prone to corruption than others.[4] All this suggests that remedies are possible.

The following presentation of surveys and other empirical evidence of the scope and effects of corruption is intended to substantiate the subversive effects that corruption has on the WTO's objective of liberalizing trade for the benefit of all. More importantly, it makes transparent the urgent need for the WTO to recognize its responsibility to share the burden of combating corruption in international trade.

Empirical evidence

Until a few years ago economists generally agreed that the propensity for international bribery by the private sector could not be meaningfully measured. Striving for maximum profit would induce all competitors to

---

[3] For an empirical review of the various adverse consequences of corruption see J. Graf Lambsdorff, *Corruption in Empirical Research – A Review*, Transparency International Working Paper, November 1999, see www.transparency.org/iacc/9th_iacc/papers/day2/ws1/d2ws1_jglambsdorff.html.

[4] For a review of recent corruption surveys, see Fredrik Galtung, 'Overview of Data and Research', in *Global Corruption Report 2001*, Berlin, Transparency International, 2001, at www.globalcorruptionreport.org.

Table 8.1 *TI Bribe Payers Index 2002*

Rank		Score
1	Australia	8.5
2	Sweden	8.4
	Switzerland	8.4
4	Austria	8.2
5	Canada	8.1
6	Belgium	7.8
	Netherlands	7.8
8	United Kingdom	6.9
9	Germany	6.3
	Singapore	6.3
11	Spain	5.8
12	France	5.5
13	Japan	5.3
	United States	5.3
15	Hong Kong	4.3
	Malaysia	4.3
17	Italy	4.1
18	South Korea	3.9
19	Taiwan	3.8
20	People's Republic of China	3.5
21	Russia	3.2
	Domestic companies	1.9

behave equally, e.g. to pay bribes in a bribe-demanding environment. Thus the playing field could be seen to be relatively even, even if it meant competing in an environment where corruption was rife.

TI's Bribe Payers Index, first published in 1999, and updated in May 2002, contradicts this notion.[5] The 2002 survey was conducted among 835 business leaders, executives at chartered accountancies, binational chambers of commerce, national and foreign commercial banks and commercial law firms, in fifteen emerging markets around the world. The results showed that companies from some countries are seen to be significantly more prone to bribe to gain business abroad than companies from other countries. Table 8.1 shows the world's top exporting countries

[5] The Bribe Payers Index 2002, Berlin, Transparency International, 14 May 2002, at http://www.transparency.org/surveys/index.html#bpi.

Table 8.2 *Bribery, by business sectors*

Business sector	Score
Public works/ construction	1.3
Arms and defence	1.9
Oil and gas	2.7
Real estate/property	3.5
Power generation/transmission	3.7
Telecoms	3.7
Mining	4.0
Pharmaceuticals/medical care	4.3
Transportation/storage	4.3
Heavy manufacturing	4.5
Banking and finance	4.7
Civilian aerospace	4.9
Forestry	5.1
IT	5.1
Agriculture	5.9
Fishery	5.9
Light manufacturing	5.9

ranked by their perceived willingness to offer bribes in the surveyed emerging market economies. A score of 10 would mean entirely corruption-free; and a score of 0 would mean relying almost entirely on corruption to enter or retain market shares when doing business abroad.

Perhaps less surprising than the differences among exporting countries' willingness to bribe are the differences between the important sectors of international trade and investment. Certain sectors, such as public works/construction, and the arms and defence industry, are particularly prone to bribery, whereas others requiring long-term immovable assets, such as agriculture, are less so (table 8.2).

Further research based on bilateral trade data bears out the hypothesis that those exporting countries and sectors that are prone to offering bribes can obtain a competitive advantage in corrupt import markets. By contrast, in clean import markets such a competitive advantage cannot be achieved by paying bribes.[6] Competition in a corrupt environment destroys the premise that the best offer in terms of price and quality will

---

[6] J. Graf Lambsdorff, 'Exporters' Ethics – Some Diverging Evidence', *International Journal of Comparative Criminology*, 1(2), 2001.

win the day. Where bribe-offering and bribe-taking determine choices, the products imported are not those that best serve the individual buyer or the public at large, but those that maximize bribe revenues. In the vicious circle of competition in bribes, the only winners, if any, are the bribe-takers. As the likelihood of increasing one's market share by offering bribes is highest in the public sector, the global costs of corruption-induced trade distortions can hardly be overestimated.

Yet the monetary costs of corruption, while no small matter for poor countries, seem almost trivial when compared with the loss of development opportunities and the destruction of human life that grand corruption has been shown to induce almost all over the globe.

Like most fast-profit-seeking activities, corruption is not without its risks. The risk associated with corruption increases with the number of transactions, the number of people involved, the duration of the transaction and the simplicity and standardization of the procedure. Since the risk does not clearly increase with the value of a transaction, large one-off purchases create a more efficient base for a kickback. This biases the decisions made by corrupt politicians and bureaucrats in favour of capital-intensive, technologically sophisticated and custom-built products and technologies.[7]

The resultant distortions in public expenditures and investment – away from education, primary health and other human development-fostering activities, towards oversized public works and arms' purchases – should be seen as one of the most pernicious crimes against humanity in our times. Such crimes of corruption cannot be contained, much less sustainably eliminated, by merely exposing individual perpetrators, shaming greed-guided transnational businessmen, or blaming developing country elites. Only a concerted, worldwide coalition of 'public-good-minded' institutions and peoples can hope to organize the systemic approaches equal to the challenge of combating transnational corruption.

As reports of grand corruption associated with oversized public works and deadly arms deals unfold in the news media and fuel the arguments of anti-globalization protesters, myriad occurrences of petty corruption exasperate businessmen and investors going about their daily transactions. If an import licence can be obtained only by bribing public officials and continuing payoffs to a phalanx of corrupt inspectors, if foreign

---

[7] S. Gupta, L. de Mello and R. Sharan, 'Corruption and Military Spending', *European Journal of Political Economy*, 17(4), 2001, pp. 749–77; P. Mauro, 'Corruption and the Composition of Government Expenditure', *Journal of Public Economics*, 19, 1998, pp. 263–79.

investors are compelled to spend inordinate amounts of time and money to 'negotiate' entry regulations, the prospect for trade-fostered development will be undermined. Numerous studies have shown that corruption, no less than other NTBs, constitutes a serious deterrent to trade that in the long run might even lead to significant reductions in trade flows.[8]

Not only trade, but also foreign direct investment (FDI), has been shown to be negatively affected by corruption. Thus for example, Wei (2000), who investigated bilateral flows between fourteen source and forty-five host countries in 1990 and 1991, ascertained that corruption had had a significant negative impact on FDI. According to his findings, an increase in the corruption level from that of Singapore to that of Mexico was equivalent to raising the tax rate by over twenty percentage points.[9] Most recently, an investigation by Lambsdorff and Cornelius (2000) showed an adverse impact of corruption on FDI for African countries.[10]

The implications are clear: investors tend to stay away from countries with high corruption levels. It is equally apparent that countries most in need of foreign investment tend to be those that suffer most from widespread corruption.[11]

More trade liberalization, more growth, more development?

According to the Global Barometer Surveys, there is a widespread view in Latin America, in major African countries and in post-Communist Eastern Europe that corruption has increased significantly in recent years.[12]

---

[8] D. Kaufmann and S.-J. Wei, 'Does "Grease Money" Speed up the Wheels of Commerce?', National Bureau of Economic Research Working Paper, 7093, Cambridge MA, NBER, 1999; J. Graf Lambsdorff, 'An Empirical Investigation of Bribery in International Trade', *European Journal for Development Research*, 10, 1998, pp. 40–59, reprinted in M. Robinson (ed.), *Corruption and Development*, London, Frank Cass and EADI, 1998; S. Djankov, R. La Porta, F. Lopez-de-Silanes and A. Shleifer, 'The Regulation of Entry', National Bureau of Economic Research Working Paper, 7892, Cambridge MA, NBER, 2000; H. G. Broadman and F. Recanatini, 'Seeds of Corruption – Do Market Institutions Matter?', World Bank Policy Research Working Paper, 2368, Washington, DC, World Bank, 1999.

[9] S. J. Wei, 'How Taxing is Corruption on International Investors?', *Review of Economics and Statistics*, 82(1), pp. 1–11.

[10] J. Graf Lambsdorff and P. Cornelius, 'Corruption, Foreign Investment and Growth', in *The Africa Competitiveness Report 2000/2001*, World Economic Forum, Oxford and New York, Oxford University Press, 2000.

[11] See various editions of Transparency International's annual Corruption Perceptions Index, at www.transparency.org.

[12] 'Corruption Data from the Global Barometer Survey Network', in *Global Corruption Report 2001*, Berlin, Transparency International, 2001, pp. 306–14, at www.globalcorruptionreport.org.

Perceptions may not be a fully satisfactory substitute for facts, but there can be no doubt whatsoever that the ascertained effects of corruption on trade and development give ample cause for alarm.

As our analyses of the available empirical evidence reveal, corrupt behaviour impedes, obstructs and distorts international trade and capital flows. Most importantly, in countries with high levels of corruption, transnational trade and investment cease to be seen as serving the public good, as indeed they by and large fail to do so. Ultimately, pervasive high levels of petty and grand corruption lead to a significant reduction in transnational trade and investment, and in extremely corrupt countries and regions may cause them to dry up altogether.

While, globally, the WTO has succeeded in stimulating the volume of world trade, corruption has been shown to undermine the presupposed positive effects of trade on development. These findings do not negate the proposition that free trade *can* induce economic growth and development. What they demonstrate is that trade liberalization does not automatically ensure development. Corruption has been shown to be a major interfering factor, at best 'merely' obstructing, at worst perniciously destroying, development opportunities. In any event, it debilitates government as a regulator and protector of the common interest, as the key actor in maintaining the social market economy.

The bottom line of the collective evidence strongly suggests that corruption poses a serious, albeit not the only, challenge to the WTO's mission and credo. Reliance on the tried and found-to-be-wanting 'more trade more development equation' has proved impossible. New corrective policies, including corruption-control measures, urgently need to be designed and implemented to strengthen the WTO's effectiveness for trade-fostered development.

3 Corruption control as a trade commitment

International efforts to contain corruption

Corruption has emerged as a central topic on the international agenda. The UN Conference on Financing for Development, held in Monterrey in March 2002, was no exception. A succession of heads of state, Finance and Development Ministers, not to mention the leadership of the World Bank and IMF, stressed the importance of controlling corruption. Differences regarding the relative contribution of trade and aid abounded, but not with respect to corruption. Here the judgement was universal: wherever corruption reigned, development aspirations would remain a hopeless dream. Indeed, if the prevalent notion of political correctness had not disallowed pre-conditionalities, the control of corruption as a *sine qua non* for increasing development aid and private investment would most certainly have figured prominently in the 'Monterrey Consensus'.

The broad anti-corruption consensus manifest at Monterrey hardly comes as a surprise. Awareness and solid documentation on the worldwide pervasiveness of corruption and its dramatically detrimental effects on developing economies and societies has been growing steadily since the mid-1990s. To date, most international organizations and agencies have at least declared their intent to contribute to the fight against corruption.

In a remarkable reversal from its non-interference stance, the World Bank declared war on corruption in 1996. Arguing for the first time that corruption is above all an economic issue and therefore its legitimate concern, the Bank has engaged in a comprehensive fight against corruption, both internally and in the countries it works with. The IMF, although opting for a less proactive approach, has taken up the fight against corruption as a central component of its lending policy.

As business has become increasingly global, it has proved to be more and more unrealistic to regard corruption as the preserve of developing countries to be addressed only by them. The 1997 OECD Convention on Combating Bribery of Foreign Public Officials in International Business Transactions was a landmark in addressing the 'supply' side of international bribery. This Convention came into force in 1999 and has since been ratified by thirty-four states (twenty-nine of the thirty OECD member countries[13] plus Argentina, Brazil, Bulgaria, Chile and Slovenia). The Convention requires all parties to criminalize the bribery of foreign public officials, and to provide mutual legal assistance to facilitate inquiries into suspected violations. Furthermore, it foresees intrusive 'country inspections' at regular intervals to help ensure that each country is playing a full role in respecting the objectives of the Convention.[14]

Several regional agreements, similar in content and aim to the OECD Convention, were initiated around the same time, or followed suit. In 1996, for instance, the Organization of American States (OAS) agreed on an 'Inter-American Convention against Corruption'. About a year later,

---

[13] As of 1 May 2002, Ireland was the only OECD member not yet to have ratified the OECD Anti-Bribery Convention.

[14] Progress reports on the implementation of the convention can be viewed at the OECD Anti-Corruption Unit web site, at www.oecd.org/daf/nocorruption.

the EU tackled the issue, enacting the Convention on the 'Fight Against Corruption Involving Officials of the European Communities or Officials of Member States of the European Union', which purports to penalize both active and passive corruption. Although rather modest, this convention has yet to be ratified by the majority of its fifteen signatories.

The Council of Europe, now an important trend-setter in international law, went much further by concluding both the 1999 Criminal Law Convention on Corruption and the 1999 Civil Law Convention on Corruption. Under the Criminal Law Convention, which entered into force in July 2002, each party commits to enacting a range of measures at the national level to counter corruption in public life, in public administration and in the private sector. Furthermore, corporations are to be rendered subject to criminal law and measures introduced to facilitate the gathering of evidence and the confiscation of proceeds. Similarly to the OECD Convention, the implementation of the Criminal Law Convention is to be monitored. For this purpose the 'Group of States against Corruption' (GRECO) was established. Its members will monitor not only this Convention but also other measures developed by the Council of Europe as part of its action plan against corruption.

These conventions constitute the most important formalized agreements of international cooperation for fighting corruption. Other international mechanisms to counter global corruption include measures taken to check money laundering, the activities of INTERPOL, and a multiplicity of mutual assistance agreements entered into between states.[15] In 2002, the noose was tightened further around international corruption. In recognition of the fact that global institutions must play their full role in containing the global menace of corruption, a UN Convention against Corruption was drafted.

Efforts to combat and control corruption must continue and become more effective. The WTO could play an important part in underpinning and assisting these efforts around the world.

What will be the role of the WTO?

Notwithstanding the commendable efforts of governments and international organizations to criminalize and thus to contain corruption, the

---

[15] For a more detailed discussion of 'International Actors and Mechanisms', see Jeremy Pope, *TI Source Book 2000. Confronting Corruption: The Elements of a National Integrity System*, Berlin, Transparency International, 2000, pp. 153 *et seq.*

rapid expansion of transnational trade continues to vastly expand the opportunities for cross-border grand corruption. And as is well known, where institutions are weak, corruption can flourish. And where the risk of being caught is small and the gain disproportionately large, corruption does flourish. This is certainly the case in the global trade arena. As the empirical evidence presented has shown, cross-border trade corruption continues to be pervasive, and the need for trade-focused corruption *prevention* policies and mechanisms remains undiminished.

What is to be the role of the WTO in combating corruption in the global trade arena? If trade is essential for development, can the WTO remain absent while corruption-fraught trade threatens to exacerbate poverty and underdevelopment? Do the WTO statutes allow a more pro-active role in combating corruption? Does the professed or implied mission demand it? How can the WTO build upon the experience of existing international anti-corruption mechanisms to expedite the development and implementation of its own, long overdue corruption-control system?

While neither the 1994 GATT agreement nor the subsequent WTO agreements explicitly address corruption and bribery, the control of corruption in international trade has been an essential, implicit element of the GATT and a constitutive component of the WTO. In TI's view, ensuring that trade liberalization comes to mean corruption-free trade is intrinsic to WTO's mandate. By virtue of its declared purpose and actual agenda, the WTO is well positioned to serve as both architect and universal guardian of global free trade. As such, it is not only ideally placed, but also obliged, to assume leadership in eliminating those obstructions to the free flow of trade that distort competition and with it an equitable distribution of the benefits of global trade. Cross-border corruption unquestionably constitutes an obstruction to free trade; it vastly diminishes the very benefits for which trade liberalization is purportedly pursued. And yet, to this day, the WTO remains the only major organ of economic governance without an identifiable corruption-control policy.

If the promises of trade-fostered development, untiringly espoused by the WTO since its foundation, and most recently emphazised as the Doha Development Agenda, are to stand any chance of serving as anything more than further fodder for 'Globalphobia', then intelligent policies and pragmatic measures for controlling trade-related corruption must start to feature prominently in the WTO Work Program. Since Seattle, scepticism, fear and outright opposition have unremittingly accompanied WTO's efforts to further expand international trade. The fear of many civil society activists – that international trade is the captive of powerful multinational corporations in an unholy alliance with corrupt government leaders – can be addressed only by designing and articulating a high-profile anti-corruption strategy driven by the WTO. It seems quite safe to predict that the manifest resistance to further trade liberalization, particularly persistent among many developing countries as well as among Southern and Northern NGOs, will not be overcome unless the link between trade and sustainable development is not only verbally espoused but also strategically supported.

Hence, one important element of such strategic support for trade-fostered development could be the design of effective WTO policies and commensurate measures to combat and thereby to significantly reduce the incidence and impact of trade-related corruption. The WTO should not hesitate any longer to commit itself to a full-fledged policy and programme of corruption control in global trade transactions.

Taking into account the scope of existing international and national efforts to contain corruption and with due concern for the requirements of the majority of the WTO's membership, a focus on prevention, rather than on criminalization, suggests itself. Particularly for poor countries, the prevention approach is crucial. Although misuse of resources needs to be avoided everywhere, in poor countries overpriced and misallocated investments in one area all too frequently mean doing entirely without in another area. In practice, as documented, corruption invariably promotes inflated infrastructure investments while basic needs such as primary education and health care – where the pickings for the corrupt are on a much reduced scale – tend to fall by the wayside. Morally, economically and politically, the long-term costs of postponed or forgone human development opportunities are staggering. Preventing irreparable social and economic damage should be a prime objective of the WTO's anti-corruption policy.

In terms of practicality and cost, the prevention approach seems preferable, as its implementation can be relatively inexpensive. Transparency, public awareness and a system of people-centered, voluntary and thus well-accepted rules can help stop corruption in its tracks. Prosecution and punishment are, by comparison, costly and complex, requiring a professional judicial and policing apparatus. Of course, punitive action cannot be dispensed with altogether; but the better the prevention the less formalized costly enforcement will be necessary.

Furthermore, an enforcement system raises controversial questions: what is to be the role of the WTO in an enforcement system? Is it to be 'a global corruption policeman'? Or would a cooperative framework to counter abusive and corrupt practices adversely affecting international markets be more suitable for an intergovernmental organization? Clearly such and many other key questions will need to be thoroughly considered when designing an anti-corruption system specifically suited to the requirements of the WTO. Preliminary analysis of a variety of international anti-corruption efforts, however, does suggest that a system designed to prevent corruption from occurring in the first place, rather than one relying on penalties after the event, will, without doubt, be superior, not only for poor countries but for the WTO membership as a whole.

A further important lesson to be drawn from international anti-corruption efforts is that the most recent and prominent ones are the children of – until recently deemed – strange bedfellows: the private sector and civil society organizations; governments and civil society organizations; and an occasional *ménage à trois* of the aforementioned. Indeed, coalitions of stakeholders have been at the forefront of the anti-corruption, good governance and accountability movement. Anti-corruption strategies could be conceptualized, specific corruption control tools developed and international agreements forged more or less by virtue of the fact that a broad-based coalition of business, government and civil society organizations reached agreement on what needed to be done, and how. Thus for example, the International Chamber of Commerce (ICC) combined with TI to campaign for the now highly regarded OECD Anti-Bribery Convention. Ever since, TI has participated in the OECD 'country inspections' monitoring compliance with the convention. The creativeness and results-orientation of these new coalitions is also evident in such joint products as corporate anti-bribery principles, the banking sector's initiative to curtail money laundering, known under the name of the 'Wolfsberg Principles',[16] and the rapid spread of corporate social reporting.

The moral of these developments is twofold. First, there is neither need nor justification for the WTO to go it alone in designing its anti-corruption policy and implementation mechanisms. A variety of multi-stakeholder coalitions have demonstrated that they can produce solid substantive

---

[16] In 2000, Transparency International was instrumental in bringing together eleven leading international banks to announce their agreement on the Wolfsberg Anti-Money Laundering Principles. The new guidelines on business conduct in international private banking state that: 'Bank policy will be to prevent the use of its world-wide operations for criminal purposes. The bank will endeavour to accept only those clients whose source of wealth and funds can be reasonably established to be legitimate'. The principles, signed on 30 October 2000, also deal with the identification and follow-up of unusual or suspicious activities; see http://www.transparency.org/pressreleases_archive/2000/ 2000.10.30.wolfsberg.html.

results and, most importantly, can be relied upon to ensure a comparatively wider acceptance than unilaterally produced solutions. Second, the
existing anti-corruption principles, conventions and agreements constitute an impressive body of efforts attempting to deal with some of the
negative fallout of globalization. Their practical impact on cross-border
trade corruption thus far has been limited and will most certainly not be
up to the challenges posed by further trade liberalization and concomitant opportunities for abusive practices. And even though – with some
conspicuous recent exceptions – private sector anti-corruption and accountability standards are on the increase, their cumulative effect cannot
be expected to be more far-reaching than anti-corruption conventions
and agreements.

If globalization is not to destroy itself, it must be better managed for the
benefit of all. Patchwork approaches to global problems may be considered
a highly useful field for experimentation, but corruption in international
trade and its manifold aberrations demand a holistic approach, one that
combines global reach and trade system acumen with social and political
sensitivity. Such a solution cannot be achieved without WTO leadership,
resources and the conviction that system reform must not be postponed
any longer. The opportunity for active engagement is most propitious:
governments are keen to introduce new anti-corruption rules applying
to cross-border trade, and the assistance of the WTO should be most
welcome to them.

Transparency in government procurement and services

The WTO, in contrast to its global sister organizations the UNDP, World
Bank and the IMF, has not so far identified corruption as one of its concerns, much less as one of its core responsibilities. Nonetheless, some
amendments and new agreements in preparation could become highly
useful tools for reducing corrupt practices. One potential agreement,
Transparency in Government Procurement, merits special attention in
TI's view. On the one hand, it is a prime example of the WTO's high
potential for reducing opportunities for corrupt practices in a key area of
world trade. On the other hand, it mirrors the institutional bind in which
the WTO is caught, a bind that restricts the WTO's capacity for dealing
with the global issues entailed in its mandate.

There is probably no more straightforward way of reducing corruption
in the multilateral trade system than tackling government procurement.
Annual budgets for government purchases worldwide have been estimated

by the OECD to run up to some $5 trillion.[17] A large share of these expenditures goes on essential public services, such as utilities and transport, education and health. And yet these economically and socially important investments, involving as they do major shares of countries' budgets, are often spent in shockingly wasteful ways.

Reviewing global experience, experts have found that far too many government investments and purchases are uneconomical, either not needed at all, oversized, ineffective or too costly to operate. Too often, the true cost of an investment or purchase is not made public at the outset, for fear of not obtaining the necessary administrative or parliamentary approvals if the full cost were known. Actual costs emerge only slowly during the implementation process, usually when it is too late to reverse an original decision because too much of the investment has already been implemented. The reasons for such misallocation of resources can include outright incompetence. But more often than not, unethical officials, frequently in collusion with unethical consultants, suppliers and contractors, have influenced and manipulated faulty project choices and investment decisions. There is widespread evidence that full transparency of the government decision-making processes – from the point of conceptualization of an investment or purchase until the completion of implementation coupled with appropriate monitoring throughout – will bring economic, design or operational faults to light and mobilize public opinion against such wastage of resources.

Global experience also demonstrates quite convincingly that in public procurement the use of competitive bidding under transparent conditions reduces the risk of manipulation and corruption. As a rule, competitive transparent procurement practices result in lower prices for the goods or services acquired, since the prices are determined by competition on the basis of quality and price rather than by bribery and corruption. Such open procedures are well worth the effort. Experts estimate that where corruption is systemic, it can add 20–30% to the costs and on top of that results in inferior-quality purchases.[18] In exceptional cases, the costs – or, conversely, the savings – can be much higher.[19] Thus for example, in

---

[17] OECD report, *The Size of Government Procurement Markets*, Paris, OECD, March 2002.

[18] This figure comes from Donald Strombom, *Corruption in Procurement*, USIA Electronic Journal, Economic Perspectives, Corruption: An Impediment to Development, November 1998.

[19] Dieter Frisch, former Director-General of Development at the European Commission, has observed that corruption raises the cost of goods and services; it increases the debt of a country (and carries with it recurring debt-servicing costs in the future); it leads to

the celebrated Karachi Water and Sewerage Board (KW&SB) investment project, the mutual no-bribes 'Integrity Pact', agreed by TI-Pakistan, the KW&SB and consultant bidders, resulted in a winning consulting bid 75% lower than the reserved funds allocated based on experience in World Bank-financed projects.[20]

Providing for more transparency in procurement is as much in the interest of the seller as of the buyer. Many companies offering goods or services have discovered that operating in a non-transparent market, where corruption thrives, is significantly more expensive (costly bribes), inherently unreliable (the influence and the advantage purchased by bribes cannot be enforced by legal action and with democratization the longevity of any particular regime can no longer be assumed) and increasingly risky (in terms of likely criminal prosecution, financial, personal and reputational disadvantages). They are also finding that corruption scandals can serve to tarnish the brand-names they have spent fortunes to promote. More and more companies thus welcome a market without bribery. In several business sectors with global activities, the major actors have recognized the advantage of a corruption-free competition and are in the process of negotiating 'common competition standards' which would of course be much more likely to be effective if those companies competed in a fully transparent procurement environment.

But the international procurement environment is a far cry from full transparency. Although many countries have quite good procurement rules, they are routinely circumvented and thus largely useless. Escape clauses based on alleged 'urgency' or 'emergency' are used too frequently, thus eroding the good 'open competition' principle. Furthermore, the evaluation of bids and the selection decision are usually made by a handful of officials in secrecy, allowing manipulation and inviting corruption in the process. Transparency of the decision-making process is thus of the

---

lowering of standards, as substandard goods are provided and inappropriate or unnecessary technology is acquired; and it results in project choices being made based more on capital (because it is more rewarding for the perpetrator of corruption) than on manpower, which would be the more useful for development. Frisch points out that when a country increases its indebtedness to carry out projects which are not economically viable, the additional debt does not only include the 10–20 per cent extra cost due to corruption; rather the entire investment, all 100 per cent of it, is attributable to dishonest decisions to proceed with unproductive and unnecessary projects (Dieter Frisch, in *The Effects of Corruption on Development*, a paper presented to the Africa Leadership Forum on 'Corruption, Democracy and Human Rights in Africa,' Cotonou, Benin, 19–21 September 1994).

[20] Karachi 'Integrity Pact', press release, Karachi and Berlin, 27 February 2002, at http://www.transparency.org/pressreleases_archive/2002/2002.02.27.karachi.html.

essence for avoiding manipulation and corruption. Indeed, it is the best guarantor that procurement rules are actually applied.

To devise a framework for removing the widespread distortions in public procurement constitutes a classic task and responsibility of the WTO. It can hardly come as a surprise, then, that a plurilateral WTO Government Procurement Agreement (GPA) has been in force since January 1996. And although it contains some basic transparency requirements, it fails to reduce the problem because it has few signatories. Developing countries in particular have refrained from acceding to the Agreement since it also contains market access or no-discrimination rules, under which importing countries cannot offer any preferences to infant industries or domestic bidders. Because fair non-discrimination rules in procurement are so central to the multilateral trading system and because the existing GPA is inadequate both in substance and number of adherents, work on a new procurement agreement has been ongoing since the first Ministerial in Singapore 1996.

The WTO Ministerial Meetings in Seattle (November–December 1999) and Doha (November 2001) had before them draft texts (submitted by the European Commission and by Hungary, Korea and the USA) for a new Agreement on Transparency in Government Procurement. Not burdened by market access clauses and thus in principle more acceptable to developing countries, the proposed new agreement also constitutes a vast improvement in terms of transparency. It explicitly requires:

• The publication of laws, procedures, judicial decisions and administrative rulings
• Timely public notification of bidding opportunities
• Information on qualification requirements
• Publication of tender documentation, including information on technical specifications and criteria for awards
• Transparent qualification and contract award decisions
• Information to the unsuccessful bidders as to why they lost and why the winning bid was chosen, and
• Independent fora and procedures for review.

Considering the rather opaque processes still in use in many countries, and the unwillingness of many bureaucrats to allow public access to information they regard as the exclusive property of the executive, these proposals will require and hopefully engender significant changes in the actual procurement practices of most countries. By curtailing secrecy and the corruption it breeds, this new agreement could make an important contribution towards reducing a major obstruction to the goal of trade-fostered development.

While all of the WTO's membership stands to profit from transparent procurement rules, there can be little doubt that poor developing and transition countries stand to gain most. With their high levels of indebtedness and their dramatically diminished volume of FDI, they need every penny that can be rescued from misallocation of resources. Yet in Doha, as in previous years, a number of developing countries managed to block the start of negotiations on the proposed Agreement on Transparency in Government Procurement – at least until the next Ministerial in 2003, possibly longer, depending on the vote on negotiation modalities to be taken then.

And while the resistance of developing countries to the proposed new procurement agreement continues unabated, Northern countries (e.g. Switzerland, the EU, the USA, etc.) have added fuel to the fire by arguing that the scope of a future agreement should cover goods and services.[21] The reasoning is varied. It includes critiques of the artificiality of separating goods and services as many procurement contracts involve both, and many service contracts have significant goods components. And it maintains that a WTO agreement on goods alone would be a step backward compared with other international agreements. Finally, the proponents of including services argue: 'There is no intrinsic reason for providing less transparency in service procurement than in goods procurement'. With services brought into the discussion, the question arises whether transparency issues relating to services ought not to be handled in the GATS, which in turn opens up a whole new Pandora's box of controversy.

Although all of these questions need clarification, they are not, in TI's view, any reason why an agreement on procurement, whether or not including services, should not be concluded. Most of the outstanding points are of a more or less technical nature and, with goodwill, could have been resolved long ago. According to some procurement experts, the work that has been done to date has addressed virtually all major issues on the subject. It should not, therefore, be difficult to move into an active negotiation, and complete that negotiation in a matter of months.

From the point of view of economic and development costs entailed in the prevailing, at best opaque, at worst massively corrupt, procurement practices, the failure to reach agreement on new rules is even

---

[21] WTO Working Group on Transparency in Government Procurement, WT/WGTGP/M/11, 19 December 2000.

less understandable. The persistence of developing countries in the view that the proposed procurement agreement with its transparency rules is mainly in the interest of industrialized countries, is to deny the reality that those very opponents of the reforms are the main victims of cross-border corruption.

The stalemate over procurement transparency is but one of a series of binds shackling the WTO. The reluctance, in some cases strong opposition, prevailing in many developing countries *vis-à-vis* further trade liberalization in general and WTO rule-making in particular, seems highly unlikely to be overcome by further perfecting proposals suspected, rightly or wrongly, of being primarily in the interests of the North. Resistance to many useful reforms, some much overdue, seems to emanate from a deep mistrust born of negative experiences with rushed or opaque decision-making processes. In the view of some insiders and many conscientious WTO-watchers, nothing short of institutional reform stands a chance of resolving the political and legislative stalemate crippling the WTO's work.

Institutional reform of the WTO: from the green room to the glass house

Since the failed 1999 Seattle Ministerial, the WTO has been under considerable pressure to reform its policy- and rule-making process and the way it interacts with the public. The 'green room' approach, in which the WTO Director General and a host governments select a few countries among which to build a consensus, no longer produces the consensus necessary to launch comprehensive trade negotiations. While industrialized country governments maintain that the 2001 Doha Ministerial preparations demonstrated some improvements in the internal processes to determine a negotiating agenda, many developing country officials and civil society organizations argue that the outcome still reflects the inequities between rich and poor countries. In their view, the Doha Ministerial Declaration proclaims an agenda heavily oriented towards the interests of the wealthy WTO members.[22]

In addition to the specific dissatisfactions and resultant complaints raised by many developing country governments and their repercussions on the organization's functioning, there is growing awareness, even among strong WTO supporters, regarding institutional shortcomings. Obviously there is something amiss when decision-making processes increasingly fail to achieve results. Even in cases where objectively there should not have

[22] See *South Letter*, 38 (3 & 4), 2001; *South Bulletin*, 24/25, 30 November 2001.

been any noteworthy difficulties – e.g. as discussed above with regard to the new procurement standards, the other so-called Singapore issues, etc. – the debate remains inconclusive for years.

And, thus, there is widespread agreement that the Uruguay Round negotiators created trade disciplines that exert unprecedented influence and propel globalization. At the same time, considerable debate rages over the question whether the WTO has proven itself capable of effectively administering these far-reaching rules and procedures in a fair, open and transparent fashion, commensurate with the unprecedented influence it exerts.[23]

Public demands for openness come at a time when other international organizations have already taken important steps toward effective public participation in decision-making.[24] But while wealthier nations have begun to consider these demands, they continue to meet resistance from developing countries, who fear that their meagre influence at the WTO would be diluted by public input or undermined by powerful Northern non-profit organizations.

The WTO's relationship with civil society has improved considerably over the past five years. Informal public information sessions help keep interested civil society organizations abreast of the content of ongoing negotiations, and document de-restriction policies help to remove some of the non-transparent nature of WTO decision-making. Nevertheless, citizens still lack adequate and timely access to the information that would enable them to comment on trade policy as it is being considered or to present their views in any meaningful way. The most egregious example of this involves the dispute settlement process, where parties to a dispute defend national policies without the benefit of public oversight or input. Lacking in all aspect of public accountability, parties have been under tremendous pressure to reform this process. Panel members have adopted informal policies of accepting *amicus* submissions, but the full WTO membership continues to resist public demands for greater transparency, accountability and participation.

---

[23] John J. Audley and Ann M. Florini, *Overhauling the WTO: Opportunity at Doha and Beyond*, Carnegie Endowment for International Peace, Policy Brief 6, October 2001, at www.ceip.org; Amrita Narlikar, *WTO Decision-Making and Developing Countries*, South Centre, Trade-Related Agenda, Development and Equity Working Papers, 11, November 2001, www.southcentre.org.

[24] Gordon Smith and Barry Carin, *Rethinking Governance Handbook: An Inventory of Ideas to Enhance Accountability, Participation, and Transparency*, British Columbia, University of Victoria's Centre for Global Studies, 2002.

4 Conclusions

With the exception of the WTO, all of the important organizations of global governance have not only recognized that corruption exerts a severe drag on economic and human development, but have also initiated programmes to conquer this major obstruction to development. Civil society organizations have demonstrated their ability to support both governments and/or private sector groups in devising strategies and tools to combat corruption and thereby proving that corruption must not be considered an unavoidable disaster. Although a considerable scope of approaches for fighting corruption can be usefully applied, full transparency of government functions represents the best way to deter and combat corruption.

Notwithstanding the commendable efforts of governments, international organizations and multi-stakeholder coalitions to contain corruption, the empirical evidence sadly shows that cross-border trade corruption continues to be pervasive, its distortive effects on trade and investment considerable and the resultant destruction of development opportunities deplorable. The need for trade-focused corruption-prevention policies and mechanisms remains undiminished. The WTO has both a unique responsibility and opportunity to contribute to a global pro-development solution. As the current trade negotiations have been proclaimed a Development Round, a major WTO initiative to tighten the noose on trade corruption is more imperative than ever.

Embarking upon any major innovation will not be an easy undertaking for the WTO. Its present state is not well prepared for taking the global lead on controlling international corruption. The discrepancy between the claim of formal equality of all members and the habitual resort to non-transparent, informal negotiation and decision-making circles has produced a quagmire of suspicion and mistrust in which even the most propitious proposals become bogged down. Many of WTO's internal blockages, and its seemingly irrational resistance to reform, might be overcome only by improving internal transparency and institutionalizing equitable opportunities for all members to participate in decision-making. This clearly implies substantial institutional reform as a prerequisite for, or at least a parallel undertaking to, any significant initiatives and innovations.

9

The impact of EC enlargement on the WTO

PATRICK A. MESSERLIN

1 Introduction

The enlargement of the existing European Community (EC15) will lead
to the largest-ever consolidation of preferential trade agreements (PTAs)
since the creation of the GATT in 1947. It will involve ten Central European countries (CECs), and almost half of the 141 PTAs notified to the
World Trade Organization (WTO, the GATT successor) and in force will
disappear.[1] This large-scale consolidation of European PTAs will restore
WTO supremacy in a very significant way. It is important to note that
this evolution is fair in the end for WTO and GATT because successive
GATT Rounds have profoundly contributed to intra-EC liberalization by
inducing the EC to lower its MFN tariffs as well as its internal tariffs –
hence reducing the risks and the magnitude of PTA-related inefficiency
costs for EC member states.

However, this large-scale consolidation requires three words of caution.
First, all the above EC-related PTAs will not disappear all of a sudden. The
timing of CECs' accession to EC15 is not clear yet, and the Doha Round
may be concluded well before most accessions. Almost all CECs' accessions
will be a lengthy progressive process because of the unusually large (by
EC15 standards) differences in levels of development between the EC15
and the various CECs. (This was the case, but to a smaller extent both
in terms of development differentials and relative population sizes, with
Greece, Portugal, and Spain which benefited from long transition periods,
particularly in agriculture.) As a result, the Doha Round negotiations may

---

[1] The ten CECs are: Cyprus, the Czech Republic, Estonia, Hungary, Latvia, Lithuania, Malta,
Poland, Slovakia and Slovenia. As of April 2002, there were eighteen PTAs between EC15
and the CECs, eighteen PTAs between the CECs themselves and twenty-eight more PTAs
(mostly between CECs and EFTA countries, echoing the PTAs between EC15 and the CECs)
which will be included in the consolidation process. These data leave aside the fact that
certain CECs have currently their own versions of the GSP and of other WTO Agreements.

witness only a few CECs behaving as quasi-EC member states, whereas the other candidate CECs may still define their trade policies individually.

Second, the EC15 trade policy in goods is almost fully 'communitarized', meaning that not only tariffs, but also NTBs, such as quotas, are defined at the EC15 level.[2] However, even today, it is hard to know whether EC15 quotas are mere aggregates of individual member state quotas (as in fisheries) or whether they are genuinely defined at the EC15 level. Such knowledge would help to give a better sense of how CEC NTBs would be integrated in the trade regime of the enlarged EC, and to what extent they will perpetuate the CEC pre-accession protection pattern.

Finally, seven more European countries are (potential) candidates for EC accession: Albania, Bulgaria, Romania, Bosnia-Herzegovina, Croatia, Macedonia and the Federal Republic of Yugoslavia (the chapter refers to these seven countries as 'the Balkans'). Under the Stability Pact initiative, the Balkans have been induced to sign preferential bilateral trade agreements between themselves. As of early June 2002, nine agreements have been signed, twelve more were expected before the end of 2002 (seven more may follow when Moldova is fully included in this group). Hopefully, this avalanche of bilateral agreements will be subject to a consolidation process leading to an integrated 'Balkan economic space' with a very open multilateral policy.

Beyond these institutional aspects, the impact of EC enlargement on the WTO raises five major questions of substance dealt with in five sections below. First, what is the relative current market openness of the EC15 and CECs? This aspect will largely drive the positions of the enlarged EC (E-EC) in the Doha Round – both because enlargement will impose new adjustments on CEC economies and because it will have some impact on the ease with which the EC15 may fulfil the commitments it has taken under the Uruguay Round. Second, what are the forces that are likely to determine the E-EC trade policy in goods during the Doha Round? Third, what are the forces which could shape the E-EC commercial policy in services? Fourth, what are the forces which could influence the E-EC commercial policy in the 'constitutional' area – competition, preferential trade agreements, environment and labour? A brief concluding section evokes the common challenges in terms of governance faced by the E-EC and the WTO – both international institutions with large memberships and increasingly addressing issues of 'deep' economic integration.

---

[2] This chapter uses the term 'trade' policy when looking at goods, and 'commercial' policy when looking at services and 'constitutional' issues.

All these issues raise the question of whether the CECs, once they be-come EC member states, will reinforce or erode the current EC15 trade and commercial policies. The overall conclusion is that most CECs (in-cluding the largest ones) are expected to join the non-liberal camp of the E-EC more often than its liberal side, whereas the relative sizes of the EC15 and of CECs will make compensations imposed by CEC re-protection af-fordable for the EC15. As a result, while refocusing the E-EC on market access issues, the European consolidation of trade agreements described above will not lead to a more forthcoming E-EC in the Doha negotiations. Difficulties should be the strongest in certain sectors with huge pending problems in CECs (steel, clothing, agriculture, etc.) which will nurture increasing tensions between the E-EC and emerging or developing coun-tries (often perceived as close competitors by CECs). Moreover, the CECs may busily use anti-dumping and similar instruments of protection for eroding *ex post* the liberalizations that they were not been able to block during the Doha Round.

While reminding how key will be some EC15 decisions – such as shift-ing to a more trade-friendly 'two-track' farm policy or introducing the notion of 'limited reciprocity' in trade relations with ACP countries – the above issues also offer the opportunity to provide three suggestions on WTO operations. First is that negotiations in market access in services should be accompanied by reference papers defining the multilateral ba-sic competition rules in widely defined services sectors, and that they should include the possibility of an 'opt-in' option for countries initially reluctant to liberalize (subjected to certain limits if one worries about the overall consistency of the Round). The rationale for such an approach is to allow the more open-minded countries to constitute a first wave of trade liberalization, without being blocked by reluctant countries. Second is that a WTO Competition Agreement is not necessary. In services, refer-ence papers will do the job. In goods, tariff concessions from developing countries could be traded against commitments by industrial countries to prosecute export cartels which currently are the main anti-competitive practices – or, alternatively, to launch negotiations on a WTO ban on export cartels. Lastly, the WTO dispute settlement mechanism could be eased with the introduction of qualified majorities *à la* EC for the different WTO broad topics (for instance, trade in goods, trade in services, IPRs). In turn, these changes could induce reassured WTO members to improve the WTO negotiating process *per se*, in order to make it more efficient and to sharpen its focus on trade liberalization.

2   Market openness in the enlarged EC at the dawn of the Doha Round

A strict condition of accession to the EC is that all EC15 trade barriers shall be adopted by the candidate countries without any modification (the so-called *acquis communautaire*). Thus comparing the existing level of protection in the EC15 and in CECs gives a sense of the adjustments that CECs economies will have to undertake when adopting the *acquis*, and of the consequences for the EC15 in terms of compliance to its commitments in the Uruguay Round. This section focuses on farm and industrial products (services are examined in section 4).

Comparing the level of protection in the EC15 and CECs

Table 9.1 gives an overall view of the level of protection (1999–2000) for a sample of thirty-nine countries including the EC15, four CECs – the Czech Republic, Hungary, Poland and Romania – and Turkey.[3] The first three CECs are good proxies for the other CECs, while Romania is taken as a proxy for the Balkans. Table 9.1 allows us to compare the European countries between themselves, and the European countries and the rest of the world. The second comparison is essential because both the risks of PTA-related trade diversion and the magnitude of their related welfare costs depend on a country's trade and commercial policies *vis-à-vis* its trading partners subjected to the GATT–WTO MFN provision. As a first approximation, one can say that the higher the MFN trade barriers are, the larger the PTA-related welfare costs are likely to be.

Table 9.1 compares EC15 and CEC trade regimes through three indexes which aim at giving an idea of the existing 'best practices' in trade policy (Laird and Messerlin, 2002). The openness index captures the level of protection as usually defined in the WTO – applied tariff rates, frequency of NTBs, anti-dumping measures, etc. The irreversibility index focuses on the key GATT concept of tariff bindings and of its possible circumvention by instruments of contingent protection, such as anti-dumping. The simplicity index captures what makes a country's trade regime friendly,

---

[3] Turkey is a case of its own, mostly for political reasons, but also because of its strong comparative advantage in labour-intensive goods, such as clothing and agriculture, which are very sensitive to the EC15. The trade regime of Turkey is relatively stabilized by its customs union with the EC15 – though a too-long denial of membership by the EC may induce Turkey to request a more flexible type of PTA, such as a free-trade area (FTA) (in order to conclude a FTA with the USA).

Table 9.1 *Aggregate indexes in agriculture and industry, selected countries*

	Agriculture			Industry		
Regions	Simplicity	Irreversibility	Openness	Simplicity	Irreversibility	Openness
A An overall view						
All countries	7.0	7.8	6.9	7.0	7.3	8.1
Industrial countries	7.2	7.8	7.5	7.8	7.7	9.4
Developing countries	6.9	7.9	6.6	6.6	7.1	7.4
B A view by region						
North America	7.3	8.0	9.2	7.8	8.1	9.6
Latin America	7.7	8.8	6.9	6.5	7.4	7.4
Europe[a]	5.1	6.2	6.7	6.7	6.2	8.7
Pacific Asia	8.2	8.9	7.4	7.5	8.1	9.0
South-East Asia	7.0	9.0	4.9	6.1	6.8	5.9
Africa	6.8	6.7	6.0	7.3	7.3	6.9
C The Enlarged EC (E-EC)[b]						
EC15	4.8	6.8	7.0	6.6	6.3	9.6
CEC[c]	5.6	5.7	8.1	6.5	6.5	8.6
Czech Rep.	6.8	8.5	8.7	7.2	7.8	9.3
Hungry	5.2	3.5	8.6	6.0	5.8	7.6
Poland	4.8	5.0	7.1	6.4	5.8	8.9
Romania	4.8	7.5	3.5	6.2	5.5	7.5
Turkey	3.8	5.5	6.3	4.6	5.0	7.8
All countries except E-EC	7.2	8.1	6.8	7.0	7.4	8.0

Source: Laird and Messerlin (2002); unweighted averages.
[a] Europe includes Iceland, Norway, Switzerland, in addition to countries listed in the text.
[b] Enlarged EC = EC15 plus CEC.
[c] CEC = Czech Rep., Hungry and Poland.

or not, to traders, such as the number of tariff lines, the share of non-*ad valorem* bound tariffs, etc. The index thus covers components of trade policy which are largely decided outside of the WTO forum, directly in the capital cities – hence reflecting 'unilateral' decisions.

Table 9.1 shows that the EC15 and CEC trade regimes differ markedly. The openness index in agriculture is better for the CEC than for the EC15, whereas the contrary prevails in industry. The irreversibility index shows no systematic differences between the EC15 and CEC in agriculture, whereas the EC15 trade policy in manufacturing is clearly more irreversible than the corresponding policies in the CEC, with the exception of the Czech Republic. The simplicity index suggests that CECs generally have a simpler trade policy than the EC15 – in both agriculture and industry. (The exception of Turkey in manufacturing is due to the fact that Turkish tariffs were still converging towards EC15 levels during the late 1990s on which table 9.1 is based.)

Table 9.1 also reveals substantial differences between the EC15 – hence, the E-EC because of the *acquis communautaire* principle – and the non-E-EC WTO trading partners on the eve of the Doha Round. The EC15 trade policy lags behind the average performance of the whole sample of WTO countries in terms of simplicity and irreversibility in both agriculture and industry, and it lags behind the average performance of the industrial countries for all the indexes, except openness in industry.

Adjusting to E-EC protection: expected CEC reactions

As CECs adopt EC15 trade barriers under the *acquis communautaire* principle, the above description leads to the conclusion that, when acceding to the E-EC, most CECs will increase on average their protection in agriculture, and decrease it in industry and services, whereas the Balkans will decrease their average protection in all three activities (Francois and Rombout, 2001). What could be the reaction of CEC producers to these expected changes in the level and structure of protection? At a first glance, CEC farmers should be pleased and lobby for enlargement, whereas the opposite attitude should be expected from CEC providers of goods and services. However, things appear more complicated (see the series of the Sussex European Institute papers on the mixed feelings in Central Europe about the accession to EC15).

CEC farmers are generally inefficient, and they need massive restructuring. As a result, they may be unable to enjoy the huge benefits from the EC15 Common Agricultural Policy (CAP15) which may remain largely unchanged until 2005–6. First, most CEC farms are small, hence unable to get much from the existing CAP15, which is based on instruments (subsidies to acreage or based on cattle head) largely biased in favour of large farms. (The top 4 per cent of EC farms get 21 per cent of EC total support to agriculture, and have an earning per person which is more than twice the EC average wage. The top 17 per cent of EC farms get 50 per cent of EC total support, and have an earning per person which is 10 per cent higher than the EC average wage (ABARE, 2000). Second, CEC farmers will compete in E-EC markets with highly subsidized EC15 farmers. Lastly, as CEC land is cheap by EC15 land price standards, it can be easily and quickly bought by rich EC15 farmers who could then become the main beneficiaries of EC enlargement. In this context, it is thus not surprising that farmers from relatively farmland-abundant CECs, such as Poland, have very mixed feelings about enlargement, which will be exacerbated by the 'discounted' CAP to be implemented in these countries (see section 3).

In industry, reducing CEC MFN tariffs to the EC15 level may still impose serious adjustment costs on CEC industrial firms. CEC industrial tariffs tend to be higher than EC15 ones (see below). The existing PTAs between EC15 and CECs may not have created enough competition in the CECs because, even if EC15 firms are efficient by world standards (an implausible assumption in the highly protected EC15 industries), they may still have charged high prices in CEC markets protected by high CEC MFN tariffs. There are many reasons for believing that there is a lack of sufficient competition in the small CEC markets, from the fact that small markets do escape the attention of many operators to the existence of NTBs imposed by CEC authorities on imports from the EC15. The number and magnitude of these adjustments is likely to be reflected in the use of the anti-dumping instrument by the CEC, once they become E-EC member-states (see section 3).

Two final remarks are needed. First, if the Doha Round fails, the above changes will be permanent. They are large enough to induce a substantial shift of CEC resources to agriculture, away from industry and services. Such profound changes in the level and structure of protection is not new in EC15 history. For instance, Portugal was unfortunate to join the EC at a time when EC quotas on textile and clothing imports were particularly tight – triggering a rush of public and private investment in the Portuguese textile and clothing industry which could not survive a limited erosion of EC protection later on, generating an economically calamitous and socially costly boom–bust cycle in Portugal.

Second, acceding to the EC15 imposes a second shock to CEC economies – the first having been caused by the opening of the CEC economies associated with the shift from central planning to a market economy. This second shock is likely to be of smaller magnitude than the shock of the early 1990s. But it remains to be seen how it will be perceived, and whether it will trigger deep changes in public policies in CECs – that is, whether rumours about more active 'industrial' policies that can be now heard in certain CECs (Poland, for instance) will rapidly fade away or not.

CEC accessions: the impact on the EC15

For EC15 member states, enlargement *per se* will not change the level and structure of protection because of the *acquis communautaire* principle – hence its impact on EC15 welfare will be very limited, even if one assumes that strong dynamic forces will emerge from the enlargement process (Baldwin, Francois and Portes, 1997). CEC accessions will have an impact on the EC15 situation in the WTO to the extent that they will require compensation when CEC protection is increased to the EC15 level. The impact will differ markedly according to the sectors.

In industry, the burden of compensation on the EC15 will be minor for two reasons. First is because CEC industrial tariffs tend to be higher than EC15 ones, as mirrored by average applied tariffs which range from 5.2 per cent (EC15) to 6.8–14.3 (depending on the CEC) to 19.5 per cent (Romania). Second, when industrial tariffs are smaller in CECs than in EC15, the compensations to be granted by the E-EC will represent a limited burden for the E-EC, because CEC trade flows are very small compared to the overall size of the EC15 economy.

In agriculture, compensation will be more frequent, as suggested by the estimated 1999–2001 consumer support equivalent-based tariffs which range from 9 per cent (Hungary) to 13 per cent (Poland), compared to 51 per cent for the EC15 (OECD, 2002). However, as in manufacturing, the small size of CEC trade flows with the rest of the world (relative to the EC15 economy) implies that compensation will not impose a large burden on the EC15.

But agriculture raises a specific issue. The differences in the EC15 and CEC level of protection in agriculture are large enough to raise the basic question of the E-EC ability to fulfil the combined commitments agreed by the EC15 and CECs under the WTO Agreement on Agriculture. The magnitude of these difficulties differs according to the type of trade barrier.

Export subsidies raise the most difficult issue. The EC15 has very little room for manoeuvre left because it has already reached the limits of its own export subsidy commitments for several products, and because CECs have scheduled low levels of export subsidies in the Uruguay Round. Another difficult issue for the E-EC is import quotas. Adding EC15 and CEC commitments would make E-EC quotas larger than the current EC15 quotas by 15 per cent for milk, 50 per cent for cereals and beef and 150 per cent for chicken. However, the EC15 hopes to use the 'netting out' technique (that is, adding EC15 and CEC quotas while subtracting their bilateral component) to reduce post-accession quotas. (The EC15 has already used this technique for the last enlargement in 1995, although it is still pending final WTO approval.)

The Uruguay commitments on the other trade barriers in agriculture raise less serious problems for the E-EC. Concerning tariffs on farm products, most CEC accessions will require compensation because many CEC tariffs are lower than EC15 tariffs – by 20 per cent for Hungary, 50 per cent for the Czech Republic and almost 100 per cent for Estonia. Concerning domestic support, the EC15 has enough reserves in unused support under the current definition of the AMS to be able to fulfil E-EC aggregated commitments (except if the AMS definition is narrowed, an unlikely event in the absence of the Doha Round).

3 Trade in goods: market access issues in the Doha Round

This section examines the main forces which will forge the E-EC trade policy in goods during the Doha Round. It tries to assess whether the EC15 agenda for the Doha Round will evolve under the influence of the CECs, although it is not an exercise about predicting the end-results (such an exercise is impossible, if only because one does not know which CECs will be E-EC member states by 2006–7, assuming this horizon as the end-year of the Doha Round). The overall conclusion is that the European consolidation of trade agreements described in the introduction will not lead to a more forthcoming E-EC in the WTO negotiations, in particular with respect to emerging and developing countries often perceived as close competitors by CECs (for a more optimistic view, see Johnson, 2001).

Agriculture

In sharp contrast to the situation in the EC15, agriculture is still a relatively large domestic sector (in terms of value-added and employment) in most

CECs. This is the case even for those CECs with no substantial comparative advantage in this sector (only Bulgaria, Poland, Romania and Turkey are seen as potentially large producers of a wide range of farm products in the future), and despite the fact that during the 1990s farm outputs substantially declined in most CECs as they began to import farm products from Argentina, Australia and Brazil. In 1996, the gross agricultural product in the CECs and the Balkans amounted to 7 per cent of GDP (compared to 1.7 per cent for the EC15), whereas farm jobs represented 22.5 per cent of total employment in the CECs and the Balkans (compared to less than 5 per cent for the EC15).

There is only a limited match between the main beneficiaries of existing protection in the EC15 and CECs. This important observation suggests limited opportunities for farm coalitions uniting farmers from the 'Western' (EC15) and 'Eastern' (CEC) parts of the E-EC. Based on the producer support (expressed in *ad valorem* tariff equivalents) by product estimated by OECD (2002), the most protected products in the EC15 are milk, sugar and meat (beef and poultry). The most protected farm good in all the CECs is poultry, with sugar in Poland, beef in the Czech Republic and milk in Hungary (and with products with a large negative protection, such as beef in Poland, other grains in the Czech Republic, or maize in Hungary).

The crucial problem is that enlargement occurs at a bad time to the extent that it will complicate enormously the reduction of European protection in agriculture. The many CEC farmers will insist on protection precisely at the time when EC15 farmers are rapidly losing their political clout in EC15 (if only because of the dramatic decline in their numbers). As a result, enlargement may delay further farm liberalization which was (slowly) starting in the EC15.

The current EC15 position on farm issues is torn by conflicting decisions on the future of the CAP15. In 1999, the Council rejected the option of renationalizing farm aid on the basis that the Treaty of Rome did not consider farm policy as a social policy (one of the few policies that the Treaty leaves under member state responsibility). Rejecting renationalization logically meant the CAP15 extension to CECs – either in its current form, or under a reformed version to be implemented in both the Western and the Eastern E-EC. But at the same time, the Council agreed that the annual transfers of EC15 to CECs will not exceed 3.4 billion euros during the pre-accession period (of which 0.5 billion euros are specifically for CEC farmers) – a decision which does not allow extending the level of subsidies of the current CAP15 to CECs farmers.[4] (Doing so would require much larger transfers: available estimates of budgetary costs fall within the range of 5–15 billion euros for the CAP15 extension to the Czech Republic, Hungary, Poland and Slovakia, and 9–23 billion euros for its extension to all the CECs.) Interestingly, the CAP15 reform, which would be compatible with the level of EC15 transfers to the CECs decided by the Berlin Council, has never been officially examined.

In the absence of a serious CAP15 reform, farm trade issues between the EC15 and the CECs would be hard to manage. In fact until 2000, farm products were largely excluded from the bilateral Europe Agreements between the EC15 and the CECs. In 2000, the EC15 tabled bilateral trade agreements eliminating export refunds and import tariffs on EC15-CEC trade for certain farm goods, such as pigmeat, poultry, cheese, fruits and vegetables – that is, all products not among the main beneficiaries of the CAP15 support system. Following these 'double-zero' agreements, the EC15 has tabled 'double-profit' bilateral trade agreements aimed at extending the double-zero agreements to 'sensitive' EC15 farm products (wheat, beef, dairy).

All these proposals have not been well accepted by the CECs. As of July 2002, only Hungary had signed double-zero and double-profit agreements.[5] There are two main reasons for this slowness. First, liberalized CEC farm products will be subject to controls for compliance with EC15 norms and standards. The extent to which such controls will constitute technical barriers to trade and to substitute for EC15 border protection remains to be seen. Second, in exchange for this limited trade liberalization, production quotas will be imposed by the EC15 on CEC farm products covered by these agreements – raising the question of the level at which

---

[4] The Commission tried to justify the Council's double standard by arguing that EC15 farmers have faced (and will continue to face) income losses due to farm price decreases, whereas CEC farmers will not. This justification does not recognize the fact that 'intervention' prices of agricultural products are as high as EC15 prices in certain CECs (Poland, Slovenia), and sometimes even higher. It also ignores the fact that such an argument implies that any 'new' EC15 farmer (whether he be the heir of a retiring EC15 farmer or an entrant into farming activities) would not be eligible for aid – and that is not the case. In its 'Issues Paper' (30 January 2002), the Commission envisages the introduction of direct payments equal to 25 per cent of the EC15 level in 2004, 30 per cent in 2005 and 35 per cent in 2006, with full parity for Western (EC15) and Eastern (CEC) E-EC farmers in 2013 at the earliest.

[5] It is often said that, following these agreements, CEC tariff-free farm exports to the EC15 would increase from 37 to 77 per cent. However, this increase is less a measure of trade liberalization than an indication of the restrictiveness of the CAP15 for the rest of agricultural products.

these quotas would be fixed. CECs wanted base years to be picked from the late 1980s, a proposal rejected by the EC15 which argued that such quota levels would reflect the distortions of non-market economies – forgetting that the base years 1986–8 were adopted by the Uruguay Round precisely because they mirrored a peak in the distortions generated by OECD farm policies. (The base year question is not a minor issue because of the sharp decline in farm output after the CEC shift to a market economy: for instance, CEC pork production declined by one-quarter during the 1990s.) The conflict is particularly acute between the EC15 and Poland, the major CEC producer of most of the products involved, and most CECs do not see the benefits from such agreements when accession is said to be close.

The EC15 stalemate about the reform of the CAP15 leaves two forces on a collision course. On the one hand, the EC15 is clearly not ready to extend the existing CAP15 to the CECs, simply because it cannot afford the budgetary consequences of such an extension. On the other hand, the CECs seem irresistibly attracted to mimic the CAP15. This strategy is a trap for CEC farmers because closing CEC farm markets will reduce the much-needed incentives for CEC farmers to become more competitive, leading to increasingly uncompetitive situations (for instance, in 1999–2000, pork was more costly to produce in Poland than in France).

Unfortunately, the logic of the Doha Round – the deeper the CAP15 reform will be, the lower the CEC-related compensations to be paid by the E-EC will be – is unable to impose a strong push on the E-EC. This is because the small size of CEC trade makes compensation likely to be a small burden for the E-EC. Hence, the E-EC trade policy in agriculture will continue to be driven by the situation prevailing in the EC15, where the rapidly diminishing power of the farm lobbies is being strengthened by a coming crowd of CEC farmers.

The only way for the EC15 (and E-EC) to escape this deadend would be to adopt a 'two-track' CAP – one for large farms and one for small farms. The CAP for large farms would insist on a progressive elimination of subsidies granted to large farms (see section 2) and on the parallel removal of the constraints on their production. In contrast, the CAP for small farms will focus on meeting farm income targets through decoupled subsidies.

Such a two-track CAP has many advantages. It is the only one which will be compatible with an integrated European farm market (that is not the case with re-nationalized CAP subsidies which will be equivalent to intra-EC barriers to the extent that they will be different, as one can expect). It solves most of the farm problems that the EC15 (and E-EC) face in the WTO because only large farms are involved in world trade (small farms tend to focus on the local market). And it permits governments to provide income targets to small farms which can be expressed in terms (say x per cent) of the national income. In the E-EC context, this last feature has the advantage not only of modulating the degree of farm support among E-EC member states (a way to minimize the costs of the whole system) but also to introduce incentives for modernization of small farmers in the Eastern E-EC (the CECs, once they are member states).

Manufacturing

In manufacturing, the E-EC will be in a situation which the EC15 has known only marginally since its creation – direct competition between a substantial number of the new E-EC member states and the emerging or developing economies. One should thus expect the E-EC to be in a more defensive position in the Doha 'Development' Round than would have been the case with the EC15. Several CECs (particularly, Poland) have substantial industries which are still state-owned and/or in bad shape. However, the relative sizes of CEC and EC15 industries may imply that the CEC influence in the E-EC will be limited in most of the industrial goods. Even the few industries where one could expect a strong CEC influence suggest nuanced situations, as illustrated by steel or clothing.

Steel is an important industry in three CECs (Poland, Czech and Slovak Republics) and in Romania. Despite a substantial drop – by 10 to 30 per cent – of CEC steel outputs (except in Slovakia) during the 1990s following the elimination of outdated capacities, today aggregate steel output of these four CEC is still equivalent to the Italian or French steel productions (the second and third largest EC15 producers, respectively).

However, a coalition of CEC steel-makers powerful enough to have a strong say in E-EC steel matters is unlikely. What CECs are looking for is structural adjustment through the integration of their most competitive plants with giant steel-makers – whether they be from the EC15 or from the USA (US Steel has a strong base in Slovakia and Poland). Such a search for consolidation can only erode CEC willingness to act jointly. Moreover, Central Europe is an attractive region for building competitive greenfield steel mini-mills, eroding further the potential for such a coalition. In sum, the key decisions on further steel liberalization by the E-EC are likely to stay in the hands of EC15 firms. In fact, this conclusion was tested by the March 2002 steel crisis. Following the US safeguard action, the EC15 instantly imposed its own safeguard measure on steel imports – including on those from the CECs, a decision that shifts the adjustment burden of the crisis from EC15 steel-makers to CEC ones (which include US Steel).

In clothing, during the 1990s, the CEC benefited from the 'delocalization' of EC15 plants because CEC labour was relatively cheap and – more crucially – because EC15 quotas on CEC clothing products were much more generous than on exports from developing economies under the Agreement on Textiles and Clothing (ATC). The first advantage (labour costs) is rapidly fading away – making the final elimination of ATC quotas in 2005 a crucial issue for the CEC clothing industry, already under the pressure of delocalization of clothing plants to the Balkans and to other emerging economies.

In this context, CEC textile lobbies may be decisive for delaying the EC15 commitments under the ATC (as of 2002, the EC15 has not yet eliminated ATC quotas on almost all its 'sensitive' clothing products). However, the success of these efforts may ultimately depend upon a key parameter of the situation in 2005–7 – China's situation. If China implements fully (or to a large extent) its WTO accession commitments, it will represent such a large market for EC15 exporters of all kinds of goods and services that the wider interests of European exporters to China will outweigh the narrower interests of the E-EC clothing industry.

Contingent protection

The above discussion suggests that, if CEC influence is unlikely to be powerful enough to change dramatically the EC15 trade agenda, CECs can contribute to change it significantly when there is a strong enough opposition in the EC15 to further liberalization in labour-intensive goods of key interest for developing countries – making the E-EC significantly less supportive of a Doha Development Round. Of course, this impact will depend upon the pace and sequence of effective accessions. Countries such as Estonia (or, to a lesser extent, the Czech Republic) are unlikely to change the EC15 positions – because these countries are less or as protected as EC15, and because of the small size of their economies. Things are different with Poland or Turkey, and things could be even more different if all the CECs accede almost at the same time.

As the CEC cannot change the existing *acquis communautaire*, the only way for CEC firms to modify current EC15 tariffs will be to use the instruments of contingent protection available in the EC15 trade regulations, in

·particular anti-dumping tariffs and measures. When doing so, CEC firms may find allies in the EC15 sectors addicted to such instruments, such as chemicals, textiles or steel. But they may also expand the use of contingent protection to a few more sectors, in particular clothing – substituting (as it has been so often the case) price undertakings (minima prices) or quantity undertakings (export quotas) to the existing quotas and other NTBs, which are to be dismantled under the ATC by January 2005.

CEC influence may be strong in contingent protection (anti-dumping) because these instruments are suited to narrow vested interests. The key criteria in such procedures (major proportion of the domestic industry, definition of the like product, etc.) are flexible enough to allow successful actions by small firms. (For instance, a narrow definition of 'like product' makes it easier for a few small firms to satisfy the condition of being a major proportion of the domestic industry.)

In the contingent protection context, the only limit to CECs' influence will be their capacity to lodge well-conceived complaints and their ability to get the required majority at the Council. The first condition requires procedural skills, which can be abundantly provided by law firms and by industry associations. Complaining CEC firms could get additional help from the Commission itself, which may be all the more forthcoming since it may feel that CEC interests were disregarded during the Doha negotiations (as a kind of compensation). The second condition is that adopting anti-dumping measures requires a simple majority in the Council – a voting regime favourable to small countries. Moreover, there is always the possibility for the E-EC to adopt 'regional' anti-dumping measures – that is, measures limited to the CEC concerned.

4   Market access in services in the Doha Round

The Doha Ministerial Declaration devotes surprisingly little space to services liberalization, although services, which represent more than half of the world GDP (60–70 per cent of E-EC GDP), are still very much protected in most WTO members. Table 9.2 shows that CEC service regulations are significantly more restrictive than those in most EC15 member states (except for railways and retail distribution). It also shows that intra-EC15 liberalization itself is still embryonic in almost all the services sectors, as revealed by the high variance in the level of the regulations enforced by the EC15 member states, and by the substantial number of EC15 member states with regulations more restrictive than the OECD non-EC15 averages.

Table 9.2 Regulatory and market environment 1998 (the scale of indicators is 0–6, from least to most restrictive)

	Air passenger	Road freight	Telephony mobile	Telephony fixed	Electricity	Railways	Retail distrib.	Average by country
European Community (EC15)								
Austria	3.2	2.8	3.5	3.0			4.1	3.3
Belgium	4.4	3.2	3.8	3.0	5.5	6.0	3.1	4.1
Britain	2.2	1.3	0.0	1.0	0.0	3.0	2.5	1.4
Denmark	4.7		3.4	2.2	5.0		2.9	3.6
Finland	3.6	1.7	2.3	0.4	0.0	6.0	3.0	2.4
France	3.2	2.5	0.8	3.0	6.0	6.0	4.7	3.7
Germany	3.0	3.0	3.2	3.0	2.1	3.0	1.2	2.6
Greece	5.5	3.6	2.4	6.0	6.0		3.8	4.5
Ireland	4.4		3.7	2.8	4.5	6.0	1.4	3.8
Italy	3.3	4.6	2.2	3.0	6.0	6.0	3.1	4.0
Netherlands	2.7	2.4	2.2	2.9	5.3		1.4	2.8
Portugal	5.1	2.3	3.4	6.0	4.2		2.6	3.9
Spain	2.9	3.0	4.6	3.0	3.8	4.5	2.5	3.5
Sweden	3.3	2.2	1.8	1.7	0.8	3.0	1.7	2.1
Candidate countries								
Czech Rep.	5.8	3.0	4.6	6.0		1.5	0.8	3.6
Hungary		3.4	4.3	6.0		3.0	1.9	3.7
Poland	6.0	2.7		6.0		1.5	3.6	3.9
Turkey	6.0	2.7	3.9	6.0		6.0	3.0	4.6

(cont.)

Table 9.2 (*cont.*)

	Air passenger	Road freight	Telephony mobile	Telephony fixed	Electricity	Railways	Retail distrib.	Average by country
Rest of the OECD								
Australia	3.3	0.8	0.9	1.3	0.9		1.1	1.4
Canada	3.6	2.0		0.8	6.0	3.0	1.3	2.8
Japan	3.1	2.1	0.4	1.1	5.0	3.0	4.1	2.7
Korea	3.8	1.1	1.6	1.9		6.0	1.3	2.6
Mexico	3.5	2.2	2.5	1.7		4.5	1.9	2.7
New Zealand	3.7	1.3	2.6	1.4	0.0			1.8
Norway	2.9	2.2	3.9	3.0	0.0	4.5	2.2	2.7
Switzerland	4.6	3.8	4.5	3.0		6.0	1.1	3.8
United States	1.2	1.5		0.3	4.3	1.5		1.7
Unweighted averages								
EC15	3.7	2.7	2.7	2.9	3.8	4.8	2.7	3.3
CEC[a]	5.9	3.0	4.4	6.0		2.0	2.1	3.8
Enlarged EC[b]	3.9	2.8	2.9	3.5	3.8	4.1	2.6	3.4
Rest of the OECD	3.3	1.9	2.3	1.6	2.7	4.1	1.9	2.5

Source: Messerlin (2001).

[a] CEC = Czech Rep., Hungary and Poland.

[b] Enlarged EC = EC15 plus CEC.

This complex situation makes it very difficult to assess the impact of EC enlargement on CEC services. In general, one should expect CEC services to be more open after accession to the EC15. But most large firms operating in the CECs originate from the EC15 or from other OECD countries (except for a few of them, such as maritime transport, railways and trucking) and these large service firms are unlikely to change their worldwide trade views because of the specific situation of their subsidiaries in the CEC. Moreover, CEC governments may not feel committed to support the views of large multinationals. On the other hand, services are often labour-intensive sectors, and competition between large firms may have an impact on small firms (such as in retail distribution). These two features may push CEC authorities to intervene and to oppose liberalization. Viewed from the EC15 perspective, expected compensations are small – if only because the Uruguay commitments in services signed by both the EC15 and CECs are very limited.

The contrast between the mandate of the Doha Ministerial Declaration and the work to be done may largely be due to the issue of how to negotiate liberalization in services. If negotiations in goods are based on a well-mastered technique of looking at the balance between given and received concessions in tariffs, generally weighted by the volume of imports involved, nothing equivalent exists in services. The EC15 experience in internal liberalization of services may provide a few key lessons in this respect, which deserve to be examined before looking at the forces which could drive the E-EC negotiating positions during the Doha Round.

How to negotiate in services: the Single Market experience

In 1985, the EC embarked on an ambitious programme of liberalization in services – the so-called 'Single Market'. However, as shown by table 9.2, this programme has not been successful. A key reason for the very slow (and reversible) pace of the Single Market is the negotiating technique used by the EC which is based on two components: mutual recognition by each member state of the other member states' regulations conditional to adopting a core of common provisions. The core (harmonization) component is defined by negotiations between EC member states on appropriate legal provisions. The outcome of these negotiations are enshrined in European 'Directives' (laws). Initially, the core component was conceived as to be limited in scope, leaving to the mutual recognition component the largest space. This approach was aimed at generating competition between member state-based regulations so that each member state would be induced to design efficient domestic regulations so that service providers based in the country could fully benefit from the country's comparative advantage in European-wide services markets.

The reality has been quite different from this initial plan. Long negotiations on Directives have systematically expanded the core component and reduced the scope of mutual recognition and slowed down the whole process of market access (because of the need for long periods of negotiations and long transition periods in liberalization). During these negotiations, each member state got ample time to insert parts of its own regulations into the core of the common provisions in order to bend it as much as possible to its favour, or even to insert 'poison pill' provisions (such as the undefinable notion of 'services of general interest') in order to limit competition as much as possible. As a result, the 'Single Market' process has been much more about regulatory convergence with still segmented markets than about regulatory competition in an enlarged and open market. The drift away from the initial conception has been exacerbated by the fact that the whole process did not benefit from any cost-benefit analyses on whether it was really necessary to adopt Directives (or not) and on the available options about the ideal doses of harmonization and mutual recognition.

Why such a drift away from the initially envisaged regulatory competition to regulatory convergence? A key reason is the rigidity of the concept of 'progressive' liberalization in the EC. In the European Single Market – as in the WTO – progressivity is defined by a unique dimension, which is the pace of implementation. A reluctant country can get more time to liberalize, but it cannot stay away from the process – sooner or later, it will have to abide by the common rules. In particular, a country has no 'opt-in' or 'opt-out' choices. As a result, a country reluctant to liberalize has strong incentives to limit as much as possible regulatory competition when negotiating the core element.

WTO negotiations in services: sectoral reference papers and the 'opt-in' option

The EC experience suggests two key negotiating instruments in the WTO context. First is the need to compile in a document the common basic conditions of competition – the Directive in the EC context, the 'reference paper' in the WTO context. Reference papers should be defined at the sectoral level because the key elements of a pro-competition framework are not the same for each service. As a result, it is important to note in passing that drafting such reference papers will eliminate incentives to include in services the contentious trade and competition link in the Doha Round (see below). For instance, the problem of public monopoly is essential in telecoms, but relatively marginal in audiovisual services. In contrast, the subsidy issue (in the sense of getting subsidies) is critical in audiovisuals, but secondary in telecoms (telecom firms have been a source of subsidies more than they have been subsidized). The mutual recognition component will then be defined by market access commitments. In fact, this structure of negotiating instruments has already been used in telecoms services, with the 1997 Agreement.

However, reference papers will not be very efficient for liberalizing services if the definition of progressivity remains too narrow. Progressivity should include the 'opt-in' alternative – the freedom for a WTO member not to participate in the first wave of liberalization and to join later on. WTO reference papers should be elaborated by the most pro-competition-minded member states, and implemented only by them. Reluctant countries could join later on the same terms, without renegotiation (except possibly on the implementation pace). The opt-in approach will seriously curb the negotiating leverage of the countries initially reluctant to liberalize, allowing the first wave of countries to focus on the best possible environment for regulatory competition. Witnessing the benefits from liberalization, reluctant countries would then, hopefully, lose their initial prejudices and hostility (for instance, today no EC15 member state could envisage returning to a public telecom monopoly regime).

At a first glance, the opt-in approach seems the equivalent in services to a preferential trade agreement (PTA) in goods. Hence, it could raise concerns on potential costs from trade diversion – all the more because services sectors are so much more permeated with monopoly situations. However, the parallel with PTAs does not seem appropriate because foreign direct investment (FDI) plays such a large role in services. Firms based in reluctant WTO members may have subsidiaries operating in liberalizing WTO members, and through them, they can participate in the liberalization process. In other words, FDI gives to the opt-in approach a strong aspect of unilateral liberalization jointly launched by the initial signatories.

Does allowing for sectoral reference papers and opt-ins raise the risk of 'Balkanising' WTO negotiations in services? The risk exists – but it has to be balanced with the danger of no liberalization at all, or liberalization outside the WTO. More importantly, this risk can be managed through several ways. For instance, it could be agreed that reference papers should be introduced at a determined level of the classification of services (so that they cover only widely defined service sectors) and that a minimum amount of WTO members (or a minimum size of the world output or trade of the service under negotiation, or any combination of these conditions) should be reached before such an agreement would be enforceable – as in the Information Technology Agreement (ITA) which is a successful precedent of the suggested approach. Determining the threshold number of signatories should help to keep a balance between the two main (opposite) effects of a threshold: reducing the costs associated with free-riding by the countries which decide not to join the agreement (the higher the threshold is, the lower these costs may be) and increasing the costs associated with a large core of common provisions (the higher the threshold is, the higher the costs from having to include in the agreement initially reluctant countries are).

The E-EC in the Doha negotiations in services

The texts summarizing the EC15 intentions for the Doha Round devote surprisingly little space to services. They reveal an EC15 approach largely permeated by the regulatory convergence approach which has dominated the European Single Market. This influence has had the consequence (important in the WTO context) of focusing on trade-offs between regulatory provisions within each service sector – hence giving less importance to cross-sectoral trade-offs between the services involved. (By contrast, regulatory competition would tend to pay more attention to trade-offs between concessions given in the various service sectors under negotiation.)

The initial EC15 position also reflects the two layers of competence in services in the Community legal regime: the layer of the services included in the Single Market (often called the infrastructure services) where the Community has some pre-eminence and the layer of the services left outside the Single Market exercise, where member states have pre-eminence and could use safeguard provisions. This distinction raises substantial problems of coalition and coordination, if only because the second layer of services consists of large key sectors (business and health services, construction, retail and wholesale trade, tourism, etc.) – some of which have already attracted a lot of attention in the WTO forum, and are politically very sensitive in the EC15 context (some of them have been explicitly excluded by the Nice Treaty from the majority voting rule).

Once enlargement is taken into consideration, the issue of competence is likely to be even more difficult, particularly in those services for which certain EC15 member states have a strong protectionist stance. In such cases, the CECs may align their position to the least open EC15 member states (and not to the 'average' EC15 position) so as to eliminate all risks of future claims for compensation. In turn, this tactic will make more difficult the emergence of a compromise about a common position among the EC15 member states because the most protectionist EC15 member states could claim to have external 'supporters' of their policy. In such cases, the WTO compensation mechanism would have the perverse impact of inducing CECs to 'maximize' their current level of protection, and to reinforce the most protectionist interests in the EC. This scenario has been illustrated by Croatia, Estonia and Latvia, which ultimately adopted the most protectionist version of the EC15 Television Without Borders Directive – instead of its 'average', more open-minded (and in fact more frequent) version.

Such difficulties could be amplified by the fact that foreign (often EC15) direct investment in CEC services has frequently led to the almost complete elimination of CEC firms in many services – including in those where CEC firms may initially have had some advantages, such as retail distribution. The question is whether dominant EC firms would want to expand to the CEC the protection they enjoy in most EC15 countries (for instance, in retail distribution) and, if so, whether CEC governments would agree to support such requests for protection.

Inconsistencies between trade and commercial policies in the WTO single undertaking

The Uruguay Round is a 'single undertaking' – meaning that all agreements will apply to all WTO members. This feature implies that there are profound interactions between liberalization in goods and in services which are often missed by WTO members.

The EC15 does not escape this general observation, as best illustrated with its approach on health issues in the WTO forum. During the Doha Ministerial Meeting, the EC15 was one of the strongest supporters of the text on TRIPS and drugs as a 'pro-public health approach in international trade' (DG Trade Communication, 6 June 2002). The problem is that the public health system of a country relies on other components than drugs – such as the services of doctors and nurses. While the EC15 was pushing hard for the Doha text on generic drugs, several EC15 member states were expanding their 'imports' of doctors and nurses from emerging and developing countries in order to decrease the costs of their domestic health regimes. Such imports generate severe disruptions in the public health regimes of the emerging and developing economies – meanwhile the EC15 refuses to include health services in WTO negotiations on behalf of 'public service'.

The CEC should be concerned by such inconsistencies. (In fact, the 1990s witnessed a decline in their production capacities of generic drugs, as a consequence of their shift to a market-based economy.) However, it is difficult to see how the past CEC experience will influence their position, including their capacity to make less inconsistent the current EC15 approach.

5   The E-EC and the 'constitutional' issues

The section examines the key 'constitutional' issues of the relations be-tween trade and competition, environment and labour, and of the future of preferential trade agreements. It suggests that CEC accessions will re-duce the priority put on these issues by the EC15, and shift the E-EC back to a greater focus on market access issues – an evolution which should be seen as positive for the WTO because it will keep it within reasonable borders (see section 6).

Trade and competition

During the Doha Ministerial, the EC15 (or more precisely, the Commis-sion's Trade Directorate which, strangely, is the major, if not the only, supporter of the link between trade and competition) pushed strongly for including trade and competition issues in the Doha Agenda – de-spite the hostility of the vast majority of developing countries, which see only small (if any) benefits from adopting domestic competition laws. Implementing such laws will be very costly because they require a fully developed legal system and highly skilled people (who are often lacking even in industrial countries (Mavroidis and Neven, 2001; Winters, 2002)). A much cheaper and faster alternative to increased competition in almost all developing country markets is to reduce trade protection and discrim-ination through traditional negotiations on market access. During the Doha negotiations, CECs understood or even shared the overall devel-oping country reluctance towards adopting competition laws and policy. This attitude largely reflects the fact that, during the 1990s, CECs had to introduce competition laws under the Europe Agreements signed with the EC15. But this has been an uneasy and frustrating task. In sum, the current EC15 stance on a widely defined trade and competition issue is likely to be eroded by CEC accessions.

The situation may be different for a much narrower, but better defined, topic which is the export cartel issue. Such cartels are mostly operated by OECD firms, and they have imposed a heavy burden (conceptually equivalent to an export tax) on developing countries – estimated to be roughly 6.7 per cent of developing country imports and 1.2 per cent of developing country GDP (Levenstein and Suslow, 2001). Doha negotiators have two ways to address the export cartel issue. The first would be to sign a Competition Agreement allowing developing country competition authorities to request the support of OECD competition authorities when suing export cartels and dealing with other anti-competitive practices. The second would consist of including export cartels in the Doha negotiations on market access on a quid-pro-quo basis: OECD countries would list the import tariffs that they would like to see reduced or eliminated by developing countries, whereas developing countries would list the export cartels that they would like to see examined by OECD competition authorities (Messerlin, 2002). What follows shows that the second alternative is more efficient than the first one.

A WTO Competition Agreement would leave most of the burden of proof to developing country competition authorities which would have to gather the basic information and arguments necessary for convincing OECD competition authorities to launch enquiries. This task will be all the more difficult because most (if not all) OECD competition laws do not oblige OECD competition authorities to look at export cartels as long as price-fixing and market-sharing have no spillovers on the competitive situation in domestic markets of these countries. The discrepancy between the level of skills that most developing countries could reasonably devote to competition matters and the highly technical work to be done leaves few chances for this approach to be workable – not to say profitable.

The cost-benefit balance of including export cartel issues in market access negotiations appears much better. WTO commitments by OECD countries to undertake actions against export cartels create the legal background (absent in most OECD competition laws) necessary for OECD governments to launch enquiries on such cartels. (In this respect, it prepares the ground for a ban of export cartels to be eventually included in a future WTO Round, if the export cartel issue emerges ultimately to be as serious as the limited information currently available suggests.) That would shift most of the technical and analytical work to be done to OECD competition authorities – developing authorities merely providing a list of the goods where export cartels are allegedly operating, and possibly responding to precise requests for additional information from OECD competition authorities. Lastly, concessions on import tariffs (by developing countries) and on export cartels (by OECD countries) are comparable in conceptual terms – which make them fit for trade negotiations.

With all these arguments in mind, would the E-EC adopt a position different from the one that the EC15 would have adopted in the absence of enlargement? In answering this question, it would have been interesting to know whether CECs have faced cases of export cartels originating from EC15 (a key information, *en passant*, for fully assessing the costs of the preferential trade agreements between the EC15 and CECs before their accession), whether such cases have been investigated by the EC Competition Directorate (or not) and by the CECs own competition authorities (or not).

In the absence of such information, one can simply note that export cartels make export markets artificially attractive. CEC firms which could be competitors of EC15 firms involved in export cartel practices in third markets have thus to determine whether it is more profitable to join the export cartel involved, or to compete with it. Their answer will depend on many parameters (the joint profit-sharing formula enforced by the cartel members, the relative production costs between CEC firms and cartel members, the degree of vertical integration created by the cartel operation, etc.). This complexity suggests that CECs are unlikely to have a strong, unique position on this issue, hence that the E-EC final view may be close to the position supported by the EC15 firms which are members of such cartels. This position is still unknown. It will decide the fate of the trade and competition link.

Trade and environment (and labour)

The EC15 has been the staunchest supporter of introducing environment and labour issues in the Doha Round. Its (apparent) success with the environment issue in the Doha Ministerial Text contrasts sharply with the almost complete failure to include labour. However, as CEC accessions raise acute problems in the domains of environment, technical regulations and work safety regulations (and labour movement), they can substantially reshape the E-EC position during the rest of the Doha Round negotiations.

The estimated costs for the CECs to fully comply with the EC15 *acquis communautaire* in all environmental matters are huge. For instance, introducing the 320 EC15 environment-related Directives alone during the next twenty years would cost annually 4–8 per cent of GDP ($6 billion–$13 billion) to Poland, and half these percentages to the Czech Republic (Mayhew, 2000). Implementing the EC15 Directives on standards and work safety rules in transport alone would cost an additional 3–4 per cent of GDP in Poland (Mayhew and Orlowski, 1998). By requiring costly investments to meet EC15 technical and environmental regulations (which may be excessive in some respects), the alignment to the EC15 *acquis communautaire* will impose large costs of forgone consumption on the CECs.

Of course, the WTO will not impose the EC15 Directives on the rest of the world. But the sheer magnitude of the costs related to these matters is likely to make the E-EC less demanding in the WTO forum – compared to today's EC15 position – for several reasons. Western (former EC15) E-EC member states will have a better appraisal of the costs that environmental constraints can impose on emerging and developing economies because they will finance part of such costs in the Eastern (former CEC) E-EC. Eastern E-EC member states may be split between two views. On the one hand, they may convey the message that such requirements impose heavy constraints on emerging economies. On the other hand, if the Western E-EC insists on a strict enforcement of these norms in the Eastern E-EC, CECs may insist on imposing the same costs on non-E-EC emerging economies.

All environmental issues have the same focal point. With rapid technical progress (making difficult the emergence of a scientific consensus), the best approach for addressing such issues is to rely on individually assessed risks, based on the best available scientific information to be provided by public and private sources. Country-based approaches of such issues are likely to be non-optimal – there is nothing such as an 'average French' or an 'average Polish' consumer. There are simply more or less risk-averse and risk-loving consumers in France and Poland, who should decide for themselves between alternative products with different risk intensities.[6] Public authorities have the responsibility to inform consumers about the

---

[6] All other things being constant, consumers with a stable risk aversion over time will smoke less when they are twenty years old (because of the compounding risk over years) than when they are seventy years old (at this age, tobacco-related health risks become limited compared to other health risks).

'scientific evidence' (a notion very different from the scientific consensus) which is available in the world (not simply in the importing country). But consumers should make the final choice.

This important point makes labelling a key instrument – if one can eliminate (or reduce to an acceptable level) its protectionist potential. (For instance, it has been estimated that the logo mentioning the French origin of beef has allowed French farmers to increase their sale prices by 4–8% (Chambres d'Agriculture, 2000). Such a protectionist potential would be lower if the label is voluntary, if it relies on product-based criteria (not on the indication of the origin country), if it does not impose a 'yes–no' situation (for instance, the lower the segregation threshold between GMO and non-GMO crops, the higher the costs of GMO crops) and if it is subjected to cross-monitoring by trading partners (for instance, would Polish experts be allowed to monitor the German 'mad-cow' detection programmes, and vice versa?). Many labelling rules recently adopted by the EC15 do miss one or several of these conditions, and they heavily insist on mentioning the country of origin which is irrelevant information (either the product meets certain technical standards, or it does not, and the location of production is likely to have nothing to do with that). Today, this feature discriminates against CEC producers. But once these producers have adjusted to EC15 labelling, they may be the best supporters of these labels for recouping their recent investments.

Labour issues are unlikely to emerge in the Doha Round (except as an excuse in case of failure). The CECs meet the basic standards concerning the core issues (such as freedom for unions, child labour, etc.) although they are concerned with the emphasis on this topic in the WTO framework – as best shown by the openly hostile Hungarian position concerning the US and EC15 stances during the Seattle Ministerial. By contrast, free movement of labour is a source of great difficulties in the enlargement with the EC15 requesting waivers for themselves from the *acquis communautaire* (by imposing a five–seven-year delay for implementing freedom of labour movement). However, movement of natural persons has few chances of becoming a serious issue for negotiation in the WTO framework.

The E-EC: a much more cautious approach to preferential trade agreements?

A key difference between the EC15 (and all the previous configurations of the EC) and the E-EC is that the E-EC will include a large number of countries with a GDP *per capita* close to many emerging countries in Asia Pacific and Latin America. The potential competition between the CECs and these emerging economies is unlikely to make the CECs great supporters of new PTAs between the E-EC and Mercosur or Asian dynamic economies.

Meanwhile, Western E-EC countries may be reluctant to envisage new PTAs, be they with developed countries, such as the USA or Japan, or even with emerging economies. The reason is that all the new PTAs will include countries which are (and will be) among the world's strongest competitors to EC15 producers – Japan and the USA in advanced manufactured products, the USA in services, emerging economies in food products or traditional manufactured goods, etc. As a result, opening Western E-EC markets to these exporters has the same economic consequences for EC15 producers as opening them to all WTO members – assuming that these PTAs will be substantial agreements, and not mere window dressing. For instance, a PTA with Mercosur will be almost as demanding in competitive pressure and adjustments for several EC15 farm sectors (cereals, meat, sugar) and industrial sectors (from food to leather products, cars, aircraft, etc.) as a WTO Agreement covering the same products. On the other hand, all these PTAs will have the disadvantage of offering (much) more limited trade-offs, in terms of market access for European exporters, to Western E-EC member states than a WTO deal of the same magnitude. The Mercosur economies, for example, cannot provide the same markets for E-EC exports than a world including the USA and Asia Pacific.

In sum, the cost-benefit balance of these new PTAs is likely to be less favourable for the E-EC than the balance offered by the corresponding WTO Agreements – the PTA with the USA offering probably the least disadvantageous alternative to a WTO deal (because of the size of US markets). The PTA with Chile (and possibly with Singapore) does not contradict this conclusion because it does not involve farm or sensitive industrial products. Moreover, the political benefits from PTAs are also hard to see for the E-EC (they often constituted the main gain from the PTAs signed by the EC15 until the end of the 1990s). Asian and Latin American countries have made clear that a trade agreement with Europe should not be perceived as an act of defiance against the USA – even less as an act of allegiance to Europe. Political gains to be expected are thus small for the EC, and they are likely to be counter-weighted by political frictions with the USA – which would not exist in the context of WTO negotiations. The political dimension will be even less important for the CECs, which are generally not looking for political influence outside Europe.

There is a last point to address: will EC enlargement lead to substantial changes in the existing EC15 PTAs with the ACP and Mediterranean countries? Concerning the latter, CECs are unlikely to support the momentum towards deeper integration between the E-EC and Mediterranean countries. First, they perceive the latter as direct competitors in EC15 markets for a wide range of labour-intensive farm and industrial goods (clothing in particular) and for certain services (such as tourism). Second, they have limited traditional political relations with these countries (an important rationale for PTAs in the EC15 history). Lastly, the EC15 has ruthlessly stopped CEC attempts to create preferential trade relations, such as Estonia with Ukraine, Hungary with certain Comecon countries, Slovenia with certain former Yugoslav republics, etc.

Concerning the ACP countries, the CECs are likely to support the shift from the traditional non-reciprocal approach of the Yaoundé–Lomé–Cotonou Conventions to a reciprocal approach requiring the dismantlement of all ACP tariffs on products imported from the E-EC. There are two reasons for such a position. As ACP countries are not CEC competitors in EC15 markets, the CECs are unlikely to be opposed to the complete elimination of all E-EC trade barriers to ACP exports. And as the CECs are not traditional exporters to the ACP countries (they even suffered from a bad reputation during the centrally planned period when they exported badly designed goods to the ACPs), CEC exports will suffer from ACP tariffs more than exports coming from the EC15. It is thus unlikely that the CEC will promote a more economically (and politically) sound solution by which the E-EC will request from each ACP country the introduction of a uniform tariff (a kind of 'limited' reciprocity) in exchange for a complete opening of the EC15 farm, manufacturing and services markets (Messerlin, 2001). Rather, they are likely to support the current EC15 plan of requesting complete reciprocity from the ACP countries – a plan which happens to be very costly for the ACP countries.

6 Conclusion: governance issues

During the years to 2010, the WTO will face two key governance issues. First is the imbalance between the very stringent WTO dispute settlement mechanism, which requires unanimity to undo rulings from panels and from the Appellate Body, and the very cumbersome WTO negotiating process which requires unanimity to do almost everything. Many observers have expressed their doubts on the sustainability of such a dualistic framework. Some of them have concluded that, as a result, the dispute settlement mechanism should be reined in (Barfield, 2001). However, it might be better to act on the two sides of the problem.

On the one hand, the negotiating process should be strengthened. Adopting the above-mentioned wider definition of progressive liberalization, which allows the most 'adventurous' WTO members to liberalize and giving to the initially 'reluctant' countries an opt-in option, would increase the efficiency of the negotiations at an acceptable cost for the whole system (this cost will be indirectly determined by the threshold number of initial signatories). The opt-in option is all the more important because of the 'fatigue' which characterizes today's USA and EC (and which, in the EC case, may increase, following the enlargement process, as found above). This can be counter-balanced by a new infusion of more free-trade-oriented countries, including developing countries (Botswana, Chile, Hong Kong, Mexico, Singapore and Thailand had important and positive roles in the 2001 Doha Ministerial).

On the other hand, the dispute settlement mechanism could be made more flexible. A relaxation of the threshold for rejecting a panel could be envisaged with a system of 'qualified' consensus. Panels examining well-defined GATT issues (such as tariffs, NTBs, etc.) on which WTO member commitments have been made clear by almost five decades of experience should stay under the current full-consensus rule. Panels in charge of more uncharted territories, such as certain GATS or TRIPS issues, could be subjected to a less strict rule – for instance, a consensus minus 'x' number of WTO signatories in the case of GATS issues, and a consensus minus 'z' number of WTO signatories in the case of TRIPS issues ('x' could be smaller than 'z' if one wants to reflect the current suspicion about the TRIPS agreement among many WTO members). Of course, there could be trade-offs between such changes and the necessary improvements of the WTO negotiating process – in order to keep the WTO's core focus on trade liberalization.

This approach based on 'qualified' majorities reflects the way the EC has functioned since its creation, with voting majorities ranging from a simple majority for some issues (such as anti-dumping) to unanimity for other topics (for instance, domestic taxation). The lesson from the EC experience is that a regime based on a range of qualified majorities gives a substantial degree of flexibility to the whole system, but that it also opens the door to trade-offs between the various voting rules. For instance, a WTO member could negotiate a more favourable outcome (strengthen its position in the consultation process) in a GATT-related case by threatening to withdraw its support to a GATS-related ruling, which would be of some interest for its trading partner. It is hard to say more on this point without knowing the details of the qualified majority regime which could be introduced in the WTO, because these details will influence the balance between flexibility and possible trade-offs.

The second key governance issue faced by the WTO is – paradoxically – its 'excessive' role in today's international economic affairs. As is well known, this situation is largely due to the dispute settlement mechanism to which many NGOs would like to have access in order to use it as a channel to impose their goals on their own governments and peoples. This effort to 'capture' the WTO legal system will be greatly reduced by the above suggestion of qualified majorities, all the more because such 'qualified' majorities are likely to be the rule for the topics in which NGOs are the most interested.

But the tendency to dump all the international issues on the WTO also flows from the absence of a high level of economic decision-making at the world level. After all, in the long run, the WTO should be merely seen as the 'Trade Department' of a embryonic world 'government'. The G8 meetings at the heads of state/government level have shown that they could provide the necessary impetus for certain well-defined problems, but the G8-base is too narrow for moving the WTO. It should thus be expanded to a G20 (at the same level of the heads of state/government) based on the G8 countries plus the twelve largest developing countries. Such a G20 could give the necessary boost for future WTO Trade Ministerials (and for those of other international institutions). It could also echo the above-mentioned concept of progressive liberalization: any liberalization undertaken by the G20 countries could be launched without waiting for the rest of the world (which could join later on an 'opt-in' basis).

Bibliography

ABARE, 2000. 'US and EU Agricultural Support: Who Does It Benefit?', *Current Issues*, October, Canberra, ABARE

Baldwin, R., J. Francois and R. Portes, 1997. 'The Costs and Benefits of Eastern Enlargement: The Impact on the EU and Central Europe', *Economic Policy*, April, 127–79

Barfield, C., 2001. *Free Trade, Sovereignty, Democracy: The Future of the World Trade Organization*, Washington, DC, AEI Press

Chambres d'Agriculture, 2000. 'Traçhabilité et étiquetage: un dossier en perpétuelle évolution', 887 Paris, Assemblée Permanente des Chambres d'Agriculture, April

Francois, J. and M. Rombout, 2001. 'Trade Effects from the Integration of the Central and Eastern European Countries into the European Union', Working Paper, 41, Brighton, Sussex European Institute

Johnson, M., 2001. 'EU Enlargement and Commercial Policy: Enlargement and the Making of Commercial Policy', Working Paper, 43, Brighton, Sussex European Institute

Laird, S. and P. A. Messerlin, 2002. 'Trade Policy Regimes and Development Strategies: A Comparative Study', Washington, DC, InterAmerican Development Bank, mimeo

Levenstein, M. and V. Suslow, 2001. 'Private International Cartels and their Effects on Developing Countries', background paper for the World Development Report 2001, Washington, DC, World Bank

Mavroidis, P. C. and D. Neven, 2001. 'From the White Paper to the Proposal for a Council Regulation: How to Treat the New Kids on the Block?', *Legal Issues of Economic Integration*, 28(2), 151–71

Mayhew, A., 2000. 'Enlargement of the European Union: An Analysis of the Negotiations with the Central and Eastern European Candidate Countries', Working Paper, 39, Brighton, Sussex European Institute

Mayhew, A. and W. Orlowski, 1998. 'The Impact of EU Accession on Enterprise Adaptation and Institutional Development in the EU-Associated Countries in Central and Eastern Europe', London, European Bank for Reconstruction and Development, mimeo

Messerlin, P. A., 2001. *Measuring the Costs of Protection in Europe: European Commercial Policy in the 2000s*, Washington, DC, Institute for International Economics

 2002. 'Le Doha Round et les relations entre commerce et concurrence: des solutions alternatives à l'introduction du droit de la concurrence dans l'OMC', Seminar on Trade and Competition, Paris, Direction de la Prèvision, Ministry of Economics, January

OECD, 2002. *Agricultural Policies in the OECD Countries: Monitoring and Evaluation*, Paris, OECD

Winters, L. A., 2002. 'Doha and the World Poverty Targets', Brighton, University of Sussex, mimeo

INDEX

Printed in the United States
By Bookmasters